The search for the origins of language was one of the most pressing philosophical issues of the eighteenth century. What has often escaped notice, however, is that music figures prominently in this search. This study analyzes instances of thinking or reasoning about music and music theory as they appear within the logical and narrative structure of contemporary texts, including writings by Rousseau, Diderot, Rameau, and Condillac. These can only be properly understood as part of an interdisciplinary project, as situated within a field of larger cultural issues and concerns. The author is interested in the ways in which music functions within this discursive framework to facilitate links between language and meaning, and between conceptions of an original society and an ideal social order.

New perspectives in music history and criticism

Music and the origins of language

New perspectives in music history and criticism

GENERAL EDITORS
JEFFREY KALLBERG AND ANTHONY NEWCOMB

This new series will explore the conceptual frameworks that shape or have shaped the ways in which we understand music and its history, and will elaborate structures of explanation, interpretation, commentary, and criticism which make music intelligible and which provide a basis for argument about judgements of value. The intellectual scope of the series will be broad. Some investigations will treat, for example, historiographical topics – ideas of music history, the nature of historical change, or problems of periodization. Others will apply cross-disciplinary methods to the criticism of music, such as those involving literature, history, anthropology, linguistics, philosophy, psychoanalysis or gender studies. There will also be studies which consider music in its relation to society, culture, and politics. Overall, the series hopes to create a greater presence of music in the ongoing discourse among the human sciences.

Music and the origins of language

Theories from the French Enlightenment

DOWNING A. THOMAS

CAMBRIDGE
UNIVERSITY PRESS

CAMBRIDGE UNIVERSITY PRESS
Cambridge, New York, Melbourne, Madrid, Cape Town, Singapore, São Paulo

Cambridge University Press
The Edinburgh Building, Cambridge CB2 2RU, UK

Published in the United States of America by Cambridge University Press, New York

www.cambridge.org
Information on this title: www.cambridge.org/9780521473071

First published 1995
This digitally printed first paperback version 2006

A catalogue record for this publication is available from the British Library

Library of Congress Cataloguing in Publication data

Thomas, Downing A.
Music and the origins of language: theories from the French
Enlightenment / Downing A. Thomas
     p. cm. – (New perspectives in music history and criticism)
Includes bibliographical references and index.
ISBN 0 521 47307 1 (hardback)
1. Language and languages – Origin – History – 18th century.
2. Music and language.
3. France – Intellectual life – 18th century.
I. Title. II. Series.
P116.T47 1995
401–dc20 94-29938 CIP

ISBN-13 978-0-521-47307-1 hardback
ISBN-10 0-521-47307-1 hardback

ISBN-13 978-0-521-02862-2 paperback
ISBN-10 0-521-02862-0 paperback

mais que c'est encore un tissu d'hiéroglyphes entassés les uns sur les autres

Diderot, *Lettre sur les sourds et muets*

CONTENTS

ACKNOWLEDGEMENTS

I have gathered many debts in the course of my work on this book. First thanks go to Michel Beaujour, under whose guidance I wrote my doctoral dissertation in the Department of French at New York University. I am also grateful to Anne Deneys-Tunney and Cliff Eisen, who read this study in its first incarnation and offered encouragement and helpful criticism. If I had to invent an "originator" of this work, it would be Richard Sieburth.

I want to thank Michel Noiray for his intellectual generosity and patience as I tried out ideas during the initial stages of this project. H. Wiley Hitchcock was of great help in the area of seventeenth-century music theory. For reading an early version of the first chapter, Jean-Marie Goulemot deserves thanks. I would also like to acknowledge Walter Rex for his kind encouragement in the final stages of writing. I should also mention The University of Iowa, whose Old Gold Fellowships supported work on this book during my first summers in Iowa City. Cynthia Gessele and Thomas Christensen offered timely advice while I was caught in the quagmire of translation. Finally, I am grateful to Penny Souster for so energetically and graciously supervising the production of this book, and to Jeffrey Kallberg for his support of this project. I cannot thank Dina Blanc enough for reading the entire manuscript twice, if not more, and for her help at every stage.

An earlier version of part of chapter 5 was published in *The Eighteenth Century: Theory and Interpretation*, vol. 35, no. 1. I thank Texas Tech University Press for their kind permission to use that material here.

Unless otherwise noted, the translations are my own. As is standard practice, I have not placed ellipsis points at the beginning or end of quoted passages in most instances and have altered initial letters of quotations according to the syntax of the sentences in which they appear.

Introduction

Music was a favorite topic of the *siècle des lumières*: the list of writers who touch upon music – whether novelists, *philosophes*, pamphleteers, or essayists – is virtually endless. As Condillac noted in his *Essai sur l'origine des connaissances humaines*, "music is an art of which every man thinks himself a judge."[1] Writers of all molds not only discussed and judged musical compositions, but also recognized recent music theory, particularly that of Jean-Philippe Rameau, as entirely unprecedented in its scope and analytic vision. In the "Discours préliminaire" to the *Encyclopédie*, d'Alembert comments that "of all these arts, music is perhaps the one that has made the most progress in the past fifteen years."[2] A fashionable topic of polite conversation and controversy in high society, music also held out the promise of becoming a truly "philosophic" art. Indeed, the history of philosophical reflections on music through the end of the eighteenth century shows the importance of music in the conception and development of aesthetics: from d'Alembert's enthusiasm for music's recent progress, through Kant's view of music as a (secondary) art arousing indeterminate ideas incommensurate with cognition, to the "infinity" and "inexpressible longing" that characterize E. T. A. Hoffmann's conception of music as the most Romantic of all arts.[3]

---

[1] Condillac, *An Essay on the Origin of Human Knowledge*, trans. Thomas Nugent (1756; Gainesville, Florida: Scholars' Facsimiles & Reprints, 1971), 216. I have chosen Thomas Nugent's 1756 English translation of the *Essai* because of its conceptual and terminological proximity to the original, though I have slightly altered the translation clarity in a few instances.

[2] *Encyclopédie ou dictionnaire raisonné des arts et des métiers*, ed. Denis Diderot and Jean le Rond d'Alembert (1751–72; Elmsford, New York: Pergamon, n.d.), 1:xxxij. The original pagination and volume numbers have been used throughout. See also d'Alembert, *Preliminary Discourse to the Encyclopedia of Diderot*, trans. Richard N. Schwab and Walter E. Rex (Indianapolis: Bobbs-Merrill, 1963). References to this translation will be noted only when it has been consulted.

[3] *E. T. A. Hoffmann's Musical Writings: "Kreisleriana," "the Poet and the Composer," Music Criticism*, ed. David Charlton, trans. Martyn Clarke (Cambridge: Cambridge University Press, 1989), 96. See also Immanuel Kant, *Critique of Judgment*, trans. Werner S. Pluhar (Indianapolis: Hackett, 1987), 196–201.

Eighteenth-century writers brought reflections on music into every conceivable form of discourse: claims about music are scattered throughout Rousseau's works; d'Alembert and his fellow mathematician Leonhardt Euler both wrote treatises on music theory while praising and criticizing various aspects of Rameau's influential system; Condillac brought music theory into his epistemology; Dr. Ménuret de Chambaud wrote about the therapeutic influence of music on the body; Diderot discussed the question of musical representation in a number of texts including the *Lettre sur les sourds et muets*; and Lafitau pointed to the role of music in the rituals of native Americans in his *Mœurs des sauvages Américains*. One might wonder why so many authors chose to discuss music, and in such varied contexts. How did eighteenth-century writers perceive the cultural dimensions of music? What place did music occupy for these writers among the many signifying practices which define a culture? What questions about culture did the meaning or purpose of music raise for the Enlightenment? What questions did music and music theory allow the *philosophes* and their contemporaries to answer? In short, what was at stake in the prominence given to music and music theory during this period? This study will focus on the appearance of music in a larger discursive field; in particular, I will examine the place of speculation on music in the theories of the origins of language and culture that were developed by eighteenth-century epistemology and, what we would call today, "anthropology."

The complex interweaving of music with other modes of discourse and inquiry has prompted a certain amount of critical interest in recent years, but has resulted in very few satisfying studies. Perhaps this is not surprising if one considers that no single discipline or critical discourse has been prepared or willing to discuss these kinds of questions. One explanation for this shortcoming is the long-standing balkanization of the disciplines. There is also the difficulty of the lack of shared approaches and terminologies. In order to get around these difficulties, I need to find a critical stance that will allow me to define and legitimate the object of this study. It will be necessary to examine the disciplines and discourses – both those of the twentieth century and those of the eighteenth – that will help to define the questions I want to ask, particularly those which take music as their object.

To begin this project, then, I will need to reflect on a shift in the meaning of "musicology." It is only in the last twenty years or so that the academic discipline of musicology has extended its scope beyond an almost exclusive focus on the great composers and great musical compositions of the Western tradition. Subfields, such as ethnomusicology, were considered minor appendages to the more important and

2

central mission of traditional musical scholarship.[4] Recent work in musicology testifies to some important changes in the field.[5] In the chapters that follow, I want to continue that work by emphasizing a less disciplinary and less particularizing meaning of "musicology." I would argue that the writings I have undertaken to study – which could be called instances of thinking or reasoning about music, or musico-logy in the larger sense – can only be properly understood as part of an interdisciplinary project, as situated within an integrated field of larger cultural issues and concerns. By restoring or creating an expansive meaning for the term "musicology" – which I apply by deliberate anachronism to eighteenth-century writings – I want to recognize the important ground-breaking work that is being done now in the field of musicology and at the same time, as an "outsider," take the risk of upsetting the boundaries of a long-established set of disciplinary-practices. It is important to study music as the cultural and ideological form that it is, as part of larger concerns encompassing cultural identity, history, and meaning.

A considerable amount of scholarship has been devoted to the relationship between music, music theory and criticism, and French culture during the eighteenth century.[6] Yet with respect to the wide-ranging discourse of eighteenth-century musicology – a practice, if not a term, which existed and flourished during the period – very few

---

[4] Today, musicologists are re-examining some of the hierarchies and values upon which the study of the great Western composers was founded. Bruno Nettl plays upon this idea by imagining an ethnomusicologist from Mars who runs into the strange concept of Mozart at the Music Building. See Bruno Nettl, "Mozart and the ethnomusicological study of Western culture: an essay in four movements," *Disciplining Music: Musicology and its Canons*, ed. Katherine Bergeron and Philip V. Bohlman (Chicago: University of Chicago Press, 1992), 137–155. Needless to say, literature's canon of writers has been the subject of a similar re-evaluation in recent years.

[5] Leo Treitler, Lawrence Kramer, Susan McClary, Richard Leppert, Wayne Koestenbaum, and Rose Rosengard Subotnik, among many others, have opened the field to new directions.

[6] See Belinda Cannone, *Philosophies de la musique: 1752–1789* (Paris: Aux Amateurs de Livres, 1990); Catherine Kintzler, *Poétique de l'opéra française de Corneille à Rousseau* (Paris: Minèrve, 1991); Béatrice Didier, *La Musique des lumières* (Paris: Presses Universitaires de France, 1985); and John Neubauer, *The Emancipation of Music from Language* (New Haven: Yale University Press, 1986). Two other recent publications are useful for their bibliographies: Cynthia Verba, *Music and the French Enlightenment: Reconstruction of a Dialogue: 1750–1764* (Oxford: Clarendon Press, 1993); and Jean-Jacques Robrieux, "Jean-Philippe Rameau et l'opinion philosophique en France au dix-huitième siècle," *Studies on Voltaire and the Eighteenth Century* 238 (1985), 269–395. For a rapid overview of texts central to the question of the origin of music as it was raised in early modern Europe, see Philippe Vendrix, *Aux origines d'une discipline historique: la musique et son histoire en France aux XVIIe et XVIIIe siècles* (Geneva: Droz, 1993), 149–205.

scholars have offered anything but the most cursory historical over-view. The vast majority of available studies on eighteenth-century music and its cultural context can be classified under two large head-ings: anecdotal and historical accounts of the various musical *querelles*, particularly the *Querelle des bouffons*; and studies in the history of ideas that follow the transformation of musical and aesthetic doctrines over the course of the century. The *Querelles des bouffons* has been well documented.[7] Béatrice Didier has pointed out the resemblances be-tween the earlier dispute pitting *Lullistes* against *Ramistes*, the *Querelle des bouffons*, and the disagreements which opposed supporters of Gluck and Piccini towards the end of the century.[8] Together, the *querelles* formed three waves of reaction against the very real influence of Italian music and conceptions of musical theater in France, and more generally against any marked change in compositional style. Although the French/Italian dichotomy remained in effect for all three *querelles*, the matter was complicated by the fact that composers were shuffled from one side of the quarrel to the other. Early in the century, Rameau was accused of exploiting "Italian" elements in his com-positions, thereby corrupting the traditional simplicity of Lully's music; with the *Querelle des bouffons*, however, Rameau was attacked by supporters of Italian opera as the representative, par excellence, of "sophisticated French music."[9] Lully, too, who in the eighteenth century stood for the very essence of French music, was himself Italian and part of the "authorized" importation of Italian culture under Mazarin, né Giulio Raimondo Mazzarini. The *querelles* were thus the symptom of ongoing uncertainties, dating from the very first operas in France, about the origin of French lyric theater and its ties to Italian music and politics.

In 1752, the polemic can be seen, at its most virulent, as a national-istic reaction to what is imagined to be a cultural invasion from the other side of the Alps, and to the enemy within – Rousseau and his invectives against the French tradition in the *Lettre sur la musique française*.[10] In this text, for which he came close to being imprisoned in

---

[7] Essential primary and secondary material on the *Querelle* includes the collection of pamphlets entitled *La Querelle des bouffons: textes des pamphlets*, ed. Denise Launay (Geneva: Minkoff, 1973); A.-R. Oliver, *The Encyclopedists as Critics of Music* (New York: Columbia University Press, 1947); and Louise Richebourg, *Contribution à l'histoire de la Querelle des bouffons* (Philadelphia: n.p., 1937).

[8] Didier, *La Musique des lumières*, 175–201.

[9] *Ibid.*, 176. See also Cannone, *Philosophies de la musique*, 17–18, 134.

[10] It is interesting to note in this context that this musical "infiltration" was not entirely metaphorical, and that the circulation of music in Europe did in fact serve political purposes. Neal Zaslaw notes that "travelling virtuosi had long served as spies, for, when they were good courtiers as well as good musicians, they frequently had easy access to the private chambers of those in power" (Neal Zaslaw, "The first opera in

Vincennes, Rousseau goes as far as to assert that "the French have no music and will never have one."[11] The very presence of Italian opera was seen as a threat to the French musical tradition, as an attack on the memory of Lully and on Rameau. Through a process of generalization, the entirety of French culture was felt to be under fire. The père Castel, from the other side of the polemic, felt it necessary to pull out all the stops to defend French music as "a proper, national, specifically French music, even Gauloise if you wish; music of our own making [*de notre crû*], of our soil."[12] Here, music is represented as part and parcel of *la francité* through its association with three inviolable symbolic elements of Frenchness: ancestry, wine (*notre crû*), and the territory of France itself.

At its most benign, however, the *Querelle des bouffons* can be considered as a kind of social game in which two opposing groups – the supporters of Italian music, known as the "coin de la reine," and the pro-French "coin du roi" – battled each other through virtuosic letter-writing. Yet this *guerre de plumes* also had more far-reaching consequences. Béatrice Didier remarks that the 1752 *Querelle* "is also at the origin of the entirely new development of musical criticism."[13] Commentary on music appeared regularly in the *Correspondance littéraire* and *Le Mercure de France*, especially after the mid-century, and periodicals devoted exclusively to music also began to emerge.[14]

A second category of critical studies draws attention to the larger question of the historical transformation of musical aesthetics during the eighteenth century. These studies claim that eighteenth-century aesthetics must be seen as a transitional phase between the doctrine of imitation inherited from the neo-classical seventeenth century, and the aesthetics of the absolute that would later characterize the Romantic age. In my view, commentators have often distorted their accounts by adhering to a very schematic view of eighteenth-century conceptions of music as nothing but a passage – a kind of no-man's-land – between the servile imitation of which it was still a part, and the liberation of expression. During the eighteenth-century, from this viewpoint, music progresses from being tied to language for its

Paris: a study in the politics of art," in *Jean-Baptiste Lully and the Music of the French Baroque: Essays in Honor of James R. Anthony*, ed. John Hajdu Heyer [Cambridge: Cambridge University Press, 1989], 8).

[11] "Les François n'ont point de musique et n'en peuvent avoir" (Jean-Jacques Rousseau, *Ecrits sur la musique* [Paris: Pourrat, 1838], 322). For a detailed analysis of the political context of the *Querelle des bouffons*, see Robert Wokler's article, "Rousseau on Rameau and revolution," *Studies in the Eighteenth Century IV*, ed. R. F. Brissenden and J. C. Eade (Canberra: Australian National University Press, 1979), 251–283.

[12] Louis-Bertrand Castel, "Lettres d'un academicien de Bordeaux sur le fonds de la musique," in Denise Launay, ed., *La Querelle des bouffons*, 1394.

[13] Didier, *La Musique des lumières*, 175.　　[14] *Ibid.*, 175.

meaning (operatic or dramatic music being the most highly valorized) to the free play of forms exhibited by instrumental music. I want to offer a more nuanced reading of this history. While I would agree that conceptions of music and of aesthetic experience changed drastically during the eighteenth century and that instrumental music played an important role in these changes, I would take issue, first, with the particular teleological vision that appears to be valorized by many critics, and second, with the idea that the conception of music as an affective language is epistemologically incompatible with the aesthetics that developed in the late eighteenth century. The title of John Neubauer's study, *The Emancipation of Music from Language*, reveals his view of music history as a continual progress towards "emancipation": Rameau, Diderot, Chabanon, and Euler *"were groping* for a justification of instrumental music but *were held back* by their insistence on determinate meaning and content."[15] Admirable for its scope and clarity, Neubauer's study nonetheless tends to see early- to mid-century theories as insufficient or incomplete because, in his view, they limited the possibilities of artistic forms and restricted the experience of the listener/viewer in ways that the absolute aesthetic of the Romantics did not. Similarly, Maria Rika Maniates concludes her otherwise excellent elucidation of Fontenelle's well-known comment on instrumental music – "Sonate, que me veux-tu?" – by suggesting that eighteenth-century aesthetics had created an "impasse" which prevented any satisfactory answer to the question of musical meaning: "having arrived at the crossroads, the French aestheticians lose their way ... absolute music must find philosophical understanding. But no philosopher of this period crystallizes a vocabulary adequate to deal with the idea of embodied or innate musical meaning."[16] Another commentator, Jean-Michel Bardez, does not hesitate to assert that their "rejection of non-imitative music is proof of a complete lack of understanding."[17] Bardez implies that eighteenth-century writers did not understand the "truth" of music and could not yet understand its "real" function.

My point here is that some commentators' views of eighteenth-century music and music theory merely echo the assumption that genuine art must ultimately forgo all attachments to language, meaning, and content in order to enjoy autonomous self-referentiality. However, no form of expression, as Rose Rosengard Subotnik has argued, can "escape a fundamentally ideological condition of exist-

---

[15] Neubauer, *The Emancipation of Music*, 182; emphasis added.

[16] Maria Rika Maniates, "'Sonate, que me veux-tu?': the enigma of French musical aesthetics in the 18th century," *Current Musicology* 9 (1969), 136.

[17] Jean-Michel Bardez, *Philosophes, encyclopédistes, musiciens, théoriciens* (Geneva: Slatkine, 1980), 2.

ence."[18] Christopher Norris has remarked that the desire to show the necessary and "innate" autonomy of art goes hand in hand with claims for a separate, autonomous discourse for aesthetics, existing beyond politics and specific ideological interests.[19] It would be possible to show that absolute aesthetics, like the *ut pictura poesis* of neo-classical representation, is bounded by and implicated in particular beliefs and aspirations. Thus, in taking the telos of absolute music at face value, the commentator forgoes any meaningful critical stance with respect to the particular view of music and music history we have inherited from the late nineteenth century. My purpose in this study is not to emphasize the "departure from mimesis" per se – the subtitle to John Neubauer's *The Emancipation of Music from Language* – or to argue for an impossible objective analysis. Rather, I want to suggest that the idea of a musical "language" in the eighteenth century was a crucial element within neo-classical theories of representation and contributed to their transformation in the second half of the century. In the process, I will attempt to reveal and examine some of the cultural and thus interdisciplinary implications which are so often ignored or excluded by contemporary commentators who have viewed the interdependence of music and language as an enslavement to an outmoded theory of representation.

I want to redefine the issue of music and culture through an examination of eighteenth-century reflections on the origin, purpose, and meaning of music. In the following chapters, I will examine the intersection of eighteenth-century concepts of music and of language through the question of the origin of signs and culture. It is well known that eighteenth-century philosophers studied the origin of language as a way of pinpointing the origin of semiosis, of meaning in general. What has often escaped notice, however, is the fact that music figures prominently in this search for origins. I am interested in the ways in which music functions within this discursive framework as facilitating epistemological links between language and meaning, between the origin of culture and that of eighteenth-century Europe, and between conceptions of an original society and an ideal social order.

Although the question of origins has no national borders, the scope

---

[18] Rose Rosengard Subotnik, *Developing Variations: Style and Ideology in Western Music* (Minneapolis: University of Minnesota Press, 1991), 299n28.

[19] Christopher Norris, *Contest of Faculties: Philosophy and Theory after Deconstruction* (London: Methuen, 1985), 123–138. Similarly, John Corbett has noted that "musicology as it now exists remains a classical mode of analysis bound up in the defense of this independence, in the assertion of music as access to the 'absolute' and as timeless and apolitical" ("Free, single, and disengaged: listening pleasure and the popular music object," *October* 54 [1990], 88).

of this study has been limited to France. The breadth of my subject has
made it convenient to focus on material in the French language,
though I do not hesitate to venture beyond these constraints
whenever appropriate. There are also two other compelling reasons
for imposing these limits. First of all, systematic reflection on music
and music theory during the eighteenth century was largely dominated by the work of Jean-Philippe Rameau. Claude Palisca writes
that, whether within or outside of France, "there is hardly a theorist in
the 18th or 19th centuries who did not engage in a dialogue across the
years with Rameau."[20] Not surprisingly, it was also in France that
Rameau's theories had the greatest influence in philosophy, aesthetics,
and in the *Encyclopédie*. Secondly, though eighteenth-century philosophy of language was by no means exclusively French, it was
Condillac who set the tone for the debate on the origin of language
which would continue for several decades in Paris, Berlin, and Edinburgh.[21] Almost twenty-five years before the publication of Herder's
Über den Ursprung der Sprache (1772), Maupertuis had brought the
debate from France to the Berlin Academy with his *Réflexions philosophiques sur l'origine des langues et la signification des mots*.[22] James
Burnet, Lord Monboddo, mentions that his text, *Of the Origin and
Progress of Language* (1773), was suggested by Thomas Nugent's English
translation of Condillac's *Essai*.[23] I do not intend to assert that the
question of the origin of language "emanated" from France. Entirely
different views of language can be found in texts such as Rowland

[20] *The New Grove Dictionary of Music and Musicians*, ed. Stanley Sadie, (London: Macmillan, 1980), s.v. "Theory, theorists."

[21] It must be noted that Warburton's *Divine Legation of Moses*, part of which was
published in French in 1744 as the *Essai sur les hieroglyphes des Egyptiens*, had already
introduced the notion of an original language of gestures upon which Condillac
would so heavily depend in his description of the origin of language. Condillac
does not hesitate to acknowledge his source across the Channel (Condillac, *Essai*, 193).
Locke was also, of course, a great influence on Condillac and had already rejected the
concept of innate ideas and questioned their relationship to words.

[22] "Arens has observed that universal grammar was the dominant French concern in the
mid eighteenth century, while origin of language [sic] received only slight attention.
But in Germany, he says, the emphasis lay on origin of language since universal
grammar made a late appearance in Germany ... I hope I have shown that the
historical facts do not offer the slightest support to Arens' thesis; it is a conventional
myth. The problem of the origin of language is brought to Germany from France only
a few years after the publication of Condillac's *Essai* in 1746, by the president of the
newly reconstituted Berlin Academy, Pierre-Louis Moreau de Maupertuis (1698–
1759)" (Hans Aarsleff, *From Locke to Saussure: Essays on the Study of Language and
Intellectual History* [Minneapolis: University of Minnesota Press, 1982], 176). For an
opposing view of the importance of Condillac with respect to the question of public
and private language, see Ian Hacking, "How, why, when, and where did language
go public?", *Common Knowledge* 1.2 (1992), 74–91.

[23] Aarsleff, *From Locke to Saussure*, 148n4.

Jones' *The Origin of Language and Nations*, which argues that Celtic was the first language and which hopes to lay the foundation for a universal language by tracing all existing languages back to their origins.

The first chapter examines the governing assumption of virtually all writing on music by the *philosophes* and their contemporaries: that music was a kind of language. This assumption represented a considerable step that led reflections on music into areas of language theory and rhetoric. I explore the question of a musical language through a variety of seventeenth- and eighteenth-century texts and contexts. My discussion of the verbal paradigm – its formation and transformation – will frame the central issues that are developed in later chapters.

The second chapter examines the eighteenth-century search for the origin of language and music. Beginning with Bourdelot's and Bonnet's *Histoire de la musique et de ses effets* and with Blainville's *Histoire générale, critique et philologique de la musique*, I demonstrate that the locus of writing on origins shifted from the myths of antiquity to the hypothetical narratives of a "theoretical empiricism." Writers no longer relied on the stories of the Ancients – those of Lucretius and Pythagoras, for example – concerning the origin of music. Rather than compile the accounts of earlier authorities, they produced their own hypotheses and wrote their own stories. Although empiricists insisted that all knowledge derives from the senses, their writings on the origin of language were no less speculative than those of earlier writers. Yet the logical and discursive strategy of their "fictions" was quite different. Rather than depend upon earlier textual authorities, the empiricists based their speculations on the guiding principles that they found in a philosophy centered on sensation.

The third and fourth chapters consist of detailed readings of Condillac's *Essai sur l'origine des connaissances humaines* and Rousseau's *Essai sur l'origine des langues*. Both Condillac and Rousseau created hypothetical accounts of the origin and development of language and culture, and both devoted lengthy passages to the origin of music. I draw out the arguments of these texts and place them in context. First, conceived of as a natural sign of the passions, music predates all conventional language. As such, it constitutes a natural model for all representation – representation being the ability for one thing to stand for another – and thus paves the way for the subsequent elaboration of conventional sign systems and signifying practices. Music serves as the anthropological "missing link" in the eighteenth-century attempt to trace semiosis to its origin, to pinpoint the semiotic moment which separates culture from nature, and human beings from animals. Through its natural link to the passions (for as a natural sign, music already represents the passions), music is the triggering mechanism of representation itself – the origin of the origin of culture, as it were.[24] My contention is that what these writers described as a proto-music forms a crucial stage in their history of knowledge and society. As a signifying practice which is nonetheless still part of the natural world, a primordial system of musical tones sets the stage for conventional language and the culture that exists within language. Because of the crucial place music occupies in the narratives used to imagine the origin and history of culture, it will afford insight into the eighteenth century's conception of and attitude toward knowledge, representation, and meaning.

Maintaining the focus on music's relationship to passion and meaning established in the search for origins, I take aesthetic writings and medical texts as the subject of the final chapter. What comes to the fore in medical discourse is the effect of music on human sensibility. I examine how music's original connection to the soul, which had been elaborated in the search for origins, also appears in eighteenth-century philosophical texts concerned with medicine. Here, rather than being a signifier-symptom of passion, music is considered through its effects on passion. With regard to aesthetics, I am interested in the use of music to represent current and future forms of culture by articulating a relationship between the individual body and the community. Whereas for Condillac or Rousseau the link between music and passion was validated in a primitive scene, for Diderot that connection holds within it the future promise of culture. The relationship between the individual and the collective can take place because, paradoxically, music asserts forms of representation which shatter the classical notion of a direct, one-to-one correspondence between sign and meaning. The spectator who is actively engaged in the creation of meaning through passion becomes an implicit metaphor for the citizen. At the

---

[24] As Christie V. McDonald has pointed out, following Jacques Derrida's analysis of Rousseau's *Essai sur l'origine des langues*, the logic of origins is by nature infinitely regressive ("Jacques Derrida's reading of Rousseau," *The Eighteenth Century: Theory and Interpretation* 20 [1979], 89). Edward Said's *Beginnings*, for example, follows this logic of origins when he notes that "there is an imperative connection to be observed between the idea of a beginning and an aboriginal human need to point to or locate a beginning" (*Beginnings: Intention and Method* [New York: Columbia University Press, 1985], 5). In other words, Said claims that the idea of origins is an (ab)original idea. The search for origins, as Eric Gans has succinctly put it, is "an endeavor condemned to endless repetition because the 'origin' is 'always already' inhabited by the search for itself" (*The Origin of Language: A Formal Theory of Representation* [Berkeley: University of California Press, 1981], ix). By its very logic, then, the search for origins will always reveal another origin through a constant splintering. An origin must always reduplicate itself in another origin, as a kind of limit. This is why eighteenth-century writers located the beginning of semiosis in another (pre-linguistic) system which nonetheless already functioned as language: the origin of signs thus has an origin in music.

junction of these aesthetic and medical texts, I argue, is the issue of the connection between bodily and moral "resonance."

The links that were established between music and the passions formed the basis of a search to recover for culture the scope of meaning and the affective dimension of knowledge which characterized eighteenth-century descriptions of the origin. What I have called musico-logy thus articulated the issues through which eighteenth-century writers defined their humanity and culture.

1

Music and language

"Music is a non-signifying art."[1]

With a few exceptions, including the recent formation of a musical semiotics, official discourse on music in the twentieth century has largely resisted discussion of music as it might be related to language or meaning.[2] Composers and theorists from Webern to Babbitt have sought to place the art of musical composition in an autonomous space adjacent to mathematics where, as in the Middle Ages, it would be exclusively concerned with carefully controlled pattern-making, according to rules that are particular to music.[3] Thus the meaning of music has generally been restricted to intramusical formal relations, considered independent of any verbal content and free of ideological influence. Discussing the widespread reluctance to link music to meaning or ideology, Rose Rosengard Subotnik gives the example of Stravinksy, for whom composition was "a specimen of purely autonomous craft."[4] The academic discipline of musicology appears largely complicitous with this view. First, musicology as an academic discipline arose during a particular moment in the history of Western aesthetics when theorists reacted against eighteenth-century mimetic principles and placed great emphasis on music as an "absolute" art

---

[1] Pierre Boulez, *Points de repère* (Paris: Christian Bourgois, 1985), 18.

[2] Umberto Eco is one of these exceptions. He argues that music is another kind of language which has "different systems of articulation, freer and differently structured" (*La Structure absente*, trans. Uccio Esposito-Torrigiani [Paris: Mercure de France, 1972], 356). More recently, Jean-Jacques Nattiez, following Jean Molino, has insisted that musical meaning should not be defined by, or restricted to, linguistic meaning. He rejects the structuralist concept of a fixed code which would establish a direct and fixed correspondence between the signifier and the signified, adopting instead a modified version of Peirce's more complex theory of the interpretant. See Jean-Jacques Nattiez, *Musicologie générale et sémiologie* (Paris: Christian Bourgois, 1987).

[3] Albert Seay has likened the isorhythmic motet of the French Ars Nova to serial composition. He notes that "twelve-tone composition is, in many ways, a modern application of the principle of *color* repetition" (*Music in the Medieval World* [Englewood Cliffs: Prentice-Hall, 1975], 134).

[4] Subotnik, *Developing Variations*, 7.

which was by nature free from the constraints of determinate meaning, and detached from the contingencies of life and history. The study of music today carries with it the heritage of its early history. Second, musicology adopted a scientific and strictly empirical approach to the score – its preferred object – isolating it from all context in order to better discern its internal structures, restoring it to its original, and thus true, form. Musicology may be willing to consider music as a kind of "language," but only if this identification is strictly metaphorical – devoid, that is, of any epistemic validity. And if music is a language, then it is one that operates on its own terms, independently of any pre-existing meaning.

Linguists seem to share this view, for Benveniste is also able to draw music away from verbal or linguistic meaning by eliminating it from his theory of semiotics. In *Problèmes de linguistique générale*, he asserts that, although music does have something comparable to a syntax, it can have no semiotics since, among other things, musical notes or phrases have no meaning that can be specified in language – as do road signs, for example.[5] Music theorists and most semioticians consider music to be only a "code" – that is, a system of elements (pitches, rhythms, timbres, dynamics, etc.) which are arranged according to culturally determined rules and constraints.[6] Kristeva notes that music does not exhibit the same binary differences that structure verbal language: "while the two signifying systems are organized according to the principle of the *difference* of their components, this difference is not of the same order in verbal language as it is in music. Binary phonematic differences are not pertinent in music."[7] Furthermore, as Benveniste explains, contrary to what one might at first suspect, the simultaneities and sequences inherent in music have no relation to the paradigmatic and syntagmatic axes of language:

the axis of simultaneity in music contradicts the very principle of the paradigmatic in language, which is the principle of selection, excluding all intra-segmental simultaneity; and the axis of sequences in music does not coincide with the syntagmatic axis of language either, since a musical sequence is compatible with the simultaneity of sounds, and since this sequence furthermore is not subject to any constraint of linkage or exclusion with respect to any sound or group of sounds whatsoever.[8]

---

[5] Emile Benveniste, *Problèmes de linguistique générale* (Paris: Gallimard, 1974), 2:54–56.

[6] For more on the distinction between language and code, see Oswald Ducrot and Tzvetan Todorov, *Dictionnaire encyclopédique des sciences du langage* (Paris: Editions du Seuil, 1972), 137.

[7] Julia Kristeva, *Language the Unknown*, trans. Anne M. Menke (New York: Columbia University Press, 1989), 309.

[8] Benveniste, *Problèmes de linguistique générale*, 2:56.

Music is a code with rules governing the combination of its elements. But there is little or no affinity between these procedures or the structures which result from them, and the rules and combinations of verbal language. In addition, music has no meaning which can be translated into language; it does not share its semiotic capacity. It would appear, then, that music has become an object of study for contemporary linguists and semioticians precisely because it differs so much from language.

If this is the position taken by most musicologists and semioticians regarding modern Western music, once outside the restrictive framework of their analyses, and in other periods of Western history or in other cultures, it becomes clear that their views no longer apply. Edward Said has spoken of the tendency in Western culture since the late eighteenth century to view music as autonomous, and has pointed out musicology's complacency towards this view. Said notes

the generally cloistral and reverential, not to say insular, habits in writing about music. For the closer one looks at the geography of Western culture and of music's place in it, the more compromised, the more socially involved and active music seems, the more concealed its social energies have been beneath its technically specialized, rigorously circumscribed, and, since the seventeenth century, perfected articulations.[9]

The standard semiotic theory outlined above is not able to address music as a signifying or social practice within our culture. It cannot explain, for example, the ways in which music interacts with and grounds public occasions or other social activities in which it is included. With specific reference to language, one only has to think of the (verbal) meanings and narratives that are popularly associated with or attributed to music. These associations are found not only in daily conversation and concert-hall programs, but also in the writings and interviews of many musicians and some composers.[10] Even such seemingly autonomous works as Chopin's second Prelude have been read as articulating specific moods or emotions, not only by nineteenth-century critics such as Hans von Bülow ("the right hand bears the inexorable voice of death, though toward the end it falters and loses the measure in uncertain tones, as if saying, 'He comes not, the deliverer!'") but also by twentieth-century musicologists such as Leonard Meyer who hear "doubt and uncertainty" in the music.[11]

[9] Edward Said, *Musical Elaborations* (New York: Columbia University Press, 1991), 58.
[10] As part of his varied attempts to popularize music and music theory, Leonard Bernstein created a model for a universal musical "language" based on Chomsky's notion of innate grammatical competence. See his 1973 Norton Lectures published as *The Unanswered Question* (Cambridge: Harvard University Press, 1976).
[11] Subotnik, *Developing Variations*, 139.

Indeed, as Lawrence Kramer has argued, these discursive meanings
"are not 'extramusical,' but on the contrary are inextricably bound up
with the formal processes and stylistic articulations of musical
works."[12] This aspect of our understanding of Western music has not
been sufficiently studied by traditional musicology.

Ethnomusicologists have examined more coded or formal relationships between music and what has generally been considered extra-
musical culture. Harold Powers has observed that in some cultures
music can function referentially or signify, like a language:

First of all, music is often said to express or evoke something that might have
been conveyed verbally. In certain restricted cases, like drum or whistle
languages, something like music is even used as a referential coded substitute
for language; the Tepehua "thought" songs described by Boilès (1967) seem to
be the extreme case. But many musical cultures recognize conventionally
coded induced associations of specific musical entities with persons, events, or
things, in real life as well as in ritual or drama.[13]

Although Powers only gives examples of non-Western cultures in
this passage, similar uses of music also exist or have existed in Western
culture. Using the recent insights of ethnomusicologists and anthropologists, much could be written about the musical practices of contemporary Western cultures, or those of the past. A glance at early
Western music theory would confirm the fact that the kinds of extra-
musical associations Powers describes have always been central to
Western musical culture. The various notes of the Egyptian scale
system, for example, were directly associated with the days of the
week and the planets. Each of the Greek modes was considered to
reflect the ethical characteristics of a tribe. Plato, in *The Republic*,
reviews in detail the ethical importance and meaning of the musical
modes and banishes all but the Dorian and Phrygian, "the violent and
the willing" modes, which are useful to the State.[14] Throughout the
Middle Ages and most of the Renaissance, music theorists used
Pythagorean metaphysics to provide music with carefully detailed
meanings in political, social, and theological contexts. According to the
Pythagorean account of music's place in the world, the harmony
generated by the divine act of the Creation infused the entire universe,
expressing itself hierarchically in layers of order. This harmony bal-
anced the cosmos – the famous music of the spheres – the elements,
the soul and the body, and the political institutions of the State.[15]

12 Lawrence Kramer, *Music as Cultural Practice: 1800–1900* (Berkeley: University of
   California Press, 1990), 1.
13 Harold S. Powers, "Language models and musical analysis," *Ethnomusicology* 24.1
   (1980), 1
14 Plato, *The Republic*, trans. G.M.A. Grube (Indianapolis: Hackett, 1974), 69.
15 Neubauer, *The Emancipation of Music*, 11–17.

Music expressed and sustained a theological conception of the place of men and women within the larger machinery of the State and the universe.

This chapter will focus on a particular view of music and language which, beginning with the decline of earlier cosmological conceptions of music in the late sixteenth and early seventeenth centuries, continued through the eighteenth century. Music and language were considered throughout this period as intimately related, though the meaning of this relationship shows considerable variation.[16] In the "Discours préliminaire" to the *Encyclopédie*, for example, d'Alembert notes that "music . . . has gradually become a kind of discourse or even language."[17] Diderot also claims that "music is a language" in the *Leçons de clavecin* that he wrote with Bemetzrieder.[18] Although it was certainly not the only approach to music, what John Neubauer calls the "verbal paradigm" could be considered to form the dominant discourse on music during the eighteenth century.[19] In his *Dell'origine et della regole della musica*, Antonio Eximeno devotes a chapter to the uselessness of musical mathematics, explaining that music is most intimately related to language through a common origin. Like the Pythagorean and other conceptions of music mentioned above, the verbal paradigm integrated music into the network of meanings, into the signifying practices that make up culture. But beyond this generalized function as part of cultural practices or systems of belief, the verbal paradigm opened music to the possibility of (what we would call today) a semiotics. In Leibniz's *Nouveaux essais sur l'entendement*

---

16 One might object that language and music were considered to be related during many periods of occidental history. Yet my argument is that the seventeenth and eighteenth centuries rely on a conception of music and language which differs, at least at its inception, from that of other periods. If the Middle Ages was concerned with the setting of words to music, theorists tended to emphasize techniques in which the musical voices were organized to form, and derived their meaning from, strictly musical patterns which were essentially unrelated to the narration of a story-line. The isorhythmic motet of the Ars Nova, and Machaut's crab canon rondeau "Ma fin est mon commencement," could be cited as examples to illustrate the importance medieval music gave to formal principles (Seay, *Music in the Medieval World*, 127, 144). One might also object that certain strains of nineteenth-century poetics (Verlaine, Mallarmé) imagined language as music. Yet in this case the relation is reversed. Instead of music being thought of as a language because of narrative and rhythmic elements common to both, language attempts to de-signify itself, or rather to be able, like music, to form constellations (the word is Mallarmé's) of sound and sense, which would belong to a higher and more naturalized order of meaning than does ordinary language.

17 *Encyclopédie*, 1:xij.

18 Denis Diderot, *Œuvres complètes*, ed. Jean Varloot (Paris: Hermann, 1975–86), 19:384.

19 See also Kevin Barry, *Language, Music and the Sign* (Cambridge: Cambridge University Press, 1987).

humain, "Théophile" considers the prospect of a musical language: "we must consider that one could speak, that is, make oneself understood by vocal sounds . . . if one used musical *tones* for this purpose."[20] In his *Traité du récitatif*, published in 1707 and reissued throughout the eighteenth century, Grimarest suggests that vocal music has already become a type of communication: "vocal music is a kind of language that men have agreed upon to communicate their thoughts & feelings with more pleasure."[21] Considered by these writers as a language, music became much more than the semantically neutral code to which Benveniste refers.[22] For the seventeenth and eighteenth centuries, it offered the possibility of representation and communication, and these possibilities gave music a particular role in culture. The theorists who described this role offer valuable insights into the interrelations of art and theories of culture. The verbal paradigm would make music speak at the same time that it would rationalize and regularize a discourse on music.

One way to explain the existence of the verbal paradigm for music would be to call it a version of logocentrism. I do not think that this answer is sufficient. At the risk of digressing for a moment, I want to attempt to explain my reasons for objecting to it. Indeed, it would be difficult to begin a study such as this one without discussing Jacques Derrida's approach to Western metaphysics. If during the seventeenth and eighteenth centuries music was thought of as a kind of language (so the argument could be construed), then perhaps this is tantamount to saying with Derrida that, despite other upheavals in philosophy, voice and reason (*logos*) remain inextricably linked: "within this logos, the original and essential link to the *phonè* has never been broken . . . the essence of the *phonè* would be immediately proximate to that which within 'thought' as logos relates to 'meaning,' produces it, receives it, speaks it, 'composes' it."[23] In the philosophical tradition of

---

20 Gottfried Wilhelm Leibniz, *Nouveaux essais sur l'entendement humain* (Paris: Garnier-Flammarion, 1966), 235.

21 Jean Léonor le Gallois de Grimarest, *Traité du récitatif* (1740; New York: AMS Press [1978]), 120.

22 The examples I have given are by no means exhaustive. Many others addressed the question of music and language in more or less detail: Turgot in his *Discours sur l'histoire universelle* and Maupertuis in his *Dissertation sur les différens moyens dont les hommes se sont servis pour exprimer leurs idées* (see *Varia linguistica*, ed. Charles Porset [Bordeaux: Ducros, 1970]); Charles de Brosses in his *Traité de la formation méchanique des langues* (Paris: Saillant, Vincent, Desaint, 1765); and Court de Gebelin in his *Histoire naturelle de la parole ou Origine du langage, de l'écriture et de la grammaire universelle* (Paris: n.p., 1772). Music appears more or less prominently in each of these texts as part of an effort to pin down the question of the origin of signs.

23 Jacques Derrida, *Of Grammatology*, trans. Gayatri Chakravorty Spivak (Baltimore: The Johns Hopkins University Press, 1976), 13. "Or dans ce logos, le lien originaire et essentiel à la *phoné* n'a jamais été rompu . . . l'essence de la *phoné* serait immédiatement

17

the West, according to Derrida, the voice is accorded a privileged status as immediately close to truth, presence, and being. Following Derrida, it would be possible to claim that music, like language, is given the metaphysical attributes of truth, presence, and being because of its close relation to voice. Insofar as music and language are both dependent on the voice, they are also, *a priori*, linked to thought or meaning (*logos*). Music's privileged relation to voice – as lyric – associates it, moreover, with the most intimate confines of subjectivity. One could argue, then, that the connection of voice and *logos* to which Derrida refers is what allows music access to meaning within the framework of Western epistemology, and to be considered, as d'Alembert writes, "a kind of discourse or even language."[24]

Derrida's interpretation offers an elegant and persuasive explanation for the verbal paradigm; yet it does not account for the waxing and waning of this paradigm. It thus would be necessary to account for the shift to an aesthetic ideology for which language must be left behind and which argues for the unmediated formal play of music. The overarching compass of logocentrism cannot be expected to fully explain the meanings of particular discourses on music. For when Derrida discusses the persistence of logocentrism, he is referring to the history of Western metaphysics as a whole, a grand narrative which cannot always be expected to correlate with events on a smaller scale. The Derridian view I have outlined, which reads the history of Western metaphysics up to the present as a history of logocentrism, produces a systematic reading where a more detailed approach to the linking of music and language in eighteenth-century discourse is also required. Even if one were to entertain the possibility of a deconstructive reading of the history of music and the voice, it would still be necessary to explore the particularities of musical understanding during a given period, particularities that may escape or be left unaccounted for by the overarching systematization of a deconstructive reading. Thomas Kavanagh has remarked on the current appeal of all-encompassing visions: "the contemporary preoccupation with theory has had as one of its effects the displacing of interest away from what is specific to any individual work and toward presuppositions and systemic cogency of the theoretical constructs that allow us to carry out our analyses."[25] Echoing Kavanagh's comments, I do not wish to take a position against theory, for of course to do so would also

proche de ce qui dans la 'pensée' comme logos a rapport au 'sens,' le produit, le reçoit, le dit, le 'rassemble'" (Jacques Derrida, *De la grammatologie* [Paris: Editions de Minuit, 1967], 21).

24 *Encyclopédie*, 1:xij.
25 Thomas M. Kavanagh, Introduction, *The Limits of Theory*, ed. Thomas M. Kavanagh (Stanford: Standford University Press, 1989), 2–3.

be a theoretical stance. I simply want to insist that the global explanation is acceptable only as a global explanation, not as a substitute for understanding the contingencies of individual moments and texts.

Commentators have frequently judged referential or expressive theories of a musical "language" as inferior or misguided. Contemporary critics and musicologists see instrumental music as the telos of all music, and non-representational aesthetics as the welcome replacement for outmoded mimetic paradigms for the arts. While this position undoubtedly reveals what aesthetic theory has come to expect from music, it also forces our reading of eighteenth-century discourse on music. Upon closer inspection, it is possible to argue that eighteenth-century conceptions of music do not always abide by the polemical categories and historical narratives invented by Romantic and post-Romantic theorists in order to stake a claim for their aesthetics of detachment from meaning or from ideology. The simple opposition of representational versus absolute music that is the touchstone of most critics even to this day is part of an outmoded polemic which necessarily disregards the complexity of eighteenth-century writings on music – the texts of Rousseau, Diderot, and Condillac that are the focus of this study. Furthermore, as Christopher Norris argues, the organicist vision of an absolute art is, like the mimetic art it condemned, "a version of aesthetic ideology in so far as it ignores the ontological difference between word and world."[26] Norris takes issue with the notion that "art can actually *achieve* that state of 'unmediated expressiveness' that often features in high-Romantic claims for the superiority of symbol over allegory, or for metaphor as a trope that transcends the limitations of other, more prosaic devices like metonymy."[27] By claiming that non-mimetic or non-representational theories transcend the traditional bounds of art, commentators ignore the fact that absolute music is itself ideologically bound. Furthermore, the ideology that promotes absolute music is, *a priori*, complicitous with the views of music theorists and semioticians who would isolate music from language because of its lack of semantics. Such thinking in most cases also blinds the critic to the wider cultural significance of music theory. My intention is not to argue against absolute music or to praise mimesis. Both could be said to exhibit a version of what Christopher Norris, after Paul de Man, calls "aesthetic ideology." I hope to show that commentators' assumptions about aesthetic detachment have led them to ignore the possibility of a more contextual reading of music and its discourses, to put forward absolute music more or less unaware

---

[26] Christopher Norris, *What's Wrong with Postmodernism* (New York: Harvester Wheatsheaf, 1990), 217.

[27] *Ibid.*, 216–217.

of their own "ersatz jargon of authenticity."[28] Although we no longer have a trivium and a quadrivium, and although we do not understand music as rhetoric or representation – at least not when we are in a professional capacity – eighteenth-century philosophers and aesthetic theorists assumed and cultivated the verbal paradigm as part of the ways they wrote about their culture, its origins, and its projected future. Borrowing Michel Foucault's concept of an archeology of knowledge, I want to undertake a study of writings on music, a study of the implications of music as voice (and of the voice as music) in eighteenth-century discourse. By revealing the theoretical work that music performs for eighteenth-century culture, I want to convey the unavoidably "engaged" character of musicology and theory.

Although I will refer to musical practices in the following pages, I am more specifically concerned with the theory that attempted to account for these practices, both real and ideal. Musical composition and performance were undoubtedly undergoing radical change during the seventeenth and eighteenth centuries. These changes have been well documented by musicologists. My interest lies with the discourses that gave meaning to the musical object which in turn contributed to a larger context of cultural practices and visions. Although music came to be understood as a kind of language, the emergence of a verbal paradigm for music was accompanied by conceptual shifts within representation, that is within the idea of a direct correspondence between the sign and the external world.[29] The emergence of the verbal paradigm for music, I argue, eventually led to a change in the concept of representation that underlay that paradigm.

The verbal paradigm for music resulted from changes in the way musical composition was conceived and carried out. In the late sixteenth century, a conceptual shift occurred in the relationship between language and music. Towards the end of the reign of Charles IX, the Académie de Poésie et de Musique led by Jean-Antoine de Baïf attempted to re-create and to re-enact what they imagined to be the Greek *mousiké* – sung verse, composed and performed by the poet – in

---

[28] *Ibid.*, 215.

[29] Critics have often confused two senses of the term "correspondence" when speaking of the relation between language and the world. I use the term here to mean a sending or a referral, and not a similarity. As Umberto Eco has pointed out, the sign should not be understood, as it often is, as functioning through resemblance, equivalence, or identification between expression and content (*Sémiotique et philosophie du langage*, trans. Myriem Bouzaher [Paris: Presses Universitaires de France, 1988], 33). Eco notes that the sign is that which opens up onto something else, generates other meanings (59–60).

a verse form that Baïf called *vers mesuré*.[30] Taking humanism to its
theoretical limits, Baïf's group sought to force the strictly quantitative
meter of Greek and Roman poetry onto the French vernacular. Pat-
terned directly on these poetic meters and reduced to a bare harmony,
the accompanying music would superimpose its rhythms onto the
newly created vernacular meters. In this way, both language and
music, acting as doubles, would be conflated into rhythm, which
became the central focus of the linear, melodic music composed by
académiciens such as Le Jeune and Lassus. Unlike earlier polyphony,
which according to Baïf distorted the text, the new music would in
principle act as a perfect catalyst for the textual meters; both music and
language would become transparent to each other, disappearing into a
reincarnated *mousiké*. Although Baïf and his followers had little influence on later composition, his strict coupling of music and language
remained a point of reference for theoretical discussions of music into
the eighteenth century. In his *Histoire générale, critique et philologique de
la musique* (1769), for example, Blainville sees Baïf's experiments as the
origin of a new conception of music: "it is therefore to this so estimable
man [Baïf] ... that we owe the first glimmers of music and poetry."[31]

By the mid seventeenth century, large-scale medieval and Renaissance polyphony and the compositional techniques which underlay
them – those same techniques which Baïf had rejected, such as *cantus
firmus* and mensuration canons – were considered arcane and antiquated. In his *Compendium musicae*, Descartes notes his disapproval of
these practices: "I do not believe that artificial counterpoint, as it is
called, in which one uses such an artifice [imitation] from the beginning to the end, belongs any more to music than acrostics and retro-
grade poems belong to poetics; this art, like our music, was invented to
excite the movements of the soul."[32] Thorough-bass texture replaced
traditional, equal-voice counterpoint, and this new kind of polyphony,
in which a melody stood out against the bass, took precedence.
Marking this change, Descartes likens an older practice in which
composition was dictated by the "artifical" rules of counterpoint to a
formalist poetics such as that of the *grands rhétoriqueurs*. The reliance
on a musical formalism of set procedures and preconceived schemes

[30] In the *New Grove Dictionary of Music and Musicians*, Winnington-Ingram notes that "no
real distinction can be drawn between the rhythms of Greek music and the metres of
Greek poetry" (s.v. "Greece"). Claude Palisca notes that Aristoxenus (fourth century
BC) uses the term *poiétiké* to refer to the composition of music (s.v. "Theory,
theorists"). This imbrication of poetic and musical form is precisely what Baïf's
Academy sought to theorize and recapture in late sixteenth-century France.
[31] Charles Henri Blainville, *Histoire générale, critique et philologique de la musique* (1769;
Geneva: Minkoff, 1972), 85.
[32] René Descartes, *Abrégé de musique* (Paris: Presses Universitaires de France, 1988),
134–136.

which ignored the text had lost its credibility. Music, like poetry, should be closely linked to the human voice and thus to the movements of the soul. With the advent of *airs de cour* and recitative, to which Baïf's experiments can be related, seventeenth-century French theorists placed great emphasis on the solo singing voice, supported by continuo.

Although this modern music was as equally dependent on polyphony as the music of the Renaissance which relied on "artificial counterpoint," the harmony created by the figured bass was principally designed to exhibit, to drive the linear motion of the solo voice and to represent the concurrent movements of the soul. The pre-eminence of the voice could be explained by the importance of the verbal paradigm which now accounted for music's beauty and meaning: as one modern commentator explains, "music was like an image of speech, whose rhythm and accent were reinforced, sustained, enlivened."[33] Music was associated with, revealed, and even created a narrative progression: it told a story in conjunction with or in addition to the text. As Brossard remarked from the vantage point of the turn of the eighteenth century, music had become closer, even wedded, to the language it sang: "*antiquo-moderna* music is the solemn and serious music in several parts which prevailed since Guido of Arezzo until the beginning of the last century; truly *modern* music is that which we have begun to perfect over the past 50 or 60 years, making it gayer, more expressive, and better suited to the long and short syllables of the text."[34] Accompanying this shift of emphasis from the old-style harmony to the new thorough-bass composition for which the melodic line was all-important, music theory reorganized the discourse in which it defined and gave meaning to its object. Since Boethius (470?–525), music had been divided into three categories or levels of meaning – *musica mundana, humana,* and *instrumentalis.* The lowest level, *musica instrumentalis,* consisted of vocal and instrumental music, and could be used to demonstrate the ratios that governed all three categories of "music." *Musica humana,* the middle level, referred to the harmonious relationship between the body and the soul, and the balance and symmetry in the arrangement of the organs and members of the body. The highest level, *musica mundana* (the music of the spheres), directed the movements of the heavens, the earth, and its elements and seasons.[35] Marking a distance from Boethius' conceptions, an early seventeenth-century theorist rearranged these classifications which organized music into genera and species. Nicolas

---

[33] Georges Snyders, *Le Goût musical en France aux XVIIe et XVIIIe siècles* (Paris: Vrin, 1968), 20.

[34] Sébastien de Brossard, *Dictionnaire de musique* (Paris: n.p., 1705), 60.

[35] Seay, *Music in the Medieval World,* 17–20.

Bergier reduced the importance of cosmology and undertook, in theory, the realignment of music toward the voice that Brossard remarked in compositional style.[36] In his *Musique speculative*, Bergier divided music into three categories very different from those of Boethius: first, music addressing itself solely to the senses, such as the noise birds make, which is without (human) proportion or measure; second, music accessible only to the the understanding, which groups together the old *mundana* and *humana*; and third, music to be heard and understood, in other words what we commonly call music. After devoting a scant few pages to the first two categories, the rest of Bergier's treatise is devoted to the last category, vocal and instrumental music, divided into *musique rithmique, prosodique,* and *harmonique.* Not only is it clear that macrocosmic divisions have been set aside, but the object of the greater part of *La Musique speculative* is precisely those categories that refer to a linear music conceived of in conjunction with language: the *rithmique* and the *prosodique.* Bergier is careful to distinguish pleasing noise, which can be found in nature and concerns only the physical senses, from true music, which has meaning and thus affects the whole being. In the categories it creates, Bergier's treatise de-emphasizes the cosmological or mathematical concerns of the quadrivium, and relocates music within the rhetorical and the human. Bergier was neither the first nor the only theorist to question earlier theory, but his work testifies to the new discourses being developed by "modern" music theory. If composers had stopped writing music designed to express the hierarchical intricacies of the universe in order to place more attention on the movement of the voice, theorists also had to develop a discourse that would emphasize the verbal and rhetorical concerns of the new music.

Through the way in which it reorganized the categories of "musicology," Bergier's treatise testifies to the displacement of the antiquated hierarchical and macrocosmic visions that did not easily conform to new conceptions of music. Not only did performance and compositional practice change drastically in the seventeenth century, but theoreticians, who nonetheless borrowed elements from earlier metaphysical systems – whether Greek, medieval, or humanist – began thinking of music in terms that were common to language theory, rearranging and discarding the elements of earlier theories which no longer seemed admissible. The new conception of a musical language was haunted by an image of ancient performance practice – that of the singer accompanying himself on the lyre. Centered around the solo voice, the new music, rhythmic and prosodic, was seen as continuing

---

[36] See Nicolas Bergier, *La Musique speculative* (Cologne: Arno Volk, 1970). Bergier was born in 1557 and died in 1623. The date of his treatise is not known.

or re-creating the texture and spirit of ancient Greek music.[37] In *L'Art de bien chanter* (1679), Bénigne de Bacilly reinforced this image of performance by insisting that the theorbo was preferable to the viol and the harpsichord for accompanying solo voice because it did not do violence to vocal clarity.[38] Imagined to be something resembling the Greek *mousiké*, music was thought of and written as a double to language and this vocal or operatic song had become the model for all music.

The rise of a musical language and a long-standing "fantasy" about Greek civilization and the place of music in that culture naturally led to rhetorical concerns. The meanings that Greek writings attributed to music undoubtedly lent weight to the idea of perfecting a modern musical "language." Even as late as 1754, the abbé François Arnaud in his *Lettre sur la musique à Monsieur le compte de Caylus* hoped to offer musicians "a musical rhetoric," based on Quintilian: "I examine all the tropes, all the figures, that music uses, like eloquence, to please, to touch & to persuade."[39] During the seventeenth and eighteenth centuries music theorists relied on the remnants of Greco-Roman theory and accounts of performance practice in order to imagine a music of enormous rhetorical and affective force. Writers shifted their thoughts on music from cosmological speculation to theories of the universal musical proportion of *Homo sapiens* – the specifically human production of voice and melody, and the effects that these produce on the body and the soul.[40] Through the narrative and rhetorical manipu-

[37] Some writers were uneasy about the relationship between their modern music and what they imagined as Greek music. Constantly comparing contemporary music with their image of Greek monody, some theorists were not always convinced of the superiority of their own opera and instrumental music. Speaking of certain authors' desire to explain away the impressive accounts of Greek music, Rousseau notes that "the majority of these opinions are founded on the conviction that we harbor concerning the excellence of our *music*, & on the scorn that we have for that of the ancients. But is this scorn as well founded as we claim?" (Jean-Jacques Rousseau, *Dictionnaire de musique* [Paris: Veuve Duchesne, 1768], s.v. "Musique"). For Blainville also, Greek music "must have had a beauty of expression in poetic subjects which might lead us to reflect on our own" (*Histoire générale*, 36).

[38] Bénigne de Bacilly, *L'Art de bien chanter* (1679; Geneva: Minkoff, 1974), 18.

[39] L'abbé François Arnaud, *Lettre sur la musique à Monsieur le compte de Caylus* (n.p.: n.p., 1754), 3, 33.

[40] It is interesting to note that this discourse on the passions allows the seventeenth century to reappropriate the medieval category of *musica humana*. In other words, one might see shifting continuities in the ruptured categories I have described: music that arouses the passions could be considered a displacement and relocation of the conceptual framework of the older *musica humana*. Though instead of forming a category separate from what had once been *musica instrumentalis*, *musica humana*, in the new guise of affect theory, includes vocal and instrumental music. See Neubauer for an informative discussion of music and the passions in relation to seventeenth-century medicine: "indebted to the hermeticism and ancient cosmological specu-

lation of voice, music was supposed to dispose the listener in certain predictable ways. Like rhetoric, selected rhythms, intervals, modes or keys, and instrumental temperaments, could affect the balance of animal spirits of the body, which in turn could occasion the soul to experience the various passions.

Descartes' *Les Passions de l'âme* provided a model for those theorists who considered music to be the vocal expression of the passions, or affections, of the subject.[41] Descartes explained the source and functions of the passions and described in some detail the six principal passions – "admiration, love, hate, desire, joy, and sadness" – together with the secondary emotions derived from these.[42] Descartes is careful to distinguish the body-machine (*automate*) from the purely intellectual functions of the soul. Taken in the strictest sense of the term, the passions of the soul differ from other perceptions in that they are said to originate neither in the exterior objects that act upon the senses nor in the body, but rather in the soul itself. Like other thoughts, then, passion occurs in the soul; but unlike reason or will, passion is the hybrid result of outside influence. Through a complex series of physiological mechanisms involving the action of nerves and flow of animal spirits, the body affects the soul, disposing it toward certain affective states. The persistence of a given passion is due to lingering animal spirits which fortify and perpetuate it. Because the passions trespass on the soul's autonomy, its quest for self-determination, they stand for the accidents and contingencies that threaten to disrupt the stability and universality of thought. If properly managed by force of will, the passions can be directed to good use. If the soul is left to the whim of its emotions, however, it will remain "enslaved and unhappy."[43] Descartes thus stages a contest between will and passion.

In his sparse writings on music, as in his other works, Descartes insists on the distinction between the body and the soul. Like his contemporaries, Descartes finds a specifically human and partially physiological basis for harmony, although he carefully sets aside the physiological as that which simply "occasions" the soul to perceive music. In his letters to Mersenne, music takes on the same mind/body duality that appears in the *Discours de la méthode*:

> lation that Cardanus, Ficino, Agrippa von Nettesheim, Paracelsus, and Giordano Bruno had revived in the Renaissance[,] the analogy between the elements, the humors, and the temperaments was adopted not only by Fludd and Kircher but also by thinkers of a more Cartesian bent. The particular contribution of the seventeenth century was to reformulate these analogies in terms of new, mechanistic models for the circulation of the blood and other physiological processes" (Neubauer, *The Emancipation of Music*, 46).

[41] George J. Buelow, "Music, rhetoric, and the concept of affections: a selective bibliography," *Notes* 30 (1973–74), 252.

[42] René Descartes, *Les Passions de l'âme* (Paris: Gallimard, 1988), 196.   [43] *Ibid.*, 186.

the twelfth is simpler than the fifth. I say simpler, and not more agreeable; for it is important to note that all this calculation serves only to demonstrate which consonances are the simplest or if you wish, the sweetest and most perfect, but not the most agreeable ... But in order to determine what is more agreeable, it is necessary to estimate the capacity of the listener, which changes, like taste, from person to person.[44]

Consonances are more or less perfect, and this perfection can be determined through calculation. The simplicity of harmonic intervals can be judged according to the universals of mathematical knowledge. Yet whether or not these consonances are (physically) pleasing depends entirely upon the contingencies of the physical world and on the different makeup of individual human bodies. Descartes refuses to consider further the pleasure of music, the sensations that the listener finds pleasing. For according to the Cartesian system the physical and affective force of music cannot be made correlate with or correspond to the absolute knowledge made possible by dualism. The above citation seems to reveal an epistemic gap created by the terms of the philosophy which would separate the mind from the body-machine. Music theorists would attempt to fill that gap.

Although seventeenth-century "musicology" borrowed heavily from Descartes' model, it did not necessarily endorse the metaphysics to which Descartes subscribed in its entirety. In particular, music theorists tended to de-emphasize the possible adverse effects of the passions and the desirability of detachment from the body. While *Les Passions de l'âme* was principally concerned with establishing a metaphysics of passion – and a system for the understanding and management of that passion – music theorists retained Descartes' categories, seeking to specify the correlation between musical sounds and the passions. This correlation was understood by Marin Mersenne as a kind of semiotics: "the voice of animals serves to signify the passions of the soul."[45] As La Voye Mignot's mid seventeenth-century *Traité de musique* shows, the task of musicology was to locate and explain the affective semiotics of existing musical components and structures: "since the modes (as I imagine) were only invented to express the various passions of our souls, it would appear that there is some

44 "La douziéme est plus simple que la quinte. Je dis plus simple, non pas plus agréable; car il faut remarquer que tout ce calcul sert seulement pour monstrer quelles consonances sont les plus simples ou si vous voulez, les plus douces & parfaites, mais non pas pour cela les plus agréables ... Mais pour déterminer ce qui est plus agréable, il faut supposer la capacité de l'auditeur, laquelle change comme le goust, selon les personnes" (René Descartes, "A Mersenne," janvier 1630, *Œuvres et lettres*, ed. André Bridoux [Paris: Gallimard, 1953], 917).
45 Marin Mersenne, "Traitez de la voix et des chants," *Harmonie universelle* (1636; Paris: Editions du Centre National de la Recherche Scientifique, 1963), 2:8.

relationship between the six modes and the six principle passions that arise in us: that is, Joy & Sadness, Love & Hate, Hope & Fear."[46] Given the signifying capacity of the voice, it should be possible to communicate the state of the soul in melodic inflections, "all the more so since one can retain the same ratios in musical intervals that are found in the movements of the soul, of the body, of the elements, & of the heavens."[47] In Mersenne's view, music joins universal perfectibility with the contingent pleasure that Descartes could only explain as a purely heterogeneous phenomenon. The movements of the soul and those of the body, once they are expressed mathematically, Mersenne claims, exhibit analogous structures. Sensation, emotion, and thought are unified in the intervals that express them. By reproducing the same intervals that correspond to the balance of bodily humors and passions, music could be used to represent and communicate the affections. This systematic use of musical intervals would not only allow for the representation of passion. It could also generate or alter passion and have an effect on the mind as a whole: "chords order the mind ... polish it, and make it more gentle, and more tractable, as many people experience every day."[48]

Mersenne notes, however, that "no one has yet established sure rules for making beautiful tunes or songs on all sorts of subjects."[49] In order to fill this gap, he suggests the possibility of establishing a universal musical code: "it is necessary to follow & imitate the movement of the passion that one wants to excite in the audience ... [and it is necessary] to use the same intervals or degrees used by the passion that one wants to excite."[50] Mersenne hopes that this musical code could be used to construct a universal musical discourse, primarily epideictic – appealing to the affect rather than producing logical argument – through the proper ordering of the musical elements representing the passions: "just as the purpose of the orator is to persuade his audience, that of the musician is to please the multitude."[51] This musicology, like the philosophy of language at Port-Royal, proposes and seeks to develop a theory of representation within a regulated discourse. Music theory imagines a practice in which the movements of the soul would be represented in the inflections of the human voice; and this representation could be used in a social context for various kinds of persuasion, for making the human mind "more gentle, and more tractable," as Mersenne suggested.

In order to develop musical representation, theorists would have to

46 La Voye Mignot, *Traité de musique* (1666; Geneva: Minkoff, n.d.), pt. 4, p. 5.
47 Mersenne, *Harmonie universelle*, 2:92.
48 Marin Mersenne, *Questions harmoniques* (Paris: Fayard, 1985), 125.
49 Mersenne, *Harmonie universelle*, 2:97.
50 *Ibid.*, 99.   51 Mersenne, *Questions harmoniques*, 157–158.

27

carefully examine the constituent elements of musical discourse. First, the essential affective components of music – tonality, rhythm and meter – had to be reconsidered in order to define a new field of musical discourse. And secondly, once these universal elements of music had been defined and organized into a compositional "grammar," the singing voice – like the speaking voice – would have to be subject to rules homologous to those prescribed in rhetoric. Batteux insisted that music and language (together with dance) share a common rhetorical principle: "since musical sounds and the gestures of dance have a meaning, like words in poetry, the expression of music and of dance must have the same natural qualities as oratorical elocution."[52] This musical rhetoric would be necessary for the composer to build an affective melody – a certain motion together with rhythmic and pitch structures that would alter the listener's affective state in certain predictable ways. Although he never bases his arguments on extensive references to language, Descartes nevertheless reminds the reader at the end of his *Compendium musicae* that "this sort of figure in music [the cadence] is comparable to the figures of rhetoric in language," and that poetics, "like our music, was invented to excite the movements of the soul."[53] If Descartes refuses to theorize the pleasure of music – that is, the relationship between music and the body – in his letters to Mersenne and later writings, he nonetheless recognizes (at least in the *Compendium musicae*, his first work) that the movement of music engenders an analogous movement in the soul.

From this standpoint, as Johann Mattheson argues, a composition should be understood as a series of musical figures – certain rhythmic patterns and melodic motifs – comparable to the figures of rhetoric, each with a specified affective meaning:[54]

Musical disposition differs from rhetoric only in its medium, for it must observe the same six parts as does a speaker ... *exordium, narratio, propositio, confirmatio, confutatio, et peroratio* ... Even in common conversation nature teaches us to use certain tropes, certain suggested meanings of words, certain arguments or reasons, and to keep them in some order even though the speaker may never have heard of rhetorical rules or figures. This very natural mental instinct, which causes us to present everything in good order and form, has given certain clever heads the basis for their rules. Up to now the outlook in this respect has been dark in the field of music. We hope that it will

[52] Charles Batteux, *Les Beaux arts réduits à un même principe* (Paris: Durand, 1746), 270.
[53] Descartes, *Abrégé de musique*, 135–136.
[54] In Johann Kuhnau's *Biblische Historien*, for example, certain rhythmic motifs are intended to denote more or less specific states of mind; dotted rhythms, for instance, represent determination, *orgueil*, or even defiance. The major and minor modes are used in the same manner. See Johann Kuhnau, *Six Biblical Sonatas* (New York: Broude Bros., 1953).

gradually grow lighter and we shall try to make a contribution toward this goal.[55]

Rhetoric is the codified version of a natural mental disposition, brought to perfection and theorization by "clever heads." Mattheson asserts that in music as in language, we naturally use tropes just as we naturally order our thoughts according to certain structural principles which were discovered later. Yet the outlook in music has been "dark" because, unlike the case of language, no one has bothered to codify the natural rules of musical rhetoric. Since musical "figures" are based on the universal nature of sound, a musical rhetoric should form, *mutatis mutandis*, a stable and entirely cross-cultural set of procedures.

Some theorists, such as Descartes, emphasized rhythm and meter as had Baïf's Académie de Poésie et de Musique, suggesting that the most effective way to arouse passions was the varied use of mensuration: "I say that in general a slow tempo likewise excites in us slow passions, such as languor, sadness, fear, pride, etc., and that a quick tempo also gives birth to quick passions, such as joy, etc."[56] Nicolas Bergier agrees, stating that rhythm, as that which gives form to music, has the greatest influence on the passions: "rhythm is the strongest & acts as the male in music, just as melody acts as the female."[57] In Bergier's analogy, the masculine, form-giving rhythm is complemented by the weaker, feminine shapes of melody. A melody, then, must be properly *rythmé* – rhythmic – in order to move the passions. Writing at the end of the seventeenth century, Masson too emphasizes the strong effect rhythm has on listeners: "measure is the soul of music, since it moves a great number of people with such precision, & since

[55] Johann Mattheson, "Concerning the disposition, elaboration, and decoration of melodies," trans. Hans Lenneberg, in Hans Lenneberg, "Johann Mattheson on affect and rhetoric in music (II)," *Journal of Music Theory* 2.1 (1958), 194.
[56] Descartes, *Abrégé de musique*, 62.
[57] "La rime est la plus fort[e] & tient lieu de masle au chant, comme la Melodie de femelle" (Bergier, *La Musique speculative*, 98). In the sixteenth century, the words *rime* and *rythme* were pronounced the same and *rime* was considered by poetic theorists such as Du Bellay to be a kind of of rhythm. Even in the late seventeenth century, Boileau uses the word *rime* to mean "verse." In the context of Bergier's chapter, it is clear that he intends *rime* to mean rhythm: "la Rime, comme par certain act virile, introduict la forme dans les sons, en leur donnant des mouvemens prompts ou tardifs, & des temps longs ou brefs..." (98). Bergier is also taking advantage of a phallocentric metaphor that was not uncommon in philosophical texts of the period. In book three of *An Essay Concerning Human Understanding*, Locke compares the charms (and deceits) of eloquence to those of the "fair sex" and contrasts this use of language with "dry Truth and real Knowledge" (John Locke, *An Essay Concerning Human Understanding* [Oxford: Clarendon Press, 1975], 508). Thus, the male prerogative of form and essence is opposed to secondary, female "accessories."

through the variety of its movements it can arouse so many different passions, calming some & exciting others."[58]

Although certainly not in conflict with the rhetoric of rhythm and melody outlined above, other theorists maintained that, among other factors, the meantone temperaments used to tune musical instruments imparted specific affective properties to each key, in both the major and minor modes. Jean Rousseau, Marc-Antoine Charpentier, Charles Masson, Athanasius Kircher, Johann Mattheson (who believed that pitch, not temperament, was the cause of the key/affect correspon-dance), Jean-Philippe Rameau and others, drawing on Descartes' treatise on the passions, provided normative lists of the affects that were to be used to construct an affective musical discourse, and catalogued the various tonalities corresponding to these affects. Rameau, in his *Traité de l'harmonie* of 1722, explains the properties of each key: "the major mode in C, D, or A, is appropriate for songs of rejoicing and happiness; in F or B flat, it is appropriate for storms, furies & other similar subjects. In G or E, it is also appropriate for tender & gay songs; the grand & the magnificent occur in D, A or E."[59] Rameau lists the correspondences between key and appropriate subject matter (which in this citation appears specifically operatic) for the use of the composer. Accompanying and supporting the rhetoric of melody oulined by Bergier, Descartes, and Mattheson, Rameau's tonal rhetoric provided music with another means of building a predictable, affective discourse.

Yet this utopian idea of a self-evident, transparent musical idiom was already fractured from its inception, since each theorist attributed different and incompatible affects to each tonality. At the beginning of the eighteenth century, Mattheson clearly saw the difficulty of a universal musical rhetoric: "the more one endeavours to establish something positive, the more one finds which is contradictory."[60] In this same text of 1713 – *Das neu-eröffnete Orchestre* – Mattheson sets out a complete list of keys and their corresponding affects while affirming that "at the same time, everyone has complete freedom to formulate different and better descriptions according to his own feelings."[61] Descartes' theoretical separation between the body and the soul –

---

[58] Charles Masson, *Nouveau traité des regles pour la composition de la musique* (1699; New York: Da Capo Press, 1967), 6.

[59] Jean-Philippe Rameau, *Traité de l'harmonie* (1722; Madrid: Arte Tripharia, 1984), 157.

[60] Quoted in Rita Steblin, *A History of Key Characteristics in the Eighteenth and Early Nineteenth Centuries* (Ann Arbor: UMI Press, 1983), 51. I refer to Mattheson because of the interesting shifts in his position on music and affect, and because he was aware of the theoretical discussions taking place in France. Mattheson contributed to the debate on the affects in 1720, for example, by responding to an anonymous article in the *Journal de Trévoux* of 1718 (*ibid.*, 52).

[61] Quoted in *ibid.*, 44.

bodily pleasure being essentially distinct from rationality – returned as a problem for the music theorist. The analytical coordination of musical technique and affect could not be sustained at the level of individual feeling. As theorists attempted to establish positive rules for the correspondence between music and the passions, the unified subject upon which this enterprise was grounded was revealed as already fragmented. Wondering why one finds countless opinions as to the specific tonality/affect correspondances, Mattheson undercuts the universalist position by invoking the idiosyncrasies of individual dispositions: "I do not know of any other reason for this than the difference in human temperaments [*Complexionen*]."[62] Later, in his *Der Vollkommene Capellmeister* of 1739, affect lists are conspicuously absent from Mattheson's theoretical discussions.[63] Charles Masson, too, for unknown reasons, deletes from the 1699 edition of his *Traité* the specific key/affect descriptions which had made up a large section of his chapter "De la nature des modes" in the 1697 edition.[64] While the debate continued through the eighteenth century and beyond, disagreements abound on the reason for the affective properties of each tonality. Each writer had a particular agenda for the discussion of keys and affects; Jean-Jacques Rousseau, for example, would use the affects to argue against the adoption of equal temperament. The possibility of a universal, combinatorial discourse of musical affect no longer seemed possible even if music continued to be considered as discourse of affect.

The seventeenth-century concern with direct correspondences between musical structures and their so-called "extra-musical" meaning relies on the strict interdependence of compositional rules (grammar) and a system of musical figures (rhetoric). The belief in a universal rhetoric and the desire to provide an exhaustive list of musical devices or "tropes" relied on the dependability of rhetoric as part of a musical semiotics. The connection between a coherent musical discourse and affect, however, turned out to be elusive. As Timothy Reiss has argued in an article on changing conceptions of logic and rhetoric in the seventeenth century, the dependability of rhetoric was precisely what was put into question by a new scientific model of language.[65] Perhaps there is a similar hesitancy in music theory. As the writings of Mattheson and Masson testify, in any case, theorists were significantly less inclined to make the kinds of claims for their musical rhetoric that can be found in Mersenne's works. Yet, despite these difficulties, composition and "musicology" continued to

---

[62] Quoted in *ibid.*, 51.   [63] *Ibid.*, 56.   [64] *Ibid.*, 37.
[65] See Timothy J. Reiss, "Problems in logic and rhetoric," in *A New History of French Literature*, ed. Denis Hollier (Cambridge: Harvard University Press, 1989), 278–284.

be marked by a concern for affect and rhetoric. As Elaine Sisman and Mark Evan Bonds have argued, rhetoric remained an important reference in musical treatises throughout the eighteenth century and into the nineteenth. Rhetoric, in this larger framework, "is not a specific body of rules or devices," but rather a rationale of discourse.[66] In his *Anfangsgründe der theoretischen Musik*, the French-influenced Marpurg "claimed that rhetoric included every aspect of musical composition and performance."[67] Later in the century, Grétry considered the sonata to be an oration.[68] Rhetorical issues remained towards the end of the century, even as confidence in mimetic codes waned. In *De la musique considérée en elle-même*, originally published in 1779, Chabanon argues that music may have effects and exhibit a certain representational capacity, but it does not contain any natural or predetermined meaning: "a musical sound alone carries no meaning."[69] Theoretical texts after Rameau, though they may deny music the possibility of determinate concepts or meaning, continue to exhibit an interest in musical signification.

Music theory, now caught between the trivium and quadrivium, also testified to the tensions generated by the divergence of rhetoric and science. In the eighteenth century, the interest in a musical rhetoric was qualified by the hope for a new musical "science" heralded by Rameau's theories. With Rameau, music theory overtly adopted what Reiss calls the "analytico-referential" discourse of modern science, but with music as its object of study rather than as a tool of inquiry.[70] Although he disagreed with some of Rameau's conclusions, d'Alembert imagined the possibility of a science of musical composition consisting of a rationalized set of procedures.[71] Commentators have often opposed the verbal and mathematical paradigms for music, claiming that the verbal paradigm restricted musical possibilities while the mathematical approach opened music to nonrepresentational aesthetics.[72] The argument that is generally advanced

---

[66] Mark Evan Bonds, *Wordless Rhetoric: Musical Form and the Metaphor of the Oration* (Cambridge: Harvard University Press, 1991), 5.
[67] Elaine R. Sisman, *Haydn and the Classical Variation* (Cambridge: Harvard University Press, 1993), 20.
[68] Bonds, *Wordless Rhetoric*, 130.
[69] Michel Paul Guy de Chabanon, *De la musique considérée en elle-même et dans ses rapports avec la parole, les langues, la poésie, et le théâtre* (Paris: Pissot, 1785), 26.
[70] Timothy J. Reiss, *The Discourse of Modernism* (Ithaca: Cornell University Press, 1982), 21–54.
[71] Jean le Rond d'Alembert, *Œuvres et correspondances inédites* (Geneva: Slatkine, 1967), 142.
[72] John Neubauer, for example, sees mathematical approaches to music as forward-looking. He suggests that these approaches were more useful than verbal or affect theories "when confronting the new music [classical music?], which had no definite

32

associates the verbal paradigm with mimesis and the mathematical paradigm with non-representational art, with the play of "pure form." As I suggested at the outset, this binary opposition is at best an oversimplification. One could argue, for example, that the rhetorical use of music in the late eighteenth century is concerned with eloquence and persuasion, operations involving the indeterminate values of consensus or community rather than preconceived, determinate contents. In any event, I see evidence that rhetoric and science were not always components of mutually exclusive epistemologies. The two paradigms appear to coexist during part of the seventeenth and eighteenth centuries, offering two different discourses on music for varying theoretical purposes. D'Alembert, while affirming that music is a kind of language, at the same time asserts a formalist approach to music, suggesting that with more scientific knowledge of the musical object, composers could "construct" increasingly perfect compositions: "making music would be like manufacturing glasses."[73] Together with a growing confidence in the possibility of a science of music, the interest music theorists paid to rhetoric through the mid eighteenth century suggests that they hoped to join social grace with virtue through the consistency of musical representation and its effects. Although many theorists had given up on neo-classical mimesis by the end of the century, the effects of music on the emotions and its possible political and civic uses were still of the utmost concern. From this standpoint, music could continue to be useful in the formation of communities and consensus however indeterminate its emotional content, and perhaps precisely because of this indeterminacy.

Though the project of an exhaustive classification of the figures of musical rhetoric failed, the affective uses of music nonetheless brought to the fore issues of representation, communication, and the place of music in culture. The emphasis on a musical language and rhetoric reveals a considerable cultural investment in music. More specifically, as I want to argue in the following chapters, music was a site from which culture itself – its origins and functions – could be theorized, its problems recast and its ideals articulated.

representational content" (*The Emancipation of Music*, 7). Given the fact that Neubauer is concerned with the ideological stances taken by the discourses that explain what music is and what it does, one might treat with a certain amount of skepticism the assertion that one kind of music does *in fact* have representational content whereas another does not.

[73] "Il en serait alors de la musique comme de la construction de lunettes" (d'Alembert, *Œuvres et correspondances inédites*, 142).

2

Origins

Relying heavily on the book of Genesis and on biblical hermeneutics, seventeenth-century theorists sought to recapture or re-create the transparence of knowledge to expression that characterized the biblical origin. In *An Essay Towards a Real Character and a Philosophical Language* (1668), John Wilkens asserts that language was the work of divine fiat: "And 'tis evident enough that the first Language was *con-created* with our first Parents, they immediately understanding the voice of God speaking to them in the Garden."[1] Just as Adam and Eve were given language by God, they also must have received music in the same way; this is the supposition that introduces Jean Rousseau's 1687 treatise on the viol: "if we begin with our first Father after his creation, we will find that having been given the most admirable understanding of the mind & the most perfect physical dexterity, he possessed all the Sciences & all the Arts in their perfection, & consequently music as well."[2] The voice of God, music, language, and understanding are conflated, all immediately present to Adam in the Garden. Whether directly infused into Adam ("con-created") or invented by him, music is described as an emanation or a direct result of being: "one can answer that Adam sung the praises of God, & consequently that he invented Music, or that he received it through divine inspiration, like the other forms of knowledge, seeing that there seems to be no other possibility: one can reasonably say the same thing of our Savior."[3] Mersenne shows Adam singing God's praise after the Creation and uses this lyrical moment to support a theory of the origin of music. Uniting the perfection of all the arts and sciences, Adam possessed a perfect and complete understanding, and this fullness generates song. Language, music, and knowledge were all unified in a single, divine origin.

The original character, lost after the deluge, was considered a direct reflection, an imprint, of the nature of the world and reproduced the

---

[1] John Wilkens, *An Essay Towards a Real Character and a Philosophical Language* (London: John Martin, 1668), 2.

[2] Jean Rousseau, *Traité de la viole* (1687; Amsterdam: Antiqua, 1965), 2.

[3] Mersenne, *Questions harmoniques*, 136.

internal structure of all things and the logic of their interrelationships.[4] The language created along with Adam not only commanded the immediacy and fullness of being, but also served as an epistemological map extending to all realms of knowledge. Modern languages, however, had been hopelessly confused and scattered about the globe following the construction of Babel. The recovery of the original character or the creation of a philosophical character thus became an important goal for philosophy. Descartes had shown that thought was the innate gift of all thinking subjects, and the authors of the Port-Royal logic carried Descartes' insight into the realm of signs: since words are signs of thought, and since reason is universal, one must be able to find latent traces of this universal reason in every language, and to construct a universal grammar that would be one with logic. Many seventeenth-century language theorists sought to rediscover, or to artificially re-create, this language in which naming would be identical to defining and understanding.

The history of music as represented by seventeenth- and eighteenth-century music theory also refers to a loss (like language's Babel), and to a desire for perfecting a universal music.[5] In *La Musique universelle* (1658), Antoine Ducousu uses the anecdotes of the historians of Greek and Roman culture to support assertions about the power of ancient music. In order to prove music's "natural power [*naïfve puissance*] & secret energy," he relates the historians' account "that in the city of Amasya in Hellespont, Pythagoras healed a child who had almost died of drinking too much with a song in the

---

[4] For a general introduction to the many facets of language theory during the seventeenth century, see Paul Cornelius, *Languages in Seventeenth- and Early Eighteenth-Century Imaginary Voyages* (Geneva: Droz, 1965), and M. M. Slaughter, *Universal Languages and Scientific Taxonomy in the Seventeenth Century* (Cambridge: Cambridge University Press, 1982). For an introduction to eighteenth-century debates, see Aarsleff, *From Locke to Saussure*, 278–292, 146–209; and G. A. Wells, *The Origin of Language: Aspects of the Discussion from Condillac to Wundt* (La Salle, Illinois: Open Court, 1987). Sylvain Auroux's *La Sémiotique des encyclopédistes* (Paris: Payot, 1979) is a comprehensive and invaluable study of language theory in the eighteenth century.

[5] It is important to note that music history as we conceive of it today only begins to emerge, at least in France, in the early eighteenth century. The first history of music in French, Bourdelot's and Bonnet's *Histoire de la musique et de ses effets* (Paris: Cochart, 1715), wasn't published until the early eighteenth century. Perhaps the emergence of this field could be related to the notion of progress that empiricism fosters. W. D. Allen asserts, in a pan-European perspective, that the "history of music, during the eighteenth century, came to regard music as *an* art that had 'developed' in the course of time. This was a radical departure from the spirit and methods of Praetorius, who set out, in 1615, to study musical arts from a polyhistorical point of view." (Warren Dwight Allen, *Philosophies of Music History* [New York: American Book Company, 1939], 184).

Phrygian mode."[6] The Greeks had perhaps retained some of the original power and secrets of the first music. Mersenne, however, is skeptical of accounts such as that of Ducousu:

Thus, it is possible that the Ancients wrote in praise of the effects of Music, not as it was, but as it would have been, had it achieved the perfection they imagined for it, so as to incite Musicians to seek musical effects, & to form an idea of the perfect Musician, just as Cicero created an idea of the perfect Orator, & others imagined the perfect Poet, the perfect Captain, & the perfect Courtesan.[7]

Perhaps truly harmonious music perished with Adam. Perhaps even the effects of Greek music, which constituted the imaginary reference point for music theory from the early seventeenth century into the eighteenth (since no original Greek music had yet been deciphered), were only a metaphor for the music of the Creation. Even if the lost power of ancient music could be explained away as a trope, the notion of perfection, however, remained an essential part of the vocabulary of theorists such as Mersenne.[8] In the seventeenth century, the quest for perfection was framed as a search for the essential, pre-existing, universal elements of music. Just as Port-Royal found the logic behind language, theorists generally viewed the basic elements of music as universal, since all music was considered to be based on "relations [*rapports*] and proportions."[9] Since these elements came to be known to us through the reason of the soul, in a nostalgia for what Augustine called "eternal and unchanging" numbers, music based upon them was likewise unchanging.[10] These universal "numbers," whether at

---

[6] Antoine Ducousu, *La Musique universelle, contenant toute la pratique et toute la théorie* (Paris: Robert Ballard, 1658), 5.

[7] Mersenne, *Questions harmoniques*, 196.

[8] Many writers imagined that music had been restored to its ancient grandeur with Lully. Those who spoke of the history of French music refer to the dark ages which preceded Lully's arrival in France: "in opera, we have *Lully*, a man beyond compare, a man whose equal we would seek in vain in the sixteen centuries that preceded him" (Le Cerf de la Viéville, *Comparaison de la musique italienne et de la musique française* [1705–06; Geneva: Minkoff, 1972], 197). Blainville would later reproduce a similar view of music history, speaking of Michel Lambert, a composer and older contemporary of Lully, as "the first man in France who brought music out of the shapeless mass of counterpoint, who created pleasant songs..." (Charles Henri Blainville, *L'Esprit de l'art musical ou reflections sur la musique* [1754; Geneva: Minkoff, 1974], 32). There is clearly an effort to recapture or to re-create what Blainville called "pleasant songs," expressing a specifically human order through the language of song, as opposed to the abject order of counterpoint. This effort would continue to shape music theory throughout the next century.

[9] Bergier, *La Musique speculative*, 16.

[10] Augustine, *On Music*, trans. Robert Catesby Taliaferro, in *Writings*, vol. 2 (Washington, DC: Catholic University of America Press, 1947), 361.

the surface or latent in the structure, were present in the musics of every culture throughout the world:

> for the Canadians use our intervals, & they often sing in this way – F, C, E, D, C – without further raising or lowering [the tone]. And if one looks to all other nations, one will find that they use our intervals because these intervals are natural. One would have to say the same thing of chords as of intervals, since the octave pleases everyone.[11]

Christian Huygens takes this universalizing logic to its limits in his essay entitled *La Pluralité des mondes*, which was republished several times in France early in the eighteenth century. Huygens asserts that if one accepts the cosmology of Copernicus, then there must be other planets which are inhabited like our own. He goes on to suggest that the people of other planets probably also have music, a music which must necessarily be built according to universal principles: "all consonances are composed of a certain relation which is always the same ... that is why one finds the same intervals in every Nation, whether they move their voices in conjunct steps, or whether they leap from note to note."[12] Huygens sees music as the same throughout the world because he locates the essence of music in sounds and proportions that are naturally reproduced in the human voice. With these universal musical elements as given, it could be possible to tap them in order to create a code, supported by mathematical principles, yet capable of forming a universal "language." It is this aspect of music – its combinatorial possibilities – which explains the presence of a lunar tone-language in both Francis Godwin's *The Man in the Moone* and in Cyrano de Bergerac's *L'Autre monde*. In his music theory, Mersenne went as far as to calculate "all 720 possible permutations of Ut Re Mi Fa Sol La" in view of creating the perfect song.[13] Mersenne's exhaustive research into the universals behind musical practice reveals concerns similar to those of Leibniz, who hoped to devise a "characteristic by which all concepts and things can be put into beautiful order, and ... one whose signs or characters serve the same purpose that arithmetical signs serve for numbers."[14]

From Wilkens to Jean-Jacques Rousseau, from Leibniz to Condillac, an epistemological shift occurred, displacing interest from the dream

---

[11] Mersenne, *Questions harmoniques*, 136.

[12] "Toutes les consonances consistent dans un certain rapport qui est toujours le même ... c'est pourquoy l'on trouve les mêmes intervales de tons chez toutes les Nations, soit qu'ils conduisent leur voix par des degrez de sons conjoints, soit qu'ils aillent comme par saut" (Christian Huygens, *La Pluralité des mondes*, trans. M. Dufour [Paris: Moreau, 1702], 144–145).

[13] H. F. Cohen, *Quantifying Music* (Dordrecht: Reidel, 1984), 112.

[14] Gottfried Wilhelm Leibniz, *Philosophical Papers and Letters*, ed. and trans. Leroy E. Loemker (1956; Dordrecht: Reidel, 1970), 222. See also Cornelius, *Languages*, 101.

of recapturing or re-creating an original and universal language to the "anthropological" search for the origins of signs and culture. Rather than locate the spark that unites sign and meaning, voice and know-ledge, in divine fiat, the eighteenth-century search for origins sought to evoke the self-determination of human language and culture. The eighteenth-century witnessed a proliferation of essays on the question of origins. The notion of a common humanity was no longer based on the singular perfection of an ideal characteristic, but rather on the assumption of the universal use of signs and speech among humans. In the *Essai sur l'origine des langues*, Rousseau noted that, as the first social institution, "speech differentiates man from the other animals."[15] Buffon, who attacked Rousseau in his *Histoire naturelle*, nevertheless agrees that language defines humanity and, consequently, that the beginning of semiosis announces the end of animality and marks the "birth" of *Homo sapiens*: "the most solitary savages, like other men, make use of signs and speech."[16] The search for origins was thus an attempt to locate the moment at which signifying practices and symbolic systems emerge, the moment at which culture separates from nature. The idea of the origin was a way of "resolving" the difficulty of universality (of generality) and particularity which became apparent when Europe began to explore and colonize, coming in contact with different practices and beliefs. As Pierre Estève argued in 1753, the very idea of a universal language was no longer plausible:

Since from the specific genius of Peoples are born the various idioms, one can conclude first of all that there will never be a universal idiom. How could one give to all Nations the same customs, the same sentiments, the same ideas of virtue and vice, & the same enjoyment of images, when their difference, or rather that of the climates that they inhabit, is the central principle of their existence.[17]

In the place of language as a singular, universal object to be re-discovered or re-created, eighteenth-century "paleoanthropology" sought to describe the structural identity of a single origin in order to explain cultural difference.

As an alternative to a religious episteme which favored divine origins (although certainly not always opposed to it, since many

[15] Jean-Jacques Rousseau, *The First and Second Discourses together with the Replies to Critics and Essay on the Origin of Languages*, ed. and trans. Victor Gourevitch (New York: Harper & Row, 1986), 240. English quotations from both the second *Discours* and the *Essai sur l'origine des langues* will be taken from this edition, hereafter cited as *Discourse* or as *Essay*, according to which text is being cited. In a few cases, I have altered the translations slightly for the sake of clarity.
[16] Georges Louis Leclerc, comte de Buffon, *Histoire naturelle*, ed. Jean Varloot (Paris: Gallimard, 1984), 156.
[17] Pierre Estève, *L'Esprit des beaux-arts* (Paris: Bauche Fils, 1753), 1:32–33.

writers posited a second, "secular" origin after the flood, thereby avoiding a direct confrontation with the first), eighteenth-century writers adopted the conceptual framework of empiricism, creating narratives that would link language, society, and culture to a common origin in human experience. As analogues of the story of the Creation, origin narratives created the security of a stable, singular reference point. Under the influence of Locke's *An Essay Concerning Human Understanding*, these writers asserted that the use of signs was that which initiated thought, memory, communication, and hence the development of culture. Considered as a placeholder for ideas, language allowed for their circulation and exchange, creating the means through which thought itself arose. As Condillac suggested in his early work, ideas existed only through the collection and manipulation of signs: "the ideas are connected with the signs, and it is only by this means, as I shall prove, they are connected with each other."[18] Vico claimed that the common origin of cultural institutions, which was the object of his "scienza nuova," was inscribed, and should be discovered, *in* language: "the vulgar tongues should be the most weighty witnesses concerning those ancient customs of the peoples that were in use at the time the languages were formed."[19] It was by studying the links between signs and culture that eighteenth-century writers precipitated the search for origins. Through this search, they hoped to be able to understand and shape contemporary conceptions and uses of language, and to form a critique and redemptive vision of the social order that is articulated in language. This chapter will examine how music provides important genealogical links for these narratives of the development of language and culture.

As Tzvetan Todorov has shown, at the foundation of all speculations about the origin of language is a search for a *motivation* in the relationship between the signifier and the signified.[20] Stories about the origin of language seek to explain the possibility of meaning itself. By what virtue can a given sign be said to indicate that which it signifies, and how could it have been possible for human beings to invent a language of signs in the absence of divine intervention? How is it possible for language to bridge the gap between sound and idea? The eighteenth-century Jesuit writer Yves André finds the question of the origin of language paradoxical and virtually insurmountable:

[18] Condillac, *Essay*, 7.
[19] Giambattista Vico, *The New Science*, trans. Thomas Goddard Bergin and Max Harold Fisch (Ithaca: Cornell University Press, 1968), 65.
[20] Tzvetan Todorov, *Théories du symbole* (Paris: Editions du Seuil, 1977), 266–267.

How many marvels of an infinitely more elevated kind, in its original institution [that of speech], in its essential purpose as the bond of our society, in the laws of Nature, which are always ready to serve it at the first command, & principally in the surprising property – which will always seem so paradoxical, although so familiar – of delivering from one mind to another thoughts that it [speech] does not contain?[21]

He notes further that "in order to create all the conventions necessary for the establishment of a language, one must already have one."[22] Finally, unable to resolve the question without recourse to God, he concedes that "man received with his being the gift of speech."[23] This interfacing of the spoken word (*la parole*) and being, as Jacques Derrida has held, is an essential preoccupation of Western metaphysics. Speech is the transmitter of thoughts, and what are thoughts if not the fleeting moments of being? The spoken word cannot be distinguished from the being which it manifests and by virtue of which it exists, and, in the view of Yves André, being can only be derived from God. The circle of this logic is thus closed.

Frain du Tremblay's *Traité des langues* is similarly reasoned. After chiding Epicurus, Lucretius, and Vitruvius for the fantasies they invented to explain the origin of language, he declares that: "speech is the means by which men agree on everything; thus they would not be able to agree on speech itself without speech. If it would be impossible to make glasses without seeing, it would likewise be impossible to make a language without speaking."[24] He concludes these otherwise unsurmountable difficulties by reassuring the reader that there is a way out of the logical loop: "as Christians, we do not need extensive research in order to find the origin of all languages."[25] Since words are in and of themselves indifferent to meaning, God was required to assign meaning to words: "all Adam's thoughts joined with certain sounds which signified them."[26] Frain du Tremblay considers it impossible to conceive of the development of language without having recourse to an external origin.

Other eighteenth-century writers, setting aside the presupposition of the divine implantation of language in the soul, looked elsewhere for its origin. Attempting to explain the apparently arbitrary or unmotivated nature of the sign, these thinkers directed their attention to the diachronic analysis of language and to the human experience that

---

[21] Yves Marie André, *Œuvres* (Geneva: Slatkine, 1971), 101.

[22] *Ibid.*, 103.

[23] *Ibid.*, 104.

[24] Jean Frain du Tremblay, *Traité des langues* (Paris: Delespine, 1703), 23–24.

[25] *Ibid.*, 29.

[26] *Ibid.*, 35.

shaped it.[27] The epistemological shift can thus be described as a move away from the re-creation or recovery of objects of universal truth towards the creation of narratives of universal applicability. Taxonomy and universal *mathesis* give way to histories and anthropological narratives. Following the examples of Locke and Newton (both figure prominently in Condillac), the search for the origins of thought and its apparatus in the experience of the senses became the hallmark of an entire generation of philosophers: "our first aim, which we ought never to lose sight of, is the study of the human understanding; not to discover its nature, but to know its operations ... We must ascend to the origin of our ideas, we must unfold their formation."[28] Renouncing the Aristotelian or Cartesian quests for essences ("not to discover its nature"), Condillac asserts that only the steps or operations involved in the development and combination of ideas can be known. Knowledge must be derived from empirical evidence since all ideas are the product of experience. This position reveals the indelible mark of Locke's *Essay Concerning Human Understanding*:

Let us then suppose the Mind to be, as we say, white Paper, void of all Characters, without any *Ideas*; How comes it to be furnished? Whence comes it by that vast store, which the busy and boundless Fancy of Man has painted on it, with an almost endless variety? Whence has it all the materials of Reason and Knowledge? To this I answer, in one word, From *Experience*: In that, all our Knowledge is founded; and from that it ultimately derives it self.[29]

The origin and development of ideas is also the history of human experience, both of which are intertwined with the origin and development of language. Condillac even goes as far as to assert, moving beyond Locke, that there are no ideas without language: "I am convinced that the use of signs is the principle which unfolds all our ideas as they lye in the bud."[30] Language, as a carrier of ideas, or as that which gives substance to ideas, becomes the focus of commentators. Sylvain Auroux has described this common ground of Enlightenment "semiotics": "whatever the particular study in which it is invested might be – theory of knowledge or etymology – the search for the origin of languages describes the *ternary organization of the linguistic sign* ... In every case, it is a question of determining what founds the connection between ideas, sounds, and objects."[31] Since in the

[27] The *Encyclopédie* shows the diversity of views on the subject. While Nicolas Beauzée, in the article "Langue," defended the biblical version against the paradoxical stance of Rousseau's second *Discours*, Jaucourt's "Langage" entertains the empiricist hypothesis.

[28] Condillac, *Essay*, 5–6.   [29] Locke, *Essay*, 104.

[30] Condillac, *Essay*, 11. "Je suis convaincu que l'usage des signes est le principe qui développe le germe de toutes nos idées" (Condillac, *Essai*, 103).

[31] Auroux, *Sémiotique*, 41.

sensationalists' view the whole of human culture, insofar as it consists of an immense web of signifying systems and practices, is derived from the knowledge of language (that is, from a privileged use of signs), essays on the origin of language necessarily delve into the origin of concomitant social practices – from the family to agriculture, laws, and the arts. Culture thus becomes implicated in the search for the origin of ideas in language – a point which is evident in the difficulty Rousseau has, in his second *Discours*, in distinguishing language and social organization, and in determining which came first: "I leave to anyone who wishes to undertake it, the discussion of this difficult problem: which was the more necessary, an already unified Society for the institution of Languages, or already invented Languages for the establishment of Society?"[32] The difficulty was that of deciding which came first, and above all, from where.[33] In this search for origins, natural theology, materialism, and of course empiricism suggested lines of reasoning that tended to converge. If all things came from the natural world, then human society must also be based on natural principles. Language, too, must be derived from the natural sounds produced by our vocal organs, and structured by the ideas imparted to us by our surroundings. If language could be shown to have links to the natural world at its origin, then the culture which seems to exist everywhere there is language would also be fundamentally natural. The question of the degree to which nature and culture participated in the formation of signs, and the degree to which Western culture had strayed or deviated from its "natural" origin, are questions which obsessed the eighteenth century. Even if modern languages were wholly conventional sign systems, perhaps at the beginning, at the origin of language and shortly thereafter, the sounds of words were organically linked to the things they signified; perhaps language could be found to be motivated, if traced back to its origin. Charles de Brosses sought to establish this claim, through the new science of etymology:

the system of the first construction of human language & of the assignment of names to things is not, therefore, arbitrary and conventional as is commonly thought. Rather, it is a true system which is necessarily determined by two

---

[32] Rousseau, *Discourse*, 157–158.

[33] Salvemini da Castiglione in his *Discours sur l'origine de l'inégalité*, published the year after Rousseau's, renounces the search for origins as impossible: "admit that the first institution of languages is beyond human forces" (G.F.M.M. Salvemini da Castiglione, *Discours sur l'origine de l'inégalité* [Amsterdam: Jolly, 1756], 76). He responds to Rousseau by retreating into the doctrine of divine inspiration, eliminating the specifically human origin Rousseau had set out to explore: "therefore, men were never without reasoning, without language, without society" (Salvemini da Castiglione, *Discours*, 85). In the *Encyclopédie*, Beauzée takes a similar position (s.v., "Langues").

causes. The first is the make-up of the vocal organs which can only render certain sounds that are analogous to their structure. The other is the nature and properties of the real things to be named. This second cause makes it necessary to use for the names of things sounds that depict them, establishing between the thing and the word a relation by which the word can excite an idea of the thing.[34]

For de Brosses, the "system" of language comes from necessary and natural conditions. Vocal sounds reveal the structure of the organs that produce them, and the objects of nature require mimetic representation in language in order to assure the passage from word back to object. In this account of the origin of language, as in Rousseau's, the objects of nature seem to be already pregnant with gestures, signs, language, which merely need to be articulated: "most root words would be sounds imitating either the accent of the passions or the effect of sensible objects: onomatopoeia would constantly make its presence felt."[35] The hypothetical situation of two children having never learned any signs and left to develop on their own, which Condillac proposed, allows language to develop from its origins as the expression of the natural world through the body of the speaker:

their mutual converse made them connect with the cries of each passion, the perceptions which they naturally signified. They generally accompanied them with some motion, gesture or action, whose expression was yet of a more sensible nature. For example, he who suffered, by being deprived of an object which his wants had rendered necessary to him, did not confine himself to cries or sounds only; he used some endeavours to obtain it, he moved his head, his arms, and every part of his body. The other struck with this sight, fixed his eye on the same object.[36]

This *langage d'action* or body language, the expression of the children's perceptions and relations to the external world, is treated as the result of the natural imprint of objects on the body and on the voice. Rousseau's characterization of onomatopoeia, which "would constantly make its presence felt," is particularly apt in describing this vision of linguistic development in which objects make themselves felt in language. For some writers the cries and gestures were the natural signs for these objects. For others, they reproduced an intersubjective relationship to these objects. Consequently, our own language should furnish hidden links to the experiential world through the history of its origin and that of the culture that is contained in and grows out of language. Even if it was necessarily conventionalized by human

---

[34] De Brosses, *Traité*, 1:xiij–xiv.
[35] Rousseau, *Essay*, 248.
[36] Condillac, *Essay*, 172.

intervention, all language could nonetheless be seen as originally, and thereby essentially, motivated.[37]

These remarks apply equally well to theories of the origin of music. As with language, the eighteenth-century writings on music reflect a preoccupation with the opposition between nature and culture. As a classical theorist of the arts, Batteux insists that "Nature is the sole object of all the arts."[38] Yet art maintains a precarious, even contradictory balance between the imitation of nature, and the distance inherent in representation; art is "more perfect than Nature itself, without, however, ceasing to be natural."[39] Jaucourt, in his article "Imitation" for the *Encyclopédie*, displays the anxiety of the theorist for whom art might prove to be unnatural: "nature is always true; art risks being false in its imitation only when it takes a distance from nature, whether by caprice or through the impossibility of getting close enough to it."[40] Eighteenth-century music theory is extremely concerned with deciding what is or is not natural about music – determining the ways in which art constitutes the perfection of nature, or on the contrary (as with Rousseau, for example) finding the point at which art oversteps its bounds to become a perversion of nature.[41] Rameau fervently believed that the physical nature of the *corps sonore*, or resonant body, not only determined the harmonic structure of Western tonality, but also inscribed within us – as physical beings – an instinct for this tonality. He described this instinct in the *Observations sur notre instinct pour la musique*:

What is it that drives these beautiful preludes, these felicitous caprices, executed as soon as they are imagined, principally on the organ? In vain would the fingers be proficient in every possible tune, and able to obey the imagination instantly, guided by the ear, if the ear's guide were not of the simplest sort. This guide of the ear is none other, in fact, than the harmony of a first *corps sonore*, which no sooner strikes it than it senses everything that can follow from this harmony, and return to it.[42]

Throughout his writings, to counter opposition from Rousseau and from d'Alembert, Rameau repeatedly insists that "music is natural to us" and that it is found in the harmony of the *corps sonore*.[43] Yet for so many eighteenth-century theorists, the suspicion is that the artfulness of music composition might at any moment stray from nature: "music

---

[37] For a more detailed discussion of language and motivation in the eighteenth century, see Auroux, *Sémiotique*, 48–53.
[38] Batteux, *Les Beaux arts*, 8.   [39] *Ibid.*, 8.   [40] *Encyclopédie*, 8:567.
[41] On eighteenth-century notions of civilization as perfection and perversion, see Jean Starobinski, *Le Remède dans le mal* (Paris: Gallimard, 1989), 11–38.
[42] Jean-Philippe Rameau, *Complete Theoretical Writings*, ed. Erwin R. Jacobi (n.p.: American Institute of Musicology, 1968–69), 3:272.
[43] *Ibid.*, 150.

speaks to me in tones: this language is natural to me: if I do not understand it, then Art has corrupted Nature rather than perfecting it."[44] For eighteenth-century theorists, these questions encouraged reflection on contemporary cultural practices, and offered the possibility of locating the original shape and meaning of culture itself. The eighteenth-century search for the origins of music is directed by two compulsions: the fear of the corruption of nature by civilization through its (perversion of) representational practices; and the desire to determine a natural basis for these practices and to perfect them.

As commentators have noted for the second *Discours*, Rousseau's consideration of hypothetical past events – in particular, the moment at which private property emerges – serves to explain a present state of affairs. Likewise, considerations of the origin of music derive present compositional practices and uses of music from a natural origin, and through the necessary and natural course of events leading away from that origin. On the one hand, voice was given a transcendent relation to meaning, and a continuity is thereby established from simple vocal sounds to language and to opera. On the other hand, the ostensibly neutral, physical components of music – rhythm and sound – were put to use by those writers who felt the need to locate a pre-cultural moment at which the purely physical or physiological could be said to generate the cultural. By combining the transcendent and the "material," the empiricist explanation claimed an authority which had hitherto been the exclusive property of theology. Empiricism, with its emphasis on the natural or material transcendence of vocal sound and meaning, replaced the theology of divine infusion.[45] The natural human faculty of voice provided clues as to how the signifying practices of language and of music were derived from a common natural base – the primordial utterances, cries, vocalizations which established the first social bonds. These reflections on the physiological and conventional aspects of voice (such as articulation and what we would call "pitch") necessarily brought musical considerations into the scope of the many essays on the origin of language. Questions arose in these essays which had previously been absent from theoretical treatises on music. At what point did sounds become motivated – at what point, and how did culture intervene to reappropriate natural sound for its purposes? At what point in human history did sound differentiate into

---

[44] Batteux, *Les Beaux arts*, 262–263.

[45] Anthony Vidler, who has studied the implications of the return to origins in eighteenth-century architecture, notes that there is a "gradual fusion of the anthropological and religious models of origins." Much of eighteenth-century culture reveals borrowed theological elements. Vidler claims that within this discourse Adam becomes the first freemason ("The return to the origins: rituals of initiation in late eighteenth century France," *The Princeton Journal* 1 [1983]: 120).

linguistic units on one hand, and musical units on the other? At what moment did the "cry of nature" [*vagissement de la nature*] become song?[46]

It is perhaps not surprising that the invention of vocal signs is seen as a catacylsm for so many eighteenth-century writers. Breath, sound and articulated sound inaugurate history or provide juncture in many myths of the origin.[47] In the Bible, after the creation of the earth and the heavens, God animates (a word derived from the latin for breath or soul, *anima*) the world with a breath: "Yahweh God fashioned man of dust from the soil. Then he breathed into his nostrils a breath of life, and thus man became a living being."[48] According to Marie-France Castarède, the earliest myths describe the creation of the world as the exhalation of a sound: "in African cosmogonies, acoustical theories are just as widespread as in the Orient: it is from thunder, from a musical instrument, from a violent breath of air ... that the creation is precipitated."[49] Castarède also notes that for Hinduism, the creator is represented as a song.[50] I do not want to suggest that this collection of myths reveals a universal structure. What is clear with respect to the corpus of texts that concerns us here, however, is that the notion of the origin as exhalation or as sound was readily available for appropriation within a culture steeped in the Christian and Hebrew tradition.[51]

For eighteenth-century philosophy and music theory, then, articulated sound was found to be a particularly apt device for the representation of beginnings, of the origin of conventions and social practices. Generally critical of the Greek myths concerning the origin of music

---

[46] De Brosses, *Traité*, 2:5.

[47] As Auroux has noted, theological writings on language and those of Rousseau or Condillac are "far from being as opposed as they appear." Although their treatments of the origin and history of language (and, by extension, of music) are quite divergent, both are obliged to introduce "a rupture between the primitiveness of a language emerging from the non-linguistic universe and the properties of a language that is already born" (Auroux, *Sémiotique*, 58). In other words, there is a tendency for any theory of origins, whether religious or empiricist, to introduce the spark of semiosis – that which sets the ternary structure of idea/sound/object in movement – from the outside. That is precisely Rousseau's tactic in the *Essai sur l'origine des langues*: "he who willed man to be sociable inclined the globe's axis at an angle to the axis of the universe by a touch of the finger ... and it is only then that they [men] speak and cause others to speak about them" (*Essay*, 266–267).

[48] Genesis 2.7.

[49] Marie-France Castarède, *La Voix et ses sortilèges* (Paris: Les Belles Lettres, 1987), 32.

[50] *Ibid.*, 31.

[51] Jean Blanchet noted in his treatise of 1756, *L'Art ou les principes philosophiques du chant*, that the superiority of vocal music over instrumental music is proven by the fact that both life and the voice have the same source in breath (*le souffle*). See Cannone, *Philosophies de la musique*, 211.

and the marvelous feats supposedly performed by musicians, the eighteenth century was nonetheless a prolific creator of fables in its own right, which were slowly being substituted for the old myths. Music would no longer be defined by the anecdotes of the classical writers, and would no longer be a part of the quadrivium. Eighteenth-century "musicology" became involved with theories of language and of the origin of society and culture. Even aspects of Rameau's theory – a theory that is always associated with "science" by twentieth-century commentators – could be said to depend on a narrative of origins. Anthropological fiction thus became a discourse in which music examined itself and understood itself as a cultural practice. Conversely, music accomplished theoretical work for eighteenth-century "anthropology," linking together the argument and conceptual apparatus necessary to explain the origin of language. I would like to investigate this relationship by selecting a few texts as specific instances which will serve to introduce the more detailed analyses of Condillac's *Essai sur l'origine des connaissances humaines* and Rousseau's *Essai sur l'origine des langues* in subsequent chapters.

Bourdelot and Blainville

Presenting itself as something comparable to *De l'esprit des lois* in the field of music, *Histoire de la musique et de ses effets, depuis son origine jusqu'à présent* by l'abbé Bourdelot, and later revised by Jacques Bonnet, was published in 1715 – the first history of music in the French language.[52] Undoubtedly also France's first encyclopedia of music, the *Histoire* provides descriptions of the instruments and musical practices of many countries gleaned from travelers' accounts. This important work addresses not only the history of French music and other European music, but also "that of the most important Nations all over the world" (2). The authors, promising to describe the musics of the world in their stark plurality, note that "not one of our Historians has yet dared to undertake [this project]" (2):

Many Historians and accounts of Explorers tell us that Music is in use all over the Universe; yet very few instruct us on its Origin and progress, though it is very likely that there may be Peoples who have their own principles and particular characters for the composition of Vocal Music [*chant*] and for the use of musical instruments, as well as differing opinions on the origin of these (2).

Bourdelot and Bonnet begin their historical study with a question of cultural difference. They assert the possibility of divergent practices in music composition, theory, and in the use of musical instruments:

[52] For a general survey of French music historiography, see *The New Grove Dictionary of Music and Musicians*, s.v. "Historiography."

"each Nation has its own practices [*usages*]" (437). The authors note that music appears to be one of the distinguishing marks of civilization, citing the discoveries made during the voyages of Columbus and of Champlain: native Americans had developed musical practices "although these Peoples did not even have writing" (48).

While stressing the differences between cultures, Bourdelot and Bonnet initially move towards a structural interpretation of the various myths about the origin of music, justifying their research with the argument that even though these accounts are simply stories [*visions fabuleuses*] this doesn't prevent their substance [*fond*] from being true (7). Fiction, then, is an acceptable vehicle for truth, and the historian can in principle reveal the "true story" which is contained within the ornaments of fable. Despite this argument on behalf of stories and their interpretation – which implies that the many fictional variations of myths conceal a single truth that can be uncovered by careful analysis – Bourdelot's and Bonnet's history of music falls short of postulating a unified *esprit de la musique* and stresses the plurality of customs and practices: "each Nation also has its own character in vocal music & in composition, as it does for public Festivals, which depend on the difference in climates, usages, customs, mores, & in the genius of Peoples" (32). This insistence on the interdependence of cultural development and local conditions can also be found throughout Rousseau's writings. Yet unlike Rousseau, who would never have justified his statement by referring to erudition, the authors support their statement with an immense bibliography.[53] As a compilation, the *Histoire* relies almost exclusively on the anecdotes and apocryphal stories of earlier writers, patched together with a few travelers' accounts: the Bible for the origin of Hebrew music; Lucan and Strabo on Greek music; Marco Polo, l'abbé le Pelletier, and Martin Martini on Chinese music. Most of these accounts either pass over the moment of origin itself, or attribute it to outside intervention. The Phoenicians, the authors note, "claim that it was Cadmus who brought to Athens the rudiments of Music" (109). Voyagers to China report the Chinese belief that the first emperor, Fossius, was the inventor of music because of his comprehensive and innate knowledge, like that of Moses (170). The Gauls are, of course, among the first to possess knowledge of music, beginning around 2140 years after the creation of the earth (256); but nothing is mentioned about how they received or invented music. In these instances, music is either already present or brought in from the outside. Bourdelot and Bonnet simply juxtapose the his-

---

[53] In the second *Discours*, Rousseau claims to read, not in books, but directly into nature: "O Man, whatever Land you may be from, whatever may be your opinions, listen; Here is your history such as I believed I read it, not in the Books by your kind, who are liars, but in Nature, which never lies" (*Discourse*, 140).

torians' accounts of the divergent origins attributed to music. Their *Histoire*, unwilling or unable to establish a universal, empirical principle underlying these stories, resorts to the *deus ex machina* of the divine inspiration theory. Since all nations attribute the origin of music to different causes, "it is better to believe that it was given to Adam, like other forms of Knowledge [*Sciences*], during the creation of the world" (49–50). By the mid-century, the theory of divine inspiration would be largely displaced by anthropological visions. Instead of dovetailing the divine origin with the anthropological origin (mythic or fictional) in the manner of Bourdelot and Bonnet, Condillac's and Rousseau's essays on the origin of language assert that their versions are separate from but do not contradict the biblical version:

> Religion commands us to believe that since God himself drew Men out of the state of Nature immediately after the creation, they are unequal because he wanted them to be so; but it does not forbid us to frame conjectures based solely on the nature of man and of the Beings that surround him, about what Mankind might have become if it had remained abandoned to itself.[54]

In their *Histoire*, Bourdelot and Bonnet rely on the traditional scholarship of citation to construct a history of music, and on the authority of the Bible in order to resolve the cultural differences exposed by conflicting myths of origin. Moving away from the assumption of divine inspiration adopted by Bourdelot and Bonnet, separate domains are established by Rousseau for theological discourse on the one hand, and for his own "anthropological" writing on the other.

Charles Henri Blainville's *Histoire générale, critique et philologique de la musique* (1769) also distances itself from the model of historical research adopted by Bourdelot and Bonnet. Although he includes references to earlier sources – Ptolemy, Kircher, Mersenne, Rollin – he pursues his own argument as to the origin of music more or less independently of the accounts of earlier writers. Whereas Bourdelot and Bonnet simply reiterate the classical authors' enthusiastic accounts of the effects of Greek music, Blainville adopts a critical stance, suggesting that these reactions were due either to the great force of the poetry, or to wine. As for the origin of music, Blainville attributes it to inexplicable, random events: "nothing is more common in Nature than sound; however, its imitation and artificial reproduction seem to be the result of chance" (1). The epistemological value of chance is in fact similar to the divine implantation used by Bonnet and Bourdelot, and by many seventeenth-century writers, in that it explains the inexplicable through the intervention of a gratuitous event. Blainville, however, goes on to

---

[54] Rousseau, *Discourse*, 139–140. See also Condillac, *Essay*, 169–170.

describe the probable conditions in which human beings began to reproduce sound. Although Blainville tips his hat to the creation story, which is dubbed "in accord with reason" – as do Rousseau and Condillac – it would seem that he firmly places the origin of music within the sphere of human experience: "let us return to the most distant past: the gust of the winds, & the breath of certain animals would have initially given the idea of Flutes to our first fathers who, for the most part, lived in the woods & the countryside. They would have made flutes on the model that Nature itself had presented to them" (1–2). In his mention of the invention of flutes and the reproduction of natural sound, Blainville reveals a concern with the natural origin of technology. Similar to the derivation of language from the natural world found in de Brosses' *Traité de la formation méchanique des langues*, in Blainville's *Histoire générale*, nature provides the model which is mimetically adopted by culture through human activity. Blainville tells the story of the human activities that are at the origin of culture. Yet his emphasis on wind and other natural objects, which would ostensibly indicate an empiricist stance on the part of the author, reveal both something of an eighteenth-century commonplace and a mark of intertextuality. Rousseau, both in the article "Musique" of his *Dictionnaire de musique* and in a fragment on the origin of melody, notes that Kircher, following Diodorus Siculus, had attributed the inspiration for the invention of music to the sounds the wind produced in reeds growing on the banks of the Nile. Lucretius, again according to Rousseau, argued that the imitation of bird-calls led to the first songs.[55] By citing commonly received opinions in this way – and probably having read Lucretius, Diodorus Siculus, or others – Blainville hesitatingly forges his own hypothetical origin of music, displaying his erudition and appealing to authority, but avoiding the traditional direct references to Greek and Roman writers. His borrowings are generalized and abstracted from the original sources to fit into his own story of origins: Lucretius' bird-calls become simply the sounds of certain animals and Kircher's scene of resonating reeds on the edge of the Nile is reduced to the generic "gust of the winds." In this version, part erudition and part anthropological fiction, our forefathers simply came across music, discovering it in the sounds of the natural world.

---

[55] Marie-Elisabeth Duchez, in her edition of Rousseau's text on the origin of melody, gives Rousseau's sources in two footnotes; Lucretius' *De Natura rerum*, and Diodorus Siculus, who is cited by Kircher in his *Prodromus Coptus sive Aegyptiacus*, published in Rome in 1636 (Marie-Elisabeth Duchez, "Principe de la mélodie et origine des langues: un brouillon inédit de Jean-Jacques Rousseau sur l'origine de la mélodie," *Revue de Musicologie* 60.1–2 [1974], 77nn4–5). For more on Rousseau's fragment on the origin of melody, see also Robert Wokler, "Rameau, Rousseau and the *Essai sur l'origine des langues*," *Studies on Voltaire and the Eighteenth Century* 117 (1974), 179–238.

Music is already latent in the sounds of animal-calls and of the wind, requiring only reproduction, imitation, or adaptation in the hands of our ancestors. These gifts of nature, adopted by human beings, establish a continuity from nature to culture rather than a violent break.[56] Rather than finding an inherent difference at the origin of culture, Blainville claims that music is the continuation of natural sound just as culture is the extension of nature.

Another chance occurrence brings about the invention of musical instruments: "finally, as men were busy with different sorts of labor or crafts ... the objects that they used could render various sounds & from this, by a happy coincidence [*hazard*], came the instruments that we know today" (2). A second muted piece of intertextuality is woven into Blainville's history here. The story of Pythagoras' walk through the forest, as recounted in Boethius' *De Musica*, was well known and can be found in a number of eighteenth-century texts, including the article "Pythagorisme" from the *Encyclopédie*. While wandering through the forest, Pythagoras heard the harmonious sounds coming from a nearby forge; this experience led him to discover that the consonance or dissonance of intervals was determined by mathematical ratios.[57] In the *Histoire générale*, the forge scene is generalized, as were the borrowings from Lucretius discussed above – no longer hammers and anvil, but more generically the tools of "different sorts of labor or crafts" – and fashioned into an imaginary episode of protolithic discovery. First taken directly from nature, as in the example of the wind and animal sounds, music later developed from specifically human activities. Blainville stresses that because these occupations were necessary for the development and survival of the species, the music that grew out of these activities was an equally necessary and natural development: "since nothing was so necessary as the use of fibers and strings for binding, for joining various things together, and

---

[56] Continuity is precisely what disappears in René Girard's theory of the origin of culture, elaborated over the past thirty years. René Girard sees the origin of cultural forms and of collectivity itself in the sacrificial designation of an arbitrary victim in prehistoric times. In contrast to most eighteenth-century anthropological narratives, the act of designation Girard describes is violent. Following Girard, Eric Gans evokes the necessity of a violent origin in any project of generative anthropology. In order to prevent the escalation of anarchic violence, a victim is arbitrarily designated as the cause of a group rivalry: "the crisis can only come to an end upon the designation of a unique (or quasi-unique) victim if the aggressive acts of the collectivity toward this victim do not lead to the internal division of the collectivity itself. These acts are, as we have seen, themselves acts of appropriation which would naturally lead to the sparagmos of the body ... At a moment when all are about to carry out such a gesture, the fear of conflict is such that the gesture is aborted. This abortive gesture, which *designates* its object without attempting to possess it, is then the first *linguistic* act" (Gans, *The Origin of Language*, 35).

[57] Seay, *Music in the Medieval World*, 19.

since these strings always make sounds depending on their tension ...
nothing was more natural to men than to fit these strings onto instruments" (4). Blainville begins with the more or less concealed authority
of bibliography – the earlier writers whose conjectures he repeats – but
transforms them, creating his own narrative describing an empirical,
natural origin of culture. From the sounds of reeds growing in nature
to the coincidental discoveries of sounds within man-made objects,
music derives from fortuitous, yet natural, events. The *Histoire générale*
represents the origin of music as an unfettered progression. The result
of simple, random, and natural events, music is molded directly on the
sounds of nature and developed as an organic part of human activities
and culture.

The emergence of anthropological narrative

The differences that separate the two texts discussed above – those of
Bourdelot/Bonnet and Blainville – from the essays of Condillac and
Rousseau are remarkable. In Condillac's essay, as in that of Rousseau,
gone is the simple juxtaposition of the opinions of the ancients that we
have seen to make up the fabric of Bourdelot's text, as are the muted
intertextual echoes found in Blainville. In the *Essai sur l'origine des
langues*, Rousseau's argument follows a separate course, and references to Greek writers or to the Bible are used as *exempla* to support the
line of reasoning, not to replace it. One might argue that a certain
distrust of traditional history, clearly present in Voltaire's article "Histoire" for the *Encyclopédie*, leads to the replacement of the notion of
history as collection, anecdote and doctrine, with history as continuous auctorial narrative, as a story of origins.[58] For the study of the
origin of music and language, the conjectural history that Rousseau
posits in the second *Discours* is deemed more instructive than the
histories handed down by earlier authorities: "Let us therefore begin
be setting aside all the facts, for they do not affect the question."[59]

The starting point of the investigation has shifted from a nature out

---

[58] Whereas Rousseau dubs his text an *essai*, both Bourdelot/Bonnet and Blainville
designate theirs as *histoire*. The use of the term *essai* would seem to imply a divergence
with respect to traditional history and the adoption of a speculative historicism. There
are exceptions, however, to this general rule. Laborde's *Essai sur la musique ancienne et
moderne* – dating from the late eighteenth century and presenting, among other
things, a summa of opinions about the music of the Hebrews, Greeks, Romans, Gauls,
Chinese, Persians, Turks, etc. – more closely resembles what has been called *histoire*,
rather than what Rousseau or Condillac call *essai*. See Jean-Benjamin de Laborde,
Essai sur la musique ancienne et moderne (Paris: Ph.-D. Pierres, 1780).

[59] Rousseau, *Discourse*, 139. "Commençons donc par écarter tous les faits, car ils ne
touchent point à la question" (Rousseau, *Œuvres complètes*, ed. Bernard Gagnebin and
Marcel Raymond [Paris: Gallimard, 1959–], 3:132).

in the world, masquerading as the sounds of the wind and the calls of animals, and which imposes itself from the outside onto human experience, to the inherent qualities of the human voice and its "natural" development. In a fragment on the origin of melody, parts of which would later appear in his *Examen des deux principes avancés par M. Rameau* and in the *Essai sur l'origine des langues*, Rousseau dismisses the accounts of the ancients which privilege outside intervention:

I will not examine, with Lucretius, whether the invention of vocal music comes from the imitation of bird song, or, according to Diodorus, from the breeze in the reeds of the Nile, nor even whether echoes, after having long frightened men, could have contributed finally to their amusement and instruction. These uncertain conjectures cannot lead to the perfection of the art [of music], and I appreciate research into antiquity only when modern men can derive something from it. Besides, it is thoroughly useless to have recourse to outside influences to explain the effects when one can deduce these from the very nature of the things in question; such is the modification of the voice that is called song, a modification which must have naturally come into existence and been formed with language.[60]

Rousseau asserts the uselessness of searching for the origin of language and song elsewhere but in the human voice. As he insisted in the second *Discours*, "it is of man that I am to speak."[61] This strategy spans the difference between an imported nature (whether in the form of a divine intervention, or that of the fortuitous discovery of the sounds of nature) and a self-generating nature – that of *Homo sapiens*. In his *Dictionnaire de musique*, Rousseau again maintains that music does not derive from inanimate nature, but from human nature and activities:

Kircher, following Diodorus, derives this term [music] from an Egyptian word, claiming that it was in Egypt that *music* began to be revived after the deluge, & that it was discovered from the Sound that reeds made on the banks of the Nile when the wind blew in their stalks. Whatever the etymology of the term may be, the origin of this Art is certainly closer to man.[62]

In the fragment on the origin of melody, Rousseau argues that since "man" learns through imitation, he undoubtedly imitated the actions of other animals – "thus, he will imitate first the cries of those that surround him."[63] Yet the *Essai* begins from the premise that the importance of vocalizations lies not in the physical capacity to produce sound or to imitate it, but in the specifically human ability to use vocal sounds as signs. Animal noises are not of the same order as those made by humans:

[60] Quoted in Duchez, "Principe de la mélodie," 61.   [61] Rousseau, *Discourse*, 138.
[62] Rousseau, *Dictionnaire de musique*, s.v. "Musique."
[63] Quoted in Duchez, "Principe de la mélodie," 61.

It would also seem from these observations, that the invention of the art of communicating our ideas is a function not so much of the organs we use in such communication as of a faculty peculiar to man which causes him to use his organs for this purpose ... Animals have a structure more than adequate for this kind of communication, yet none of them has ever put it to this use.[64]

Rousseau's remarks, many of which bear the mark of Condillac's *Essai* which appeared about ten years before Rousseau began his *Essai*, foreground many aspects of the complex debate surrounding music, language, and the origin of signs. Unlike Bourdelot/Bonnet and, to a certain extent, Blainville, Rousseau and Condillac have shifted the focus of the search for the origins of language and culture from nature in the world to human faculties and culture, and from past authorities and historical research to the fictions of a speculative anthropology. As I will argue in chapter 4, the focus on the human is at the center of the contentious disputes between Rousseau and Rameau. From the standpoint of a fledgling anthropology, Rameau's discovery of the *corps sonore* could be considered a story of origins, like that of Rousseau. Yet given its focus on the natural properties of resonance that are discovered "out there" in the world, it could also be compared to the story of Pythagoras that Blainville recounts. Indeed, like Pythagoras walking through the forest, Rameau writes that he came across the *corps sonore* as a chance occurrence, as a revelation.[65] The event is not integrally related to the development of language or culture, as it is for Rousseau, but rather to the pre-existing, natural conditions of resonance that are revealed by chance in certain kinds of objects.

Those writers who sought a specifically anthropological origin of music and language, despite their many differences, adopted a common narrative. For these writers who were active, generally speaking, from the 1740s to the 1780s, a proto-language came about as vocal cries were joined with simple gestures; these movements and cries were eventually codified to form a conventional language system of gestural and vocal signs. At this point in their development, music and language were undifferentiated. In other words, speech is said to be musical. Although for very different reasons, both Condillac and Rousseau were interested in explaining how and why the human voice came to have two separate functions – speaking and singing. Rousseau and Condillac sought to account for this separation by deriving both speech and song from a hypothetical "proto-voice." If the point of departure in the search for the origin of music was set at a hypothetical state in which melody and *parole* were one, then the eighteenth-century presupposition that music is expressive of something – meaningful – by virtue of its alliance with the human voice

---

[64] Rousseau, *Essay*, 244.   [65] Rameau, *Complete Theoretical Writings*, 3:170.

comes into clearer focus. True music was always, and must always have been, vocal or operatic. Music without words was considered relatively unimportant, and music without meaning, inconceivable.[66] If the connection between *logos* and music was an issue of some theoretical importance and debate in the eighteenth century, it is not surprising that this very issue is projected back and resolved in narratives of original culture. As Michel Murat suggests, a common origin was designed to explain the history of the separation of music and language:

if the realization of an abstract, "original" structure immediately produces a history of language and of music which is partly hypothetical and partly real, it is because the structure was itself conceived as a synchronic projection of the historical facts, such that these facts could mutually guarantee their own validity. It thus goes without saying ... that music and language will necessarily be derived from a single form obtained through the neutralization of their existing differences.[67]

From this standpoint, one could claim that origins already exhibit within them the history that they produce. The projected point of historical and epistemological origin would allow theorists to reveal, first, an original indifference between language and music, and second, the beginning of a divorce that continues to the present day, though relations have not been entirely severed. This tenuous relation became a magnet for a number of other debates. The divorce between language and music, mended in descriptions of original cultural and signifying forms, also carried within it implications for the history of culture, politics, and social vitality.

A history of the voice would serve to justify current conceptions of and practices involving music; and at the same time, as I want to argue,

---

[66] Until later in the eighteenth century and especially in comparison with opera, instrumental compositions were considered relatively unimportant. Instrumental music could only acquire meaning through the imitation of voice (as in the well-known baroque "sigh," consisting of a pair of alternately stressed and less-stressed notes), or through its deliberate juxtaposition with narrative music (as in operatic overtures). Maria Rika Maniates observes that "it is not insignificant that chamber music was published in Paris at this time under such titles as *conversation* ... even some of Haydn's quartets and symphonies were published under the title of *quatuor dialogué* (Maniates, "'Sonate, que me veux-tu?'", 130). This hierarchy is entirely in line with eighteenth-century aesthetics as a whole, for which religious painting and other narrative works were of greater importance than the non-narrative still life. Even as late as 1780, Laborde maintained that "music without Poetry can generate enough interest to make tears flow, & to inspire a sweet melancholy; but it is difficult to imagine that it can give anyone a greater idea of himself, nor expand the scope of his ideas" (Laborde, *Essai sur la musique*, 1:x).

[67] Michel Murat, "Jean-Jacques Rousseau: imitation musicale et origine des langues," *Travaux de Linguistique et de Littérature* 18.2 (1980), 162.

the elaboration of this history functioned as a process of reflection on culture, its forms and their development. The unification of music and language at a utopian point of origin is the work of an anthropological discourse. The history of music was in the process of separating itself from theology, and the fledgling discourse of speculative anthropology was beginning to produce its own narratives to explain cultural practices as part of a larger order of events. For both Rousseau and Condillac, the point at which human beings began to use signs was the "moment" at which we withdrew from the animal world because the use of signs demarcates humans from other animals. The origin of conventional sound – of music and of language – becomes, for Rousseau in particular, a demonstration of human perfectibility. As he argues in the second *Discours*, the absolute dependence of our ideas on the vocal sounds which represent them is "one of the reasons why animals could not frame such ideas, nor ever acquire the perfectibility that depends on them."[68] Starobinski points out the specific importance of musical concepts (in particular, the concepts of melody and unison) for Rousseau's anthropological, social, and political theories, "so that the history of societies can be considered as a history of the voice."[69] This relationship explains why the *Essai sur l'origine des langues* constitutes an attempt to provide a fulcrum for the unresolved question of the origin of institutions and of the political order, as posited by Rousseau in the *Discours*; in fact, the two act as mirror images, reflecting the origin of vocal signs in that of social conventions and conversely, *ad infinitum*.

[68] Rousseau, *Discourse*, 156.   [69] Starobinski, *Le Remède dans le mal*, 228.

3

Music theory and the genealogy of knowledge in Condillac's *Essai sur l'origine des connaissances humaines*

Condillac is interested in the ways in which signs in general, and language in particular, allow us to combine thoughts and construct knowledge.[1] The larger aim of the *Essai sur l'origine des connaissances humaines*, first published in Amsterdam in 1746, is to rid philosophy of the metaphysics of Aristotle, which is characterized as "a kind of magic incantation [*enchantement*]," and to supplant it with a radical empiricism based on Locke's rejection of innate ideas and inspired by Newton's single principle of the conservation of movement.[2] By analogy with the Newtonian, physical universe, Condillac claims that "the brain can be acted upon only by motion" (43n).[3] As he would later clarify in the *Traité des sensations*, all the operations of the mind are based on the displacement and transformation of basic sensation: "judgment, reflection, desires, passions, and so on are only sensation differently transformed."[4] The growth of our ideas should be conceived of as a natural process deriving from sensation – a series of ever-expanding equivalencies branching out from our immediate experience of physical nature to the most complex operations of the mind. This new philosophy sets itself the task, then, of extracting all of human knowledge from sensations. Yet Condillac tempers this empiricism with an emphasis on language. He recognizes that signs are

[1] The most complete and diverse of recent studies on Condillac and language is a collection of papers commemorating the 200th anniversary of his death: *Condillac et les problèmes du langage*, ed. Jean Sgard (Geneva: Slatkine, 1982). On language and materialism, see the excellent contribution by Sylvain Auroux, "Condillac, inventeur d'un nouveau matérialisme," *Dix-Huitième Siècle* 24 (1992), 153–163. For biographical and bibliographical information, see *Corpus Condillac*, ed. Jean Sgard (Geneva: Slatkine, 1981). See also Isabel F. Knight, *The Geometric Spirit* (New Haven: Yale University Press, 1968).

[2] Condillac, *Essay*, 3. Subsequent references given in the text are to the English translation, with the original French text cited in notes when necessary.

[3] "Il ne peut y avoir dans le cerveau que du mouvement" (*Essai*, 123n).

[4] Condillac, *Traité des sensations* (London: De Bure, 1754), 7–8.

necessary for thought and seeks to reconstruct the genealogy of know-ledge through the development of language. As Sylvain Auroux has rightly commented, Condillac's sensationalism results in a "meta-linguistic empiricism."[5]

Related to this reflection on language and knowledge, several chap-ters of the *Essai* treat issues in music theory, the question of the origin of music, debates on Greek writings on music, and notions of operatic representation. Given that Condillac's object is the rehabilitation of metaphysics, one might wonder why he makes extensive reference to music and music theory in the *Essai*.[6] I want to discuss the place of music theory and, more generally, of reflection on music within the argument and conceptual framework of the *Essai* as a whole. I will argue, first, that music bridges a particular conceptual gap in Con-dillac's genealogy, the gap separating noise and meaningful sound; and secondly, that Condillac modeled his epistemological undertaking on the method of analysis that Jean-Philippe Rameau had already established in music theory.

The problem with metaphysics

The *Essai* is divided into two sections; the first, "Of the materials of our knowledge, and particularly of the operations of the mind [*âme*]" unveils the metaphysical progression of knowledge, from the simple to the more complex operations of the mind (liv). The second follows the historical progress of the faculties from their hypothetical origin.[7] Condillac's argument begins with the equation of sensation and per-ception. Furthermore, it is this sensibility that defines consciousness: "hence perception and consciousness are only the same operation under different names. Considered only as an impression on the mind [*âme*], we may continue to give it the name of perception; as it renders us sensible of its presence, we may call it consciousness" (35). Per-ception is sensation itself, delivered to and impressed upon the mind; and consciousness is the space of self-awareness in the soul, opened and activated by the sensation. Continuing in the metaphysical order of knowledge, Condillac establishes an equivalence between single perceptions and simple ideas. Complex ideas consist of an aggregate of

---

[5] Sylvain Auroux, "Empirisme et théorie linguistique chez Condillac," in Jean Sgard, ed., *Condillac et les problèmes du langage*, 182.

[6] Cf. Belinda Cannone, who puzzlingly claims that the two-fold question of music and origins "only occupies the space of a paragraph" (*Philosophies de la musique*, 47).

[7] In the "Discours préliminaire" to the *Encyclopédie*, d'Alembert repeats this division – first the metaphysical, then the historical – representing the synchronic order of the encyclopedia and the linear order of the dictionary.

perceptions. The more elaborate operations of imagination, contemplation, and memory are created through the coupling of these ideas, through "the connexion [*liaison*] of ideas" (45). Finally, memory, imagination, and the use of signs that these presuppose, make possible and generate reflection:

As soon as the memory is formed, and the habit of the imagination is in our power, the signs recollected by the former, and the ideas revived by the latter, begin to free the soul from her dependence in regard to the objects by which she was surrounded. As she has it now in her power to recall the things which she has seen, she may direct all her attention towards them, and transfer it from the present object ... Thus we sensibly perceive in what manner reflexion arises from imagination and memory (59).

Signs allow us to organize our perceptions into thoughts, and consequently confer upon reflection the ability to master presence, to create time through memory, reminiscence and imagination. The sign allows for the mastery of the moment, relieving the burden of the present through memory and by governing the mind's attention to objects in the world. To represent the continuity of knowledge – from sensations all the way to reflection – Condillac presents the *liaison* of ideas as a chain, each link securely fastened to the next: "our wants are all dependent upon one another, and the perceptions of them might be considered as a series of fundamental ideas, to which we might reduce all those which make a part of our knowledge. Over each of these series, other series of ideas might be raised, which should form a kind of chains" (46). Knowledge forms a network which, once the connections are mapped out, is eminently traceable. By following the genealogy of signs, Condillac suggests, one also discerns the links in the chain of knowledge.

Chapter 4 announces yet again the crucial role signs play in the development of knowledge: "That the use of signs is the real cause of the progress of the imagination, contemplation and memory" (51). Condillac distinguishes three categories of signs:

1. Accidental signs, or the objects which particular circumstances have connected with some of our ideas, so as to render the one proper to revive the other.
2. Natural signs, or the cries which nature has established to express the passions of joy, of fear, or of grief, etc.
3. Instituted signs, or those which we have chosen ourselves, and bear only an arbitrary relation to our ideas (51).

The role of the sign is to provide the mind with the ability to activate, to combine the raw material of sensations: "I am convinced that the use of signs is the principle which unfolds all our ideas as they lye in the bud" (11).[8] The organic metaphor should not be overlooked, as when Condillac argues that we must return to the origin of ideas in order to "unfold their formation [*génération*]" (6). The physical world furnishes human beings with the raw material of knowledge, which is only awaiting the fertile touch of the sign in order to be processed into the network of culture.

The progression of knowledge, as described in this first section, is an entirely unambiguous process in which sensation is transformed into reflection through the logical links between ideas – analogies or, again in Newtonian terms, their force of attraction – produced by our use of signs.[9] However, misconceived language – and, in particular, that of the bad metaphysics of Aristotle – has dislodged our thinking from its original and natural course of development. If we make mistakes in our judgements about the world, it is not our perceptions and ideas that are, as Descartes had held, obscure and confused – for these come directly from sensation – but our use of signs to represent them:

What makes us imagine that our ideas are susceptible of obscurity, is that we do not sufficiently distinguish them from the expressions commonly used. We say, for instance, that *snow is white*; and we frame a thousand such judgments, without ever thinking of removing the ambiguity of words. Thus because our judgments are expressed in an obscure manner, we imagine that this obscurity falls on the judgments themselves, and on the ideas which compose them: but a definition would set the whole to right. *Snow is white*, if by *whiteness* we understand the physical cause of our perception: but is not white, if by *whiteness* we mean something that resembles the perception itself. These judgments therefore are not obscure, but are true or false according to the meaning attributed to the words (24–25).

Judgement is obscure only insofar as the expressions used to convey it are imprecise and ill-defined. The problem can be corrected only by establishing an effective correspondance between language and judgement through definition. In order to do away with Aristotle and to reveal the true course of knowledge set out by nature, Condillac begins to realize that he must not only alter the existing vocabulary of philosophy, but also the imprecisions of everyday language: "I have been obliged to frame to myself, in some measure, a new language. It was impossible for me to be exact, and at the same time to employ such undeterminate signs as vulgar use has adopted" (26). This project would later seek, in *La Langue des calculs*, to map out the network of human thought by using a linguistic analogue to mathematics. Con-

---

[8] "Je suis convaincu que l'usage des signes est le principe qui développe le germe de toutes nos idées" (*Essai*, 103).

[9] For a discussion of the epistemological and methodological influence of Newton on Condillac's *Essai*, see Jacques Derrida, *L'Archéologie du frivole*, in Condillac, *Essai*, 51–53.

dillac already hints at this new language in the *Essai*: "should not words be the same in regard to our ideas in the several sciences, as cyphers are to our ideas in arithmetic?" (117–118). Language would thus offer the certitude of demonstration. Analysis is the only proper model of reasoning; and Condillac would later seek to reduce the art of reasoning to "a well-formed language."[10] *La Langue des calculs* comes to the conclusion, as Sylvain Auroux has remarked, that, as "well-formed languages," the sciences are the ultimate linguistic model.[11] As Derrida comments, this new language would spell out the natural configuration of knowledge: "in guiding its extreme formalization by the necessity of the simple, the language of calculus must reconstitute metaphysics' prelinguistic and nature base. Good metaphysics *will have been* natural and mute: in the end – physics."[12] The notion of reforming language as a system based on the precise combination of ideas stands as a way around the complicity of a badly conceived metaphysics and an imprecise vocabulary. However, Condillac insists that he does not seek to fully dismantle and replace existing languages:

When I speak however of framing words, I do not mean that we should propose quite new terms. Those authorized by custom [*usage*] appear to me generally sufficient for conversing on all sorts of subjects. I would be even prejudicing the perspicuity of language, if we were to invent words without any necessity, especially in the sciences. I therefore make use of this way of speaking – *faire des mots* – because I would not advise any one to begin with presenting terms, in order afterwards to define them, as is generally practised: but, after having placed ourselves in circumstances in which we felt or saw some object or other, we should give to that object a name authorized by custom (307–308).

It is Condillac's empiricism that distinguishes his move to perfect language from Leibniz's idealist project of a universal character. Working from the pre-existing terms of a "global logic of the real" rather than from our perceptions and their step by step contribution to knowledge, as Nicolas Rousseau points out, Leibniz "undertakes not to return to the origins of linguistic systems, but rather to simplify the categories that latin syntax manifests."[13] For Condillac, on the contrary, it is only by returning to the origin of knowledge – the object of

---

[10] "Une langue bien faite" (Condillac, *La Logique* [New York: Abaris Books, 1980], 188).

[11] Auroux, "Empirisme et théorie linguistique," 180.

[12] Jacques Derrida, *The Archeology of the Frivolous*, trans. John P. Leavey, Jr. (Pittsburgh: Duquesne University Press, 1980), 37–38. "La langue des calculs doit reconstituer, en réglant son extrême formalisation sur la nécessité du simple, le socle pré-linguistique et naturel de la métaphysique. La bonne métaphysique *aura été* naturelle et muette: la physique enfin" (Derrida, *L'Archéologie du frivole*, 19).

[13] Nicolas Rousseau, *Connaissance et langage chez Condillac* (Geneva: Droz, 1986), 126.

the *Essai* – that the terms of a new language of analysis can be defined – the *langue des calculs*. Conversely, it is only through the analysis of language that we can arrive at a complete understanding of its origin: "his project consists therefore more in determining how any current linguistic practice can illustrate and engage its own natural mechanisms of development and retrospectively insert itself in a History which then derives from Nature without any discontinuity."[14] By returning to the origin, Condillac will define the exact relation of language to the world and thus inaugurate a new era in the history of knowledge by replacing an older, Aristotelian paradigm. The search for origins thus constitutes a methodology. By way of Condillac's method, the origin and history of humanity would be "visible" and fully traceable in the language itself: "if a language is analogous, each of its states must allow for the reconstruction of its previous states ... If it is furthermore well-made, the genetic recovery of the linguistic states must correspond to the genetic recovery of correct knowledge."[15] If language and judgement were self-confirming, as in a *langue des calculs*, then the structure of knowledge – the origin and progress of ideas – could be fully exposed and understood, and perhaps its future development would thus be closer at hand.

The history of knowledge and culture

In the second section of the *Essai*, on language and method, Condillac moves away from the synchronic description of the metaphysical order of knowledge toward the diachronic analysis of the development of thought and, finally, gives a glimpse of the method that should rid metaphysics of Aristotle and Descartes. Condillac seeks to explain the history of knowledge by telling the story of the origin and development of vocal and gestural signs. By tracing out this history, the *Essai* wants to distinguish the misguided and the proper usages of signs, to differentiate language which does or does not embody incorrect notions of the world. The importance of this section for Condillac's argument is evident since, as the *Essai* insists, our faculties of knowledge and thought are in fact wholly determined by our use of signs: "we shall find that words or other equivalent signs, are so greatly necessary, that they supply, as it were in our minds, the place which is occupied by the objects without" (119). Just as Rousseau claimed that the history of society could be determined from the history of the human voice, Condillac's *Essai* affirms that the development of knowledge could be accounted for in the history of signs.

---

14 *Ibid.*, 93.
15 Auroux, "Empirisme et théorie linguistique," 181.

From this standpoint, this second section of the *Essai* on the origin of signs could be said to encapsulate the whole of the project.

The first eight chapters of the second half of the *Essai* all contain discussion of music, and chapter 5 – "Of music" – explicitly points to the origin of music and its role in the development of language: "Hitherto I have been obliged to suppose that the ancients had a knowledge of music: it is now time to give a history of this art, so far at least as it constitutes a part of language" (208). As a system of signs and as "a part of" language, music is allotted a place in the history of knowledge. Unlike Bourdelot or Blainville, Condillac completely eliminates the sounds of the wind and of other animals from his origin of language and music. The presupposition of the *Essai* is that music and language are properly considered not as sounds that materially resemble other noises found in nature, but rather as artifacts relating to the history and development of culture. Condillac supposes that two children, one of each sex, have been permanently lost in the desert and must re-invent a method of communication in order to survive. In this way, he firmly sets the origin of music, and of signs in general, within the boundaries of a purely human experience; music is a part of an anthropology, for which the sounds of the wind or of the birds are not of primary importance. This scenario – that of the two lone children – works for the *Essai* in the same way as the lifeless statue does for the *Traité des sensations*, providing an artificial *tabula rasa* from which the empirical narrative can begin again. This supposition is both a logical device that guarantees Condillac control over his argument – something analogous to the controlled conditions of a laboratory – and a fiction which, mimicking the biblical story of Adam and Eve, provides the narrative with a clear beginning.

Before discussing music per se, Condillac sets the scene for language and society. Each of the two children, Condillac informs us, having previously been entirely isolated, lived without any use of signs and consequently without the complex operations of thought that signs permit. Each child simply reacted to his or her environment, to certain "accidental signs," which are defined as "the objects which particular circumstances have connected with some of our ideas" (51). The connections between one perception and another were minimal, held together entirely by the continuity of events and disappearing with the events that brought them together. However, when the two children began to live together, "their mutual converse made them connect with the cries of each passion, the perceptions which they naturally signified" (172).[16] Passions naturally generate cries;

---

[16] "Leur commerce réciproque leur fit attacher aux cris de chaque passion les perceptions dont ils étoient les signes naturels" (*Essai*, 194–195).

instinctual bodily movements then act as supplements to these cries, clarifying their meaning:

They generally accompanied the cries with some motion, gesture or action, whose expression was yet of a more sensible nature. For example, he who suffered, by being deprived of an object which his wants had rendered necessary to him, did not confine himself to cries or sounds only; he used some endeavours to obtain it, he moved his head, his arms, and every part of his body. The other struck with this sight, fixed his eye on the same object, and perceiving some inward emotions which he was not yet able to account for, he suffered in seeing his companion suffer. From that very instant he felt himself inclined to relieve him, and he followed this impression to the utmost of his power. Thus by instinct alone they asked and gave each other assistance (172).

Condillac describes the event that inaugurates social contact; but he is also interested in this founding event as a linguistic moment. Not only does the event tell the story of the first act of cooperation, the two children instinctually helping each other in need; this passage also describes the origination of meaning *tout court*. Meaning derives from passion, defined first in the general sense of being subject to external conditions – in this case, a relation of privation to objects. Passion leads to an effort of gratuitous expression: this expression is the natural cry. The natural cry only gains meaning in the ear of the other, becoming communication. Condillac defines the cries of each passion as natural signs because they are instinctual reactions to situations of passion. Elsewhere in the *Essai*, Condillac defines the natural cries as those sounds "which nature has established to express the passions of joy, of fear, or of grief" (51); likewise, "different emotions [*sentimens*] are signified by the same sound varied in different tones" (181). A given sound is organically connected to a certain emotion. The natural cry is the result of a psychological state inflicted on the subject by circumstances. Yet Condillac suggests that the sign could not result simply from a reflex to need and that the principal mechanism of semiosis cannot thus be located in the relation of privation. The sign is the product of a human investment and as such results from and is driven by passion in relation to the other. Meaning is not simply the result of a relation to objects; it is because this relation triggers an emotion of sympathy in another being that the natural cry is noteworthy for Condillac. Condillac locates the origin of meaning in the natural cry; next, gesture serves to indicate the object of those desires crying out to be fulfilled through a supplementary effort: "he who suffered ... did not confine himself to cries or sounds only; he used some endeavours to obtain it." The primary function of the vocal is emotive; gesture then serves to link the emotion with external circumstances. In the narrative proposed by the *Essai*, these instinctual gestures will later evolve into the first language – "the language of action" – and vocal sounds will later develop into spoken language and music.

It is through the development of the natural sign, not that of the accidental sign, that music makes its mark on the history of language. At the very beginning of the couple's interaction, instinctive cries allow one of the children to define him- or herself as the subject of "language" and then serve to link the two children together in a society of intersubjective affect. As Condillac had insisted in the first section of the *Essai*, the constitution of the self, and hence of knowledge, must be concomitant with that of language. Nicolas Rousseau has pointed out how the child's utterances act to define an existence and the possibility of action:

ideas will join together in signs only insofar as, retrospectively, recurring circumstances will represent these ideas to the mind as coming from its own activity through the action of memory, and, at the same time, will open up the possibility of multiplying them at will . . . a reflexive development of which the first language will constitute both a manifestation and an instrument.[17]

Yet the self-reflexive action of memory does not fully account for the development of language. It is the children's society – "their mutual converse" – which establishes the intersubjective link of signification between the sound and the feeling, which had previously only existed as a "meaningless" reflex. One child cries out and lashes about wildly; "The other struck with this sight . . . suffered in seeing his companion suffer" (172). A simple reflex produced by the suffering or joy of one of the children, the natural cry causes the same emotions in the other. Conversely, they serve to define the self as the subject of language, in what one might consider a primordial "mirror stage."[18] It is important that a sexual difference is posited, both by Condillac and by Rousseau, at the origin of language and music. It would be possible to argue that it is the polarity or difference created by the existence of the two sexes that brings forth the signifier in Condillac's *Essai*. At the same time, the linguistic moment of socialization, of acculturation, is also one of repression, since the origin of signs also constitutes the sublimation of sexuality within the cultural order. It is therefore appropriate that the origin of language be traumatic, located as it is in suffering, or, more precisely, in the spectacle of the other's suffering.[19] It is only through the presence of another being that signification becomes possible.

---

[17] Nicolas Rousseau, *Connaissance et langage*, 235–236.

[18] In Lacanian terms, "the subject is constructed through its acquisition of language from the place of the Other" (Rosalind Coward and John Ellis, *Language and Materialism: Developments in Semiology and the Theory of the Subject* [London: Routledge, 1977], 111).

[19] "Il souffroit de voir souffrir" (*Essai*, 195).

What is not actually a language for the utterer, becomes one for the listener who compares what he/she sees and hears with his/her own activity. Nature supplies the unconscious connection – which is also the connection in the unconscious – between the emotion and the sound. Society provides the differential structures within which this meaning can continue to exist and circulate:

Indeed, man will have to begin to learn the meaning of the signs that he gesticulates, and he will be able to do this only insofar as the actions of his fellow companion appear to him as the exact reflection of those that he himself manifests in the same circumstances and under the influence of the same needs ... Thus, the activity of analysis cannot come into play and perfect itself until the moment when the human being places himself simultaneously in the position of spectator and actor with respect to this activity.[20]

The origin of society and reflection is located at this crucial moment where the children begin to establish different subject positions through their utterances. Before this moment, natural cries – which the *Essai* terms "natural signs" – are not yet signs, nor are the gestures that accompany them. Condillac confirms this in the first section of the *Essai*: "with regard to natural cries, this man shall form them, as soon as he feels the passions [*sentimens*] to which they belong. However they will not be signs in respect to him the first time; because instead of reviving his perception, they will as yet be no more than consequences [*suites*] of those perceptions" (52). These cries only become signs when the subject begins to reflect on his use of them, when she/he is able to identify the self and the other as positions of signification. Condillac thus derives the primitive social bond from a natural vocal reaction to circumstances and, more importantly, from the presence of the other child who hears, witnesses, and reacts to the scene.

As they exist before the constitution of society and self-reflexivity, the natural cries are not yet signs; yet at the same time they are always already prepared for meaning. At the origin, an unbroken chain joins sensation, passions, and cries. Vocal utterances are already organically linked to the passions as their natural signs. In relation to these natural signs, the passions have a privileged, double role: that of the signifying force – the necessary cause of the utterance – and that which it signifies.[21] The passions are understood here as the psychic events, such as joy or fear, that occur as responses to circumstances; these psychic events are structured in predictable ways and are repeatable. Needs impress themselves on one of the children, and the passions of the soul, moved by these needs, lead the child to cry out. These sounds then arouse the same passions in the other child: "he cannot hear the one [*le cri*] without experiencing in some measure the other [*le senti-*

---

[20] Nicolas Rousseau, *Connaissance et langage*, 238–239.   [21] Auroux, *Sémiotique*, 34.

ment]" (52). Neither language nor the actual capacity for language are present at the origin; these are the product not of individual makeup, but of the interactions formed by society. Yet at the origin, as Condillac depicts it, the mechanism of the passionate cry already bears an uncanny resemblance to the structure of signification that will later be set up in language. In the *Essai*'s reconstruction of the birth of signs, as Sylvain Auroux has remarked, "language always preceeds itself."[22] There is a grain of teleology in Condillac's empiricism: the patterns of language are found to be already traced in nature's designs. Nature supplies the connection between the idea (in this case, an emotion) and the sound. Henceforth, human choice will take advantage of this pre-existing connection and will later forge the arbitrary link of the conventional sign following the model provided by nature. The importance of this primary liaison is that it is the first link in a series which will form the chain of human knowledge: "thus all our knowledge would form only one and the same chain" (47). The *cris naturels* – the mechanical product of the passions – will later become the model for all further signifying. As the point of origin for all signification, the passions are, to use Condillac's terms, the seed of the seed [*le germe*] – the origin of that which triggers "this displacement of signifiers where memory and reflection, reason and freedom, gradually shape themselves."[23] Passion makes meaning possible and at the same time precedes all signification. The vocalization of the natural cry is what makes possible liaison in general, and liaison is the structural principle of all knowledge. Language is thus modeled on the reflexive vocalization of passion as it is put into social circulation. Nature supplies the model for this linkage without being able to sustain it, to prolong its duration. Only the children's interaction – their *commerce réciproque* – can introduce the connections whose accumulation defines meaning and knowledge.

Out of natural signs develop conventional signs. There is no material difference between these two categories of signs. The distinction resides solely in an act of free will on the part of the subject: "Instituted signs, or those which we have chosen ourselves" (51). Rather than being provided for by nature, as in the case of the cries of passion, these signs must be chosen. Initially, this choice is determined through the habitual familiarity of the natural sign:

[the two children] accustomed themselves at length to connect with the cries of the passions and with the different motions of the body, those perceptions which were expressed in so sensible a manner. The more they grew familiar with those signs, the more they were in a capacity of reviving them at pleasure. Their memory began to acquire some sort of habit, they were able to command

---

[22] *Ibid.*, 32.   [23] *Ibid.*, 34.

their imagination as they pleased, and insensibly they learned to do by reflexion what they had hitherto done merely by instinct. At first both of them acquired the habit of discerning by those signs the sensations which the other felt at that moment, and afterwards they made use of them in order to let each other know their past sensations (173).

As Auroux points out, the difference between the arbitrary sign and the natural sign is not one of substance, but of status.[24] Nature provides a repeated pattern – the connection between sound and idea. The children, through the establishment of a custom – a social habit – appropriate this structure and in so doing learn to use their natural cries and gestures as signs, indications, warnings. These signs then "enlarged and improved the operations of the mind, and on the other hand these having acquired such improvement, perfected the signs, and rendered the use of them more familiar" (173–174). Natural cries, once they are used as signs, begat our advanced faculties of thought, which in turn perfected our signs.

It is precisely this transition between natural signs and conventional signs that interests us. The *langage d'action* – a "language of action" consisting of contortions and violent movements – is the first true language for Condillac. Nevertheless, as I have argued, the cries of each passion, which Condillac calls natural signs, already exhibit, *ipso facto*, the signifying structure of later languages. The passionate cries confer on the *langage d'action* their newfound (as Condillac's genealogy maintains), yet built-in (as we have seen), ability to signify. The *langage d'action* then connects the vocal sounds of the passions with objects in the world: "he who suffered, by being deprived of an object ... used some endeavours to obtain it" (172). Slowly, the children become aware – unconsciously [*insensiblement*] and by force of habit – that they are linking signs and ideas of their own accord: "by these particulars we see in what manner the cries of the passions contributed to enlarge the operations of the mind [*âme*], by giving occasion naturally to the mode of speaking by action" (174). Vocal sounds, which as I will demonstrate form a kind of proto-music, have precedence in Condillac's speculative fiction. It is the vocal, not the gestural, that has the birthright of a link with the passions, institutes society, and imparts its ability to signify to all successive languages. Gestures appear as embodiments, congealed versions of the passionate cries – as *paroles gelées* – carrying the voice into the world. As the *Essai* portrays it, gesture has the paradoxical status of secondary instinct: it is the voice's crutch. The privileged status of the musical cries of passion is that of the seed, of the true origin.

The first two chapters of this second section of the *Essai* describe the

---

[24] *Ibid.*, 30.

early history of the human voice. First a disjointed and unconscious series of vocal cries gives rise to the *langage d'action*. The ability to signify gradually develops from the links to passion already present in the natural cries and from the children's constant interaction. The natural expressions of pain, joy, or unhappiness, provide the material – the gestures, and especially the vocalizations – for what later will become conventional signs: "the natural signs by which man thus manifests his affects represent the very materials that will constitute all his subsequent analytical constructions."[25] A new language emerges from the combination of these two pre-languages as speech slowly comes of age: "these languages did not succeed each other abruptly: they were a long time intermixed; and it was not till very late that speech prevailed" (180). The history of language and knowledge is one of continuous progress, growth, linkage, connection, all stemming from nature – from the imprint of sensations (of need) on the psyche, on the one hand, and from sympathy to the voice of suffering, on the other. The violent movements of the *langage d'action* and its violent contortions are little by little replaced by the "violent inflexions" of natural cries as they appear in language: "speech succeeding the language of action, retained its character ... In order then to supply the place of the violent contorsions of the body, the voice was raised and depressed by very sensible intervals" (180).[26] However, natural cries are no longer simple reflexes, but the product of a desire to communicate and, as such, socialized: "mankind meeting with too great a difficulty in devising new words, had no other means for a long time of expressing the emotions of the soul, than the natural cries, to which they gave the character of instituted signs" (180–181). Reflection and choice have taken the place of instinct, reappropriating the same material sounds as conventional signs.

Music, music theory, and epistemology

Music comes into play in order to explain this intermediate step in the history of language, where natural signs are being used conventionally, before the wholesale invention of non-motivated signs. Music, or a metaphor for music, is what allows Condillac to describe the raw tones of "the prosody of the earliest languages" – the subject of the second chapter of the second section of the *Essai*. In Condillac's depiction of the first vocal language, composed of a conventional mix

---

[25] Nicolas Rousseau, *Connaissance et langage*, 233.

[26] "La parole, en succédant au langage d'action, en conserva le caractère ... Ainsi, pour tenir la place des mouvemens violens du corps, la voix s'éleva et s'abaissa par des intervalles fort sensibles" (*Essai*, 200).

of natural signs and *langage d'action*, the voice moves in intervals and varied inflections – "the voice was raised and depressed by very sensible intervals"; "every man may experience in himself, that it is natural for the voice to diversify its inflexions" (180). Musical terminology has already slipped into Condillac's vocabulary. At the origin of language, warnings, cries for help, shouts of joy, and the lamenting voice of sadness all incorporate vocal inflections and even distinct intervals – what Condillac, and many other eighteenth-century writers, repeatedly designate as a kind of music: "at the origin of languages the manner of pronouncing admitted of inflexions that were so distinct, as a musician might notate it, making only some small changes; I shall say then that it partook of the nature of music" (182). However, if what Condillac describes as the first vocal language, which mostly consists of natural signs, is a kind of music, then the pure cry of the passions must be a pre-musical or proto-musical vocalization. The natural sounds of the voice, which exhibit all the properties of inflection and pitch which will later be appropriated by the first musical language, are a music-in-the-making. The same teleology found in the first chapter on the origin of language surfaces again. The links connecting natural, vocal signs to emotions are already structured for later signifying systems. Just as the link between the sound and the emotion pre-exists any language in the *Essai*, the distinct "musical" inflections that would later act as signifiers, are already present in passionate cries: "the natural cries necessarily introduce the use of violent inflexions; since different emotions are signified by the same sound varied in different tones" (181). It could be shown that the role of the origin is essentially that of a logical triggering device for the later history of language and music that the *Essai* intends to describe. It reveals itself as such through Condillac's inability to actually posit a zero degree of music, language, and culture. As I noted in chapter 2, the origin is a certain image of eighteenth-century culture, projected back to a mythic origin. This projection explains the fact that the primitive vocal forms described in the *Essai* are negative images of eighteenth-century language and music and, at the same time, ideal versions of those same forms. Indeed, the scene of the first conversations is uncannily operatic, bearing a striking resemblance to eighteenth-century descriptions of an ideal musical *Affektenlehre*: "Ah, for instance, according to the different manner in which it is pronounced, expresses admiration, pain, pleasure, sadness, joy, fear, dislike, and almost all the passions" (181). In its treatment of the natural cry, this passage closely resembles the description of the affective elements of music l'abbé Dubos proposes in his *Réflexions critiques sur la poésie et sur la peinture*, where he notes that "each emotion has its own tones, accents & sighs."[27] In this way, eighteenth-century musicology sought to authenticate its object by indicating a timeless origin which would validate, *ipso facto*, the musical rhetoric it was proposing, at the same time, to an eighteenth-century audience of critics and amateurs. The patterns of sound that conform to a rhetorical theory of music were thus already there at the origin, prefigured in the natural cry. Just as Condillac could derive the whole of knowledge from simple sensation, eighteenth-century opera could see an ideal image of itself reflected in the artless natural cry. Reflection on music thus helped to shape and authenticate an image of contemporary practices as well as that of their cultural origins.

Condillac gives three reasons why the first vocal language must be considered a kind of song. Each is based on the notion that this language constitutes a transitional phase, a logically required bridge between the natural, innate ability to cry out, and the conventional aspects of later sign systems. First, undeveloped organs do not produce the minute phonetic distinctions that characterize modern languages: "the crudeness of their organs did not permit them [to articulate] by such delicate inflexions as ours" (180). The discrete intervals of eighteenth-century Western music – easy to vocalize and finite in number (at least in theory, since, practically speaking, the width of any given interval would change according to the tuning system being used) – provided a model for a primitive speech. Secondly, since this language was new and unfamiliar, and since the mind was as yet "rude and uncultivated," these marked intervals and inflections – distinguishing features – were necessary to communicate ideas clearly (180). Finally, since they had such difficulty devising new words, the first societies for a time simply reused the varied musical accents of the natural cry. In his short text, *De l'analyse du discours*, Condillac indicates that music could be said to accurately describe the melodic and metric qualities of this language:

Given the necessity of asking for and giving assistance, the first men studied this [natural] language; they thus learned to use it with greater skill; and the accents, which for them were initially only natural signs, gradually became artificial signs which they modified with different articulations. This likely explains why the prosody of many languages was a kind of song.[28]

In the place of inventing different words, as he also noted in the *Essai*, the first speakers used the same sound varied through different tones.

---

[27] Jean-Baptiste Dubos, *Réflexions critiques sur la poésie et sur la peinture* (Paris: Jean Mariette, 1719), 1:674.
[28] Condillac, *De l'analyse du discours*, in Charles Porset, ed., *Varia linguistica*, 202.

Something like music seems to fit the description of what, for Condillac, must have eased nature into culture. We have seen that the natural cry is what allows for the formation of the subject (of language) at the origin of society, and sets up the structure of all further signification. These vocal sounds, this proto-music, take part in the most significant moments in Condillac's history of the development of knowledge. A primeval song-language is the transition that leads the first societies from instinctive cries to language and reflection. As Akiko Koana has noted, "thanks to this sort of intermediate sign, [Condillac] is able to explain the invention of conventional signs without presupposing the faculty of reflection."[29] The first musical language inherits, through the ancestral sounds of the natural cry, the original link with the passions that was their prerogative. Musicality, in the guise of the natural cry, transmits the authority of a natural origin to the first conventionalized language: "this prosody was so *natural* to mankind in the beginning" (182). In the context of Condillac's system, this musical language could be said to constitute an anthropological "missing link," bridging the gap between the pre-history of language and the development of conventional sign systems. The musical inflection of the voice contributed to eighteenth-century epistemology by assuring the passage from sensation to sign that the *Essai* sought to describe; in this genealogy, the vocal "music" of the natural cry acts as the threshold between nature and culture.

Chapter 5 – "Of music" – bears out this observation. In the first few paragraphs Condillac isolates the gradual development of musical sounds as they occur in language. The history of music is examined, insofar as it constitutes a part of language. This section reveals an effort which, it becomes clear, also takes place on a larger scale throughout the text – an effort to use Rameau's work in music theory to support the philosophical and methodological footing of the *Essai*.[30] Jean-Philippe Rameau's theory of the *corps sonore* was without doubt the most important event in eighteenth-century music theory. But the *corps sonore* was also seen as a milestone by writers in other fields. D'Alembert, for example, considered it a methodological paradigm which, as the most philosophically advanced and most elegant theo-

[29] Akiko Koana, "La Théorie musicale dans l'épistémologie de Condillac," in *The Reasons of Art: l'art a ses raisons*, ed. Peter J. McCormick (Ottawa: University of Ottawa Press, 1985), 450.

[30] The fact that Condillac was the censor for both d'Alembert's *Elémens de musique* and Rameau's *Nouvelles réflexions sur la démonstration du principe de l'harmonie* suggests that he had some knowledge and/or interest in music theory (James Doolittle, "A would-be *philosophe*: Jean Philippe Rameau," *PMLA* 74.3 [1959], 238n25).

retical model since Descartes, could be taken over into other fields.[31] D'Alembert discussed Rameau's theory in his "Discours préliminaire" to the *Encyclopédie* and suggested, in part because of Rameau's progress in theory, that of all the arts music was the most capable of advancement. In his *Elémens de musique*, d'Alembert compared Rameau's advances in music theory to those of Newton in physics: although it doesn't explain everything there is to know about music, the fundamental bass is the principle of harmony and melody in the same way that gravitation is the physical principle of astronomy.[32] At about the same time as d'Alembert was writing the "Discours préliminaire," Condillac singled out Rameau's theory among the many inadequate systems that he scrutinized in the *Traité des systèmes* as one that deserved more attention:

Mr. Rameau has created a system based on harmonic generation which I could use as an example. In it, he reduces everything to the harmony of the *corps sonore* ... Thus, when one observes analytically all the different combinations and movements which this harmony experiences, one will see it transformed into all phenomena which seem to have no rule other than the imagination of the composer [*musicien*]. If this system suffers from difficulties, it is because all its elements have not yet been sufficiently examined.[33]

Like d'Alembert, Condillac sees great potential in the analytic structure of Rameau's theory as a model for other forms of knowledge, and

---

[31] The most comprehensive view of Rameau published to date is Thomas Christensen's *Rameau and Musical Thought in the Enlightenment* (Cambridge: Cambridge University Press, 1993). See also Catherine Kintzler, *Jean-Philippe Rameau: splendeur et naufrage de l'esthétique du plaisir à l'âge classique* (Paris: Le Sycomore, 1983). A number of articles provide analyses of the theoretical and epistemological context of Rameau's writings and the development of his theory. See particularly Marie-Elisabeth Duchez, who gives a very detailed account of these questions and a view of the dissemination of Rameau's theories in "Valeur épistémologique de la théorie de la basse fondamentale de Jean-Philippe Rameau: connaissance scientifique et représentation de la musique," *Studies on Voltaire and the Eighteenth Century* 245 (1986), 91–130. See also Antoine Hennion, "Rameau et l'harmonie: comment avoir raison de la musique," in *Actes de Jean-Philippe Rameau: colloque international*, ed. Jérôme de la Gorce (Paris: Champion-Slatkine, 1987), 393–407. For an examination of d'Alembert's rewriting of Rameau, see Thomas Christensen, "Music theory as scientific propaganda: the case of d'Alembert's *Elémens de musique*," *Journal of the History of Ideas* 50.3 (1989), 409–427; and Françoise Escal, "D'Alembert et la théorie harmonique de Rameau," *Dix-Huitième Siècle* 16 (1984), 151–162. See also Marie-Elisabeth Duchez, "D'Alembert diffuseur de la théorie harmonique de Rameau: déduction scientifique et simplification musicale," in *Jean d'Alembert, savant et philosophe: portrait à plusieurs voix*. Monique Emery and Pierre Monzani (Paris: Editions des Archives Contemporaines, 1989), 475–496.

[32] D'Alembert, *Elémens de musique* (1779; Plan-de-la-Tour: Editions d'Aujourd'hui, 1984), 222. Though it is not central to the similarities d'Alembert perceived in the two theories, it is also interesting to note that for Newton, white light was a composite of seven colors.

[33] Condillac, *Œuvres* (Paris: Chez les Libraires Associés, 1777), 2:296n.

in particular for understanding and for perfecting the other arts. In his praise of Rameau, Condillac appears to view his own *Essai* as undertaking for metaphysics what Rameau had already successfully accomplished for music theory: "Mr. Rameau is the first who discovered the source of all harmony in the resonance of sonorous bodies, reducing the theory of this art to a single principle" (210). Condillac's *Essai* proposes a genealogy of knowledge which, like Rameau's system, reduces to a single principle: "my purpose therefore is to reduce to a single principle whatever relates to the human understanding" (6).

Relying on the *Génération harmonique* of 1737, Condillac transforms Rameau's synchronic analysis of the fundaments of harmony into a narrative of the successive discovery of musical intervals. In Condillac's history of music, out of the simplicity of the natural cry grew more complicated vocal sounds. Just as the invention of new words described in chapter two of the *Essai* was brought on by coincidence, chance events led to the discovery of new sounds and habit ingrained them into linguistic practice: "consequently they could not avoid falling now and then upon some tones, with which the ear was pleased. These were observed, and frequently repeated: and such is the first idea they had of harmony" (209).[34] The choice of sounds is dictated by pleasure. Conforming to this "pleasure principle," there is a natural order to the discovery of vocal sounds. Certain intervals would perforce be recognized and reproduced before others – more pleasing to the ear because in perfect accordance with the natural *corps sonore*, the origin of musical sound. In his *Génération harmonique*, Rameau had shown that a *corps sonore* – such as a string – produced, in addition to a fundamental sound, three others related to the first: its octave, the twelfth and major seventeenth:

the deep & predominant Sound that one believes one distinguishes alone [in the resonance of the *corps sonore*], & that we will subsequently call *Fundamental*, is always accompanied by two other Sounds that we will call *Harmonic*, & with which the Octave will be comprised.

If this fundamental sound changes in scale degree [*de Ton, de degré*], it is nonetheless accompanied by the same Harmonic Sounds; and because its twelfth & its major seventeenth always resonate with it in the same *corps sonore*, it is never separated from them.[35]

Rameau asserts that the twelfth and major seventeenth are interchangeable with the perfect fifth and the major third, since octaves are equivalent ("finally everyone agrees on the virtual equality of these

---

[34] "Le hasard ne pouvoit donc manquer d'y amener quelquefois des passages dont l'oreille étoit flattée. On les remarqua, et l'on se fit une habitude de les répéter, telle est la première idée qu'on eut de l'harmonie" (*Essai*, 216).

[35] Rameau, *Complete Theoretical Writings*, 3:29–30.

two Sounds that mark the endpoints [*termes*] of the Octave") and that these sounds form the most elemental triad of music:[36] "the *Chord* called *Perfect*, or *Natural*, & which is exactly composed of the three different Sounds $C = 1$, $G = \frac{1}{3}$, $E = \frac{1}{5}$, must crown [the theory of the *corps sonore*], since it is the Chord which affects us the most agreeably, toward which all our desires are directed, & after which we wish nothing more."[37] The intervals of the major triad are immediately derived from the harmonic overtones of the *corps sonore*, as Rameau had shown. Because of its direct derivation from the *corps sonore*, the major triad is altogether satisfying: it leaves nothing to be desired. In Condillac's scenario, these intervals are closely linked to the passions because they are pleasing and, as he would later clarify (in chapter 6), because they are closely linked to the sound of the natural cry: "for I want to know what sound is best adapted to express any particular passion? In the first place, it must surely be that which imitates the natural sign of this passion ... Next it is the harmonics [*les sons harmoniques*] of those first sounds, as being more closely connected with them" (222). The claim that Condillac advances here points to a close relationship in method between the *Essai* and the *Génération harmonique*. The principle guiding the historical development of the human voice and of language in the *Essai* is the one Rameau had established for the derivation of musical intervals, chords, and progressions. Following this principle, the harmonic progression is easy for the senses to perceive and the voice to reproduce. As such, Condillac argues, it has genealogical precedence over the diatonic interval:

Since it is a point demonstrated that the progression by a third, a fifth, or an octave immediately depends on the principle from whence harmony is derived, that is on the resonance of sonorous bodies, and that the diatonic order arises from this progression; it necessarily follows that the relations of sounds ought to be far more sensible in the harmonic succession than in the diatonic order ... The harmonic intervals were therefore the first taken notice of (209).

Describing the historic development of music in language, Condillac adopts the definitions of simplicity (harmonic) and complexity (diatonic) given by the theory of the *corps sonore*. Simple combinations of sounds, such as the interval from C to G, are necessarily discovered before complex intervals (regardless of how familiar they are, as Condillac insists), such as C to D, because the first are the direct result of the *corps sonore* whereas the second are derivative: "for example, in

---

[36] *Ibid.*, 3:31. Rameau's assertion that everyone agreed about octave identity drew a certain amount of criticism. Pierre Estève, for example, rejected this claim in his *Nouvelle découverte du principe de l'harmonie* (Paris: Jorry, 1752).

[37] Rameau, *Complete Theoretical Writings*, 3:28.

the diatonic order *D* is connected with *C*, only because *C-D* is produced by the progression *C-G*; and the connexion [*liaison*] of the two last has its principle in the harmony of sonorous bodies, of which they constitute a part" (209). Mirroring the structure of knowledge, more "abstract" musical configurations, always derived from the immutable principles of the *corps sonore*, are the result of combinations and extensions of previous material:

It is therefore highly probable that this entire progression *C-E-G-C* was not found out, till after repeated experiments. When this was once known, several others were made on the same pattern, such as *G-B-D-G*. With respect to the diatonic order, it was discovered only by degrees, and not till after many fruitless attempts, since the origin of it was not determined till very lately (210).

We have returned to the notion, encountered earlier, of analogies, connections, links between ideas and between the signs representing these ideas. The two progressions C-E-G-C and G-B-D-G are analogous – simple transpositions of each other. G-B-D-G has become possible as a transposed twin of C-E-C-C, just as the simple interval from C to G became possible because G itself is contained within C as a harmonic. The first advances in music, as Condillac's text reveals, are all the result of links and analogies. The development and structure of music, as it is represented in Rameau's theory, exhibit the principle of analogy that Condillac seeks to establish for the history and structure of our natural languages as well. If Rameau could trace the origin and development of music from a single principle, it should be possible to do the same for language and knowledge.

Indeed, if we return to the earlier sections of the *Essai* concerning the "materials of our knowledge," it becomes clear that Rameau's system is present throughout the *Essai* as an epistemological model. The structure of Rameau's genealogy of sound, from the fundamental tones of the *corps sonore* to the complex configurations of music, is reproduced in Condillac's synchronic view of knowledge: "our wants are all dependent upon one another, and the perceptions of them might be considered as a series of fundamental ideas, to which we might reduce all those which make a part of our knowledge. Over each of these series, other series of ideas might be raised, which should form a kind of chains" (46).[38] The series of fundamental ideas that Condillac situates as links between sensation and knowledge duplicates Rameau's *basse fondamentale*, or chord root, which allowed him to explain musical practice – the patterns of notes and intervals in actual

---

[38] "Tous nos besoins tiennent les uns aux autres, et l'on en pourroit considérer les perceptions comme une suite d'idées fondamentales, auxquelles on rapporteroit tout ce qui fait partie de nos connoissances. Au-dessus de chacune s'élèveroient d'autres suites d'idées qui formeroient des espèces de chaînes" (*Essai*, 125).

musical progressions – as derivative of the *corps sonore*, its theoretical basis. Condillac's spacial and visual metaphors [*au-dessus, des espèces de chaînes*] also bring the metaphysical structure of knowledge into the space of the musical score. The networks he described in the synchronic analysis of human faculties have become a temporal "series of ideas," a sweeping progression of ideas originating the vertical "harmonics" of abstract knowledge. When Condillac presses the urgency of his research – to return to the origin and to unfold the development of ideas – in addition to the organic metaphor of the *germe* (the seed) and its *génération* (its growth or development) he insistently recalls the title and purpose of Rameau's 1737 treatise.

Music theory thus supports and corroborates the epistemological and methodological order of the *Essai*. The successive discovery of intervals (the harmonic interval C-G was found before the diatonic one C-D) mimics the epistemological principle of the *Essai* as a whole – that our knowledge invariably moves from the simple to the more complex: "nature itself points out the order we ought to follow in the presentation [*exposition*] of truth: for if all our ideas come from the senses, it is manifest that the perception of abstract notions must be prepared by sensible ideas" (337). The *corps sonore* offered Condillac a theoretical model he could not refuse, one in which the most elaborated configurations of the musical language and its rhetoric were derived from a single, empirical event.

The development of knowledge in the West

From the emergence of musical sound – Condillac's own "harmonic generation" – the *Essai's* presentation of the history of music moves through Greek and Roman prosody to contemporary musical and linguistic practices. This history follows a process of refinement in which conventional sounds are substituted for natural cries – a demusicalization of language. The predisposed link between sound and passion becomes less and less important for communication: "prosody ... began insensibly to recede from music, in proportion as the reasons for its former approximation, ceased to take place" (182). Memory and reflection, as more developed faculties, take the place of the passions, of the imagination; the affective qualities of music are traded for the analytic ability of discourse; and as a consequence, convention, having little need of instinct, substitutes its signs for the built-in natural cry. The *Essai* posits an inverse relationship between lexical complexity and musicality; as the number of words multiplies, the use of vocal accent, inflection, and intervals declines. The Chinese, however, managed to keep much of the early structure of language, expressing different ideas by pronouncing the same "word" in varying tones:

"they have only 328 monosyllables; these they vary on five tones" (182). Through a substitution of geographic distance for temporal distance, Condillac catches an imaginary glimpse of original language. Instead of cultivating the wealth of possible vocal inflection, as had the Chinese, "other peoples," the Greeks and Romans, "chose rather to invent new words. Prosody with them began insensibly to recede from music" (182). Thus, the projected difference in linguistic and musical resources corroborates and explains a perceived difference in cultural development and character (the Chinese are often represented as hot-headed and passionate in eighteenth-century texts). This description might be seen as a form of nostalgia that is located in – or, projected onto – the cultures and customs being "discovered" and explored by the West.[39] The eighteenth-century search for origins could be said to harbor the more or less unconscious assertion, only partially articulated by Condillac, that the basis of our identity and history is somehow to be found in other cultures (which might be tantamount to claiming further that the truth of the other culture is original to the West). In Condillac's *Essai*, the splitting of speech and song, if unfortunate in certain respects, is a normal consequence of the perfection of our (Western) faculties of knowledge and the development of a cultural identity.

A significant portion of the *Essai* devoted to music concerns itself with this split. Whereas our speech and elocution no longer exhibit the faintest traces of their original musicality, those of antiquity were still quite musical: "That the Greeks and Romans notated their recitation or declamatory speaking, and accompanied it with the sound of instruments, is beyond all manner of doubt: it was therefore properly a kind of chant or song" (183). Likewise, "the prosody of the Romans bordered upon vocal music" (195). In addition to the distinct intervals that characterized original languages, Condillac also asserts that we can find traces of the song-like quality of original speech by examining the measured accent of ancient languages:

Some sounds therefore at the origin of languages succeeded each other with great velocity, and others very slowly . . . As the inflexions by marked [*sensibles*] intervals introduced the use of musical declamation, so the distinct inequality of syllables added a difference of time and measure to it. The declamatory speaking of the ancients contained therefore those two things, which characterise vocal melody, I mean modulation and movement (194–195).

The musicality of these languages gives them a number of advantages which are no longer within the reach of the language of

[39] On the relationship between exploration and linguistic theory in the eighteenth century, see David B. Paxman, "Abstraction in eighteenth-century language study," *Journal of the History of Ideas* 54.1 (1993), 19–36.

eighteenth-century France. First, the declamation of ancient theatre was perfectly transparent, since the music and the words coincided exactly. Modern French, on the contrary, having no long or short syllables in addition to its lack of accent makes opera confusing and often incomprehensible (196). Secondly, Roman orators could be heard and understood by large open-air assemblies. The distinct syllabic tones and the meter allowed the audience to distinguish words perfectly at a great distance:

In Latin, syllables differed by the quality of the sound; by the accent, which, independently of the sense, required the voice to be raised or depressed; and by the quantity: the French tongue wants accents, and has scarce any such thing as quantity; besides a great many of their syllables are mute. A Roman might therefore make himself perfectly heard, where a Frenchman could not be heard without difficulty, or perhaps not at all (198).

A third characteristic of ancient language is that, closer to the natural vocalizations of the origin, the musical sounds of their speech were more directly linked to the passions; and their constructions were made of "sensible images" as the *langage d'action* had been, exercising the imagination (227). Since the development of human faculties reflects that of signs, the people of emergent civilizations, although short on memory and reflection, had an extremely highly developed imagination: "persons not as yet accustomed to instituted signs, have the liveliest imagination" (214). Having more imagination than modern peoples, the ancients were more affected by harmony. Closer to the original conditions of emergent meaning, and removed from the abstraction of modern thought, the ancients were closer to the physical and passionate relation of the natural cry and of the *langage d'action*. The musical languages of antiquity, then, were more closely knit to the imagination and had "more energy and force [*plus de feu*]" than does modern French (214). A kind of entropy – a cooling down of the imagination, a movement towards abstraction and insensitivity – takes place over the course of history. Whereas the ancients were highly sensitive to music, as Condillac demonstrates through the effects it reportedly produced, "we keep ourselves as calm as we can" during a musical performance (212).[40] We have a similar relationship to our language: "in speaking of things, we are satisfied with recollecting their signs, but we seldom revive their ideas. Thus the imagination being seldom raised, becomes more difficult to enliven" (214–215). Our relationship to signs and their meaning is complex and derivative. Because of the increasing distance from the origin – from the original passionate nature of the sign – both music and language are close to becoming a mere juggling of signifiers. But if "our declamatory speak-

[40] "Nous gardons tout le sang-froid dont nous sommes capables" (*Essai*, 218).

79

ing is therefore naturally less expressive than music" and "does not imitate the passions like music," our language recoups its losses in other ways (222–223). French, even though it "has less variety and less harmony" than ancient languages, "makes us amends on the side of simplicity and perspicuity [*la netteté de ses tours*]" – "less lively" yet "more precise" (270–271).

Condillac hopes to strike a balance between these two qualities – passionate energy [*feu*] and exactitude – in both music and language. Although he asserts that "there is certainly in this [music] as in other arts, a point of perfection, from which we must not wander," Condillac hesitates to specify this point (216). Ancient music, in and of itself, is less perfect than modern music: "[let us judge] by the instruments they used, and we shall have reason to presume that the superiority is on our side" (213). Yet Greek and Roman prosody, more like song than ours, "made much nearer approaches than ours to this point of perfection" (225). However, considered as a philosophical language, modern French has the analytic exactitude that the languages of antiquity lack. Condillac attempts to temper the paradox:

In order to fix our ideas, we ought to imagine two languages; one which should exercise the fancy, to such a degree, that the people who spoke it must be perpetually blundering: the other, which on the contrary should cause such an exercise of the analytic method, that those to whom it was natural should conduct themselves even in their pleasures, like mathematicians investigating the solution of a problem (295).[41]

At the heart of the eighteenth century's drive towards the refinement of knowledge and its languages appears a desire for something quite other – illogic and imprecision. Music in some measure describes an imaginative, "delirious" understanding, located elsewhere in place and in time, which is nonetheless elemental to Condillac's epistemology and his history of knowledge.

The presence of music and music theory is crucial to the *Essai*, first as that which contributes to the genesis of signification, that which explains the transition from natural signs to conventional signs, and secondly as a confirmation of the logic of the *Essai* itself. Something like music, in the natural cry and its link to the passions, moves sensation into the realm of signification. This anthropological missing link, integrated into a philosophy of sensation and movement based

---

[41] "Il faudroit, afin de fixer nos idées, imaginer deux langues: l'une qui donnât tant d'exercice à l'imagination, que les hommes qui la parleroient déraisonneroient sans cesse; l'autre qui exerçât au contraire si fort l'analyse, que les hommes à qui elle seroit naturelle se conduiroient jusques dans leurs plaisirs comme des géomètres qui cherchent la solution d'un problème" (*Essai*, 265).

on that of Newton and Locke, allows Condillac to attack Aristotle's philosophy of essence: to explain how "judgment, reflection, desires, passions, and so on are only sensation itself differently transformed."[42] Perhaps Condillac's treatment of music also reveals a moment of hesitation in the progression of signs and knowledge. Force is lost for truth; passions give way to analysis. Reversing Condillac's argument in a sense, Rousseau would take up this notion of loss in virtually all of his writings on music. What appears in Condillac as a trade-off, represents for Rousseau an irretrievable and devastating loss.

[42] Condillac, *Traité des sensations*, 7–8.

4

Music and original loss in Rousseau's *Essai sur l'origine des langues*[1]

Rousseau did not stop at the first ideas that Condillac's writings had inspired in him: his mind, always active, criticized them, corrected them, transformed them. Duclos' Remarques, which had just appeared, suggested still others. He expounded them with satisfaction. And preoccupied with the problems that he had examined in his Discours, he even devoted a large part of the Essai to his conceptions of the state of nature and of the first epochs of humanity. From this triple inspiration has arisen a slightly confused and badly digested work.[2]

The *Essai sur l'origine des langues*, as a reflection on both language and music, holds a unique position in the work of a writer who was also music theorist and composer. In addition to a *Projet concernant de nouveaux signes pour la musique* – a proposal to simplify musical notation by eliminating the traditional staff and its symbols – Rousseau wrote the music articles for the *Encyclopédie*, published a widely read *Dictionnaire de musique*, and composed operas, motets, and chansons.[3]

---

[1] References to the *Essai sur l'origine des langues* given in the text are to Victor Gourevitch's English translation. Unless otherwise noted, when the original French is given in notes, references are to Rousseau, *Essai sur l'origine des langues*, ed. Charles Porset (Bordeaux: Ducros, 1970).

[2] Paul Fouquet, "J.-J. Rousseau et la grammaire philosophique," *Mélanges de philologie offerts à Ferdinand Brunot* (Paris: Société Nouvelle de Librairie et d'Edition, 1904), 117.

[3] In the *Confessions*, Rousseau characterizes his musical background as amateurish and styles himself as largely self-taught (Rousseau, *Les Confessions*, ed. Jacques Voisine [Paris: Garnier Frères, 1964], 192–193, 238–242). Yet, whether or not he was an important composer, whether or not the *Devin du village* deserves a place amongst the "great works of music" (which it surely does not), Rousseau's music and writings on music clearly had a decisive influence on the musicians, composers and musical public of the eighteenth century (see Wokler, "Rousseau on Rameau and revolution," 251–267). Both Gluck and Burney, for example, pay tribute to Rousseau's music and theories of music. And Rameau devoted the theoretical works of the last decade of his life to refuting Rousseau and the Encyclopedists. Tiersot argues that "if Jean-Jacques Rousseau had done nothing in his life besides composing the *Devin du village*, writing his *Dictionnaire de musique*, taking part in the musical wars between France and Italy, and had devoted the rest of his activity to publishing a few purely literary writings and

Reflections on music are also scattered throughout Rousseau's fictional and non-fictional writings. The *Discours sur l'origine de l'inégalité, La Nouvelle Héloïse, Emile,* and the *Confessions* all include references (from relatively brief digressions in the second *Discours,* to rather extensive passages in the *Confessions*) to music and/or music theory.[4] The particular complexity of the *Essai*'s intertwining of reflections on music, language, society, and political systems has left many critics perplexed.[5] Yet the *Essai* remains one of the most developed, if the most difficult (and no doubt the most commented upon) of all eighteenth-century essays concerning the origin of language and music. If Paul Fouquet, at the beginning of the twentieth century, considered Rousseau's *Essai* "confused" and "badly digested," it may reflect less on Rousseau's text than it does on the disciplinary strictures of most modern scholarship. A short overview of the history of the *Essai* and the critical debate it has elicited is in order before I move to examine the text more closely.

Published in 1781 by Du Peyrou, three years after Rousseau's death, the *Essai* has raised a great deal of scholarly controversy. When exactly did Rousseau write the *Essai*? How do the positions taken in the *Essai* compare with Rousseau's other reflections on music and language, from the period of the two *Discours* (1750–54) to the *Dictionnaire de musique* (1767)?[6] At the time of writing, there appears to be a general

---

to serving as a music copyist, he would already deserve a place in the history of eighteenth-century French music" (Julien Tiersot, *J.-J. Rousseau* [Paris: Félix Alcan, 1912], 1).

[4] Two articles concerning Rousseau's fiction and music deserve particular mention. Christie V. McDonald has studied the relationship between music and the proper name in "En-harmoniques: l'anagramme de Rousseau," *Etudes Françaises* 17.3 4 (1981), 7–21. Alain Grosrichard brings up the question of conscience and voice in the *Confessions,* in "La voix de la vérité," in *Littérature et opéra,* ed. Philippe Berthier and Kurt Ringger (Grenoble: Presses Universitaires de Grenoble, 1987), 9–17.

[5] Pierre Juliard, like Fouquet (see chapter epigraph), seems frustrated at the many contradictions present in the *Essai* and, as he sees it, at Rousseau's ultimate "failure" to determine the origin of languages in conjunction with that of society (Pierre Juliard, *Philosophies of Language in Eighteenth-Century France* [The Hague: Mouton, 1970], 24–27).

[6] The most thorough discussions of the textual and conceptual genesis of the *Essai sur l'origine des langues* can be found in Robert Wokler, *Social Thought of Jean-Jacques Rousseau* (New York: Garland Publishing, 1987), 235–378; and in Charles Porset, "L'inquiétante étrangeté' de l'*Essai sur l'origine des langues*: Rousseau et ses exégètes," *Studies on Voltaire and the Eighteenth Century* 154 (1976), 1715–1758. Jean Starobinski provides a helpful summary of the question in his edition of the *Essai sur l'origine des langues* (Paris: Gallimard, 1990), 193–200. Wokler reviews in detail the various positions taken in the debate including his own earlier interpretation, published in 1974 as "Rameau, Rousseau and the *Essai sur l'origine des langues.*" Michel Murat's article, "Jean-Jacques Rousseau," includes a rigorous study of two concepts central to Rousseau's work in music – the distinction between "natural music" and "imitative music," and the analogy between painting and music – and establishes a detailed and

consensus among commentators that the composition of what would
later become the text of the *Essai* cannot actually be said to have begun
until 1755, when Rousseau began a response to Rameau's anony-
mously published *Erreurs sur la musique dans l'Encyclopédie*. An intermediate version of this response, "Du principe de la mélodie," contains a digression on the origin of melody, parts of which are found in
the final published version of Rousseau's response, entitled *Examen de
deux principes avancés par M. Rameau*, and most of which is also included
in the *Essai*.[7] Begun in 1755, the *Essai* seems not to have been completed until 1761, when Rousseau asked Malesherbes' advice about
publishing it.[8] In 1763, Rousseau wrote a *Projet de préface* which was
intended to introduce an edition uniting a short text on l'*Imitation
théâtrale*, the *Essai sur l'origine des langues*, and the *Lévite d'Ephraïm*.[9]
Rousseau would never publish this triptych. In the *Projet de préface*, he
indicates that the *Essai* had originally been a fragment of a longer
version of the second *Discours*, which he took up again in 1755 for his
response to Rameau. This assertion, which has been cited frequently
by scholars, would seem to situate the *Essai* as an offshoot of the
second *Discours*. Based on this comment, critics have insisted on reducing the meaning of the *Essai* to one of its chapters: "for V. Gold-
schmidt, it is as though the *Essai sur l'origine des langues* had been
nothing at first but the chapter ix – which Rousseau never states."[10]
However, despite the incontestable fact that chapter 9 of the *Essai*
continued and expanded upon the discussion of the origin of language found in the second *Discours*, without a first draft of the second
Discours, as Porset notes, the textual genesis of the *Essai* "cannot be
located anywhere else but in the intermediate version of the *Examen de
deux principes*."[11] In short, Rousseau touched upon the question of
music and language in the second *Discours*, but probably only began

in part hypothetical chronology of the various chapters of the *Essai* based on comparisons with Rousseau's treatment of these same concepts in other, more accurately
dated works. Porset's article contains an extensive bibliography of the debate. Other
important contributions, mentioned in Porset's bibliography, can be found in the as
yet incomplete Pléiade edition of the *Œuvres complètes* (1:560, 3:146n2, 3:149n8,
3:154n2), and in Derrida, *De la grammatologie*, 243–278.

[7] The intermediate version of Rousseau's reply to Rameau has been published and
commented on by two scholars. See Duchez, "Principe de la mélodie", and Wokler,
"Rameau, Rousseau and the *Essai*." See also the recent review of the question in
Wokler, *Social Thought*, 235–378.

[8] See Rousseau's letter to Malesherbes, dated 27 September 1761, in Rousseau, *Correspondance complète*, ed. R. A. Leigh (Geneva: Institut et Musée Voltaire, 1965–), 9:131.

[9] Porset, "L'inquiétante étrangeté,'" 1716.   [10] *Ibid.*, 1719.

[11] *Ibid.*, 1721. Murat and Porset arrive at similar overall chronologies for the composition
of the *Essai* although Murat bases his conclusions on a diachronic analysis of certain of
Rousseau's concepts about music, whereas Porset concentrates on the different
textual versions.

the text we know as the *Essai sur l'origine des langues*, albeit in an earlier version, as a response to Rameau's tract against the positions Rousseau had taken on music in the *Encyclopédie*. Indeed, the complete title of Rousseau's text is in fact *Essai sur l'origine des langues, où il est parlé de la mélodie et de l'imitation musicale*. Furthermore, as Starobinski notes in his edition of the *Essai*, Rousseau planned to place the *Essai* directly after the *Examen de deux principes*, which in turn followed the *Lettre sur la musique française*, in a proposal he sent to Du Peyrou in 1765 for the publication of his *Œuvres*.[12] This placement, as Starobinski remarks, speaks to Rousseau's view of the *Essai* as part of a larger scheme of his works.

My point about the genesis of Rousseau's argument in the *Essai* will be important for what follows. Those critics who have singled out the *Essai* for detailed analysis have generally centered their discussion on Rousseau's treatment of language at the origin of society and culture, the chapters on music being either ignored entirely or seen as secondary, as curious but marginal accessories to the main thrust of the text. In short, as Porset explains, the *Essai* has largely remained an appendix to the second *Discours*:[13]

From Beaudouin to Starobinski ... passing through G. Lanson, P. M. Masson, R. Derathé, M. Launay, M. Duchet and some others, it is as if the *Essai* ... should be understood and could only be understood as coming from the *Discours sur l'inégalité* (no doubt because a 'cause' preceeds its 'effects'), that is, as the complement to a master-text or its appendix ... wherein [derives] the commentators' insistent reading of 'footnote' where Rousseau writes 'fragment'.[14]

Nonetheless, why should one privilege the *Essai* with lengthy and finely wrought analyses, when it is after all a text Rousseau never saw fit to publish himself? In his critique of Jacques Derrida's reading of Rousseau, Aram Vartanian stresses that Derrida must somehow "upgrade a marginal, or at least accessory, aspect of Rousseauism into one of its main preoccupations."[15] Rousseau himself claims to have felt a certain foolishness, dissatisfaction, or even shame regarding this text.[16] One might point out, however, that the subject of this "marginal" text – the origin and present state of music and language – is one which permeates a healthy number of Rousseau's "major" works as

---

[12] Rousseau, *Essai sur l'origine des langues*, ed. Jean Starobinski (Paris: Gallimard, 1990), 197.

[13] A few commentators, including Marie-Elisabeth Duchez, Robert Wokler, Michel Murat, and Catherine Kintzler, are notable exceptions to this generalization.

[14] Porset, "L''inquiétante étrangeté,'" 1752.

[15] Aram Vartanian, "Derrida, Rousseau, and the difference," *Studies in Eighteenth-Century Culture* 19 (1989), 130.

[16] Porset, "L''inquiétante étrangeté,'" 1722; Derrida, *De la grammatologie*, 380.

well, not to mention his work as music copyist and opera composer. Charles Porset has stressed the importance that Rousseau indeed does attribute to his text, despite the fact that it was not published until after his death:

> Whatever the case may be, even if, as Rousseau himself wrote, he sought to suppress his text; even if, as several commentators have observed with a measure of malice, Rousseau consistently referred to the *Discours* and not to the *Essai*, events speak differently. Not only did he overcome his "shame," forget his "dissatisfaction," and publish (or attempt to publish) his text; but, instead of making it disappear, he kept it in his possession in a portfolio, he corrected it, reworked it, had Malesherbes and Lorenzi read it, and finally entrusted it to Du Peyrou. If you insist, you could say that Rousseau "contradicts" himself; but you cannot say that Rousseau did not value his *Essai*.[17]

Starobinski, too, insists that Rousseau had carefully prepared the manuscript of the *Essai*: it was thus not a text that Rousseau neglected after its initial composition.[18]

Before opening my analysis of the text, I would like to briefly review the central questions raised by the critics and to examine Derrida's influential commentary on the *Essai*. Much has been written on the links between the second *Discours* and the *Essai*, on the possible continuities or discontinuities between the two texts. Michel Launay suggests, for example, that a difference of method separates the two texts, that in the *Essai* Rousseau no longer leaves aside "all the facts" as had the speculative history of the second *Discours*, but instead methodically supports his assertions with references to historical characters and events.[19] Revealing the continuities between the two texts on the other hand, Michèle Duchet points out that the *Essai* further develops conceptions first introduced by the second *Discours*: distinguishing two kinds of "need" at the origin of language, Rousseau "proposes a much richer and more nuanced theory of language than that of the *Discours*."[20] Duchet notes that "the chronology of the *Essai* fills the gaps found in the *Discours*, it does not contradict it."[21] Agreeing with Duchet's analysis, Trudy Ettelson sees the *Essai* as picking up where the second *Discours* had left off: "The *Essai*, then, begins by answering the main question posed in the *Second Discours*, namely, what is the exact relation between language and society?"[22]

Possibly divergent notions of *la pitié* in the *Essai* and the second

[17] Porset, "L''inquiétante étrangeté,'" 1722.

[18] Rousseau, *Essai*, ed. Starobinski, 193.

[19] Michel Launay and Michèle Duchet, "Synchronie et diachronie: l'*Essai sur l'origine des langues* et le second *Discours*," *Revue Internationale de Philosophie* 82.4 (1967), 428–429.

[20] *Ibid.*, 431.   [21] *Ibid.*, 434.

[22] Trudy Gottlieb Ettelson, "Jean-Jacques Rousseau's writings on music: a quest for melody" (Ph.D. dissertation, Yale University, 1974), 223.

Discours have provided another avenue for studying the relationship between the two texts. *La pitié*, or compassion, is a crucial concept for Rousseau: in compelling sympathy and identification, *la pitié* forms a bond of society and communication between two beings. In a note to the Pléiade edition of Rousseau's works, Starobinski asserted that the *Essai* and the second *Discours* endorse two rather different notions of *pitié*. In his view, the *Essai* does not allow for the possibility of an unreflective movement of compassion, whereas the earlier text asserts the absolute necessity of this spontaneous *pitié*.[23] Derrida argues to the contrary that the two texts are perfectly compatible on this point, that *la pitié* is always there even if the *Essai* specifies that it remains dormant before being activated by the imagination.[24] While revealing important features of the text, many of these commentaries overlook the fact that the chapters on music in the *Essai* substantially alter the tenor of Rousseau's treatment of language and culture. In no way a simple by-product of the second *Discours*, as Porset has shown from the textual evidence, the conceptual framework of the *Essai* has particular significance for the study of Rousseau's thinking on music and on culture as a whole.

Derrida was one of the first commentators to recognize the importance of Rousseau's reflections on music to the larger structure of the *Essai*. His *De la grammatologie* remains perhaps the single most influential interpretation of the *Essai* to date. Derrida's reading of the *Essai* is also based on an interpretive strategy which is rather different from those of his predecessors. Instead of beginning with an interpretation of the second *Discours*, his reading proceeds to sound out the *Essai* for traces of a preoccupation with "suppléments" – excesses that are added to or substituted for a hypothetical original plenitude – which Derrida has also found in Rousseau's other texts, particularly in the *Confessions*. Derrida's analysis shows that Rousseau attempts to represent an absolute origin, of language and culture, by supposing a chain of supplements and degradations which are appended to the original state: culture is substituted for nature, appearance for being, unhappiness for happiness, writing for speech, and so on. However, as Paul de Man notes, the logic of "supplementarity" also requires that these binary oppositions self-destruct: "Rousseau defines voice as the origin of written language, but his description of oral speech or of music can be shown to possess, from the start, all the elements of

---

[23] Rousseau, *Œuvres complètes*, 3:154n2.
[24] Derrida, *De la grammatologie*, 262–263. See the entire section entitled "Le débat actuel: l'économie de la Pitié," in *De la grammatologie*, 243–272. Charles Porset has given a succinct account of this debate in the introduction to his edition (Rousseau, *Essai*, ed. Porset, 16–24). Recently, Jean Starobinski has revised his view of the question (Rousseau, *Essai*, ed. Starobinski, 198).

distance and negation that prevent written language from ever achiev-
ing a condition of unmediated presence."[25] "While Rousseau postu-
lates a pure origin," as Christie McDonald explains, "at the same time,
he betrays the fact that the process of decay (in writing, in culture) has
always already begun."[26] Derrida's reading argues that Rousseau's use
of language contradicts or subverts the logocentrism of Western metaphysics that he appears to uphold.

Paul de Man has shown that this interpretation forces Derrida into
an awkward position. He must now read Rousseau as saying what he
doesn't mean to say, as giving evidence against his own doctrine of
original, unmediated presence. Derrida suggests that while Rousseau
ostensibly supports the classical doctrine of mimesis and the requisite
battery of binary oppositions which accompany this doctrine (such as
nature versus culture), his text reveals the contradictions, the impasse,
of the metaphysics upon which those dichotomies are based. It is to
Derrida's credit that instead of reading Rousseau as an "interesting
psychological case," as had many previous commentators, his analysis
shows that the problem is much larger in scope, involving the whole of
Western philosophy.[27] Yet Derrida's reading maintains, with other
critics, beginning with G. A. Villoteau at the beginning of the nineteenth century, that Rousseau's text has somehow been sabotaged,
whether from the inside or the outside.[28] Questioning aspects of
Derrida's analysis, for example, Christie McDonald has wondered why
Derrida denies "that Rousseau was conscious of the inconsistencies in
his thought."[29] On the question of music, Derrida remarks that the
Essai initially seems to be concerned with the origin and deteriorating
state of music: "a disquiet *seems* to animate all Rousseau's reflections
and to give them their vehemence: they are concerned *at first* with the
origin and degeneration of music."[30] However, Derrida soon sets aside
musical issues to make room for his own interpretive strategy by
attempting to close off the parts of the *Essai* that do not "directly"
concern music from those that do:

---

[25] Paul de Man, *Blindness and Insight: Essays in the Rhetoric of Contemporary Criticism*
(Minneapolis: University of Minnesota Press, 1983), 115.

[26] McDonald, "Jacques Derrida's reading of Rousseau," 90.

[27] De Man, *Blindness and Insight*, 113.

[28] Guillaume André Villoteau's *Recherches sur l'analogie de la musique avec les arts qui ont
pour objet l'imitation du langage* (Paris: L'Imprimerie Impériale, 1807) differs from
Derrida's in that it tends to regard Rousseau as a "case"; yet both authors find that
Rousseau's own text is blind to what it reveals: "it is even quite remarkable that, in
order to combat this illustrious writer to one's advantage, and to win a complete and
stunning victory over him, one only has to take hold of the arms that he offers against
himself in his own writings" (Villoteau, *Recherches*, 2:151).

[29] McDonald, "Jacques Derrida's reading of Rousseau," 93.

[30] Derrida, *Of Grammatology*, 195.

If one wants to maintain that the destiny of music is the major preoccupation of the *Essay*, it must be explained that the chapters that directly concern that subject occupy hardly a third of the work (a little more if you consider the number of chapters, a little less if you consider the number of pages) and that the rest of the essay does not deal with it at all.[31]

Contrary to Derrida's view, my contention is that music is at the heart of the *Essai*, both because, as Porset argues, the *Essai* is conceived of – at least in part – as a response to Rameau, and because music explicitly remains present throughout the text as central to Rousseau's conception of language itself. With the reservations just mentioned, Derrida's reading of Rousseau nevertheless remains a powerful and convincing one in that he insists on treating the *Essai* as part of larger philosophical and aesthetic concerns, not as a "badly digested" fragment of the second *Discours* or as a minor and thus peripheral digression on music.[32]

One last reading of the *Essai* deserves mention. Leaving aside the philosophical framework of Derrida's interpretation, Catherine Kintzler's recent reading offers perhaps the most integral analysis of the *Essai* within the context of musical and aesthetic debates. Kintzler notes that for Rousseau, "musical thought is a kind of social science [*science humaine*]."[33] However, the section of Kintzler's book that is devoted to Rousseau has a tendency to "resolve" conceptual difficulties by making them into simple terminological problems, rather than maintaining the close attention to shifts in meaning and to the problematic nature of Rousseau's dichotomous oppositions that characterizes Derrida's work.

My principal concern with the *Essai* is not to examine Rousseau's denigration of writing, nor am I specifically concerned with his attachment to a metaphysics of presence. The reading I offer is centered on the place of music in the logical and narrative structure of the *Essai*; and beyond these textual considerations, my analysis examines how Rousseau's reflections on music reveal larger concerns about the origin of semiosis, the nature of musical and linguistic signs, and the place of music in culture. It is important to note the specificity of Rousseau's approach to the origin of music, the particular way in which he connects discussion of music and his story of the origin and development of society. In the first place, as many critics have pointed out,

---

[31] *Ibid.*

[32] For a critique of Derrida's deconstruction of Rousseau and in particular of his use of the notion of "supplementarity," see Vartanian, "Derrida, Rousseau, and the difference." Other critics, though more sympathetic to Derrida's work, have also pointed out the omissions of his reading: see De Man, *Blindness and Insight*, 102–141; and McDonald, "Jacques Derrida's reading of Rousseau," 92–94.

[33] Kintzler, *Poétique de l'opéra français*, 437.

Rousseau's *Essai* re-evaluates questions of language and culture which haunt the second *Discours*. Condillac saw enormous possibilities in the perfection of languages: language would continue to be rationalized by logic, which in turn would develop through language. In the *Essai*, Rousseau takes a more somber view of linguistic "progress," maintaining that the development of languages contributes to the disaffection of individuals within society and even to oppression. Rousseau singles out the French tongue as the perfect example of a language which has become less and less sonorous and clear, and hence less and less compatible with freedom: "now, I maintain that any language in which it is not possible to make oneself understood by the people assembled is a servile language; it is impossible for a people to remain free and speak that language" (295). Rousseau identifies the departure of music from language – the musical qualities of a language being precisely those which allow it to be heard by the assembled masses – as the single most decisive event leading to the present, disastrous state of affairs. This passage, coming as it does in the concluding chapter of the *Essai*, points to the fact that reflections on music lead to and support Rousseau's re-evaluation of linguistic, cultural, and political progress.

In the second place, and as commentators have been slow to recognize, the *Essai* brings matters of eighteenth-century musical debate into focus by returning to the origin of language and music. For as is evident from a brief overview of textual sources, the *Essai* was in some measure precipitated by Rameau's *Erreurs sur la musique dans l'Encyclopédie*. I will argue that the *Essai* reveals what is at stake in music theory by pointing to the cultural, linguistic, and political implications and presuppositions of that theory. Condillac admired Rameau's theory as a successful attempt to develop a science of music based on empirical evidence, and he borrowed Rameau's discovery of the *corps sonore* in order to support his own claim to a Newtonian approach to language. For Condillac, the principle of conservation of movement would apply to the development of language and the psyche as well as to the physical realm. Rousseau, however, openly rejects the two essential consequences Rameau draws from his principle of the *corps sonore* – that music is best understood as the result of a physical action and is hence universal, and that melody is secondary to harmony, the latter being the direct product of the *corps sonore*. By returning to the origin, and by following "the very order of nature in [his] inquiries," Rousseau hopes to put together a systematic and forceful response to Rameau.[34]

---

[34] Rousseau, *Essay*, 260. Catherine Kintzler notes that Rousseau's musical thought operates in opposition, presenting itself not so much as a theory, but rather as a "counter-theory" (*Poétique de l'opéra français*, 439).

In order to understand the degree to which Rousseau's account of the origin of music is conceived as a reply to Rameau's theoretical writings, a brief excursion through Rameau's discoveries in music theory is required. The principal elements of Rameau's theory to which Rousseau objected in the *Essai* can be found in those writings which precede his direct responses to the Encyclopedists: principally, the *Génération harmonique* (1737), *Démonstration du principe de l'harmonie* (1750), and *Observations sur notre instinct pour la musique* (1754).[35] Searching for a single principle that would illuminate the theory and practice of music, and "enlightened by Descartes' Method," as Rameau stated in the *Démonstration*, "I began by reflecting on myself" as had Descartes in his *Discours de la méthode*.[36] This methodical contemplation gave immediate results: "The first sound which struck my ear was a flash."[37] His experience led him to the discovery of the origin of harmony in the resonance of the *corps sonore*. The exact relationship between the *corps sonore* and music is defined in the opening chapter of the *Génération harmonique*: "harmony, which is made up of an agreeable combination of several different Sounds, is a natural effect whose cause resides in the Air stirred up by the impact [*choc*] of each particular *corps sonore*."[38] Like Bourdelot and Blainville, Rameau pinpoints the origin of music in the sounds generated by the resonant objects of nature. Yet, whereas Blainville uncovers the origin of music through a narrative of speculative history, Rameau finds this origin in what amounts to a rudimentary laboratory experiment which he invites his readers to reproduce for themselves. What was the story of primitive man's encounter with reeds and animal gut, has become, in the *Génération harmonique*, an experiment with organ pipes and violin strings: "bow hard across [*raclez*] one of the largest strings of a Viol, or Cello; you will hear, together with the whole Sound, its Octave, its

---

[35] For the purposes of my exposition, I am necessarily creating a succinct account of what was spread over various texts and developed in different directions. As Thomas Christensen has pointed out, "the kinds of arguments and evidence [Rameau] employed in the *Traité* of 1722 were not the same as in the *Démonstration* of 1750 ... This is why it is so difficult to derive a picture of Rameau's theory from any single publication, or even worse, to take all his writings and try to reduce them to a single and static form" (*Rameau*, 41–42).

[36] "Je commençai par descendre en moi-même" (Rameau, *Complete Theoretical Writings*, 3:170). In the *Discours de la méthode*, Descartes began with a similar movement of introspection: "I stayed all day shut up alone in a stove-heated room, where I had the opportunity to reflect [*m'entretenir*] on my thoughts" (René Descartes, *Œuvres philosophiques* [Paris: Garnier, 1963], 1:579).

[37] "Le premier son qui frappa mon oreille fut un trait de lumiere" (Rameau, *Complete Theoretical Writings*, 3:172).

[38] *Ibid.*, 3:15.

double and even triple octave, its Twelfth & its major Seventeenth, which are in a proportion of 1, $\frac{1}{2}$, $\frac{1}{3}$, $\frac{1}{4}$, $\frac{1}{5}$, $\frac{1}{8}$."[39] Though in a large sense, Rameau's *corps sonore* is a story of origins, his derivation of musical sound is fundamentally different from the historical or anthropological narrative that Rousseau sought to advance. Rameau establishes a relationship, unvarying in historical or cultural terms, between the ear and the physical vibration of the string. Discounting all the octaves of the principal note, or the *fondamental* (the initial sound made by the viol string), which are all equivalent according to Rameau's theory, we are left with the fundamental tone and two of its harmonics, the sounds which make up the major triad: "the *Chord* called *Perfect*, or *Natural* ... C (1), G ($\frac{1}{3}$), E ($\frac{1}{5}$)."[40] The major triad, more or less directly emitted by the *corps sonore*, is also "the Chord which affects us the most agreeably, toward which all our desires are directed, & after which we wish nothing more."[41] The natural resonance of physical objects, captured in music, delivers a feeling of metaphysical satiety. And since any *corps sonore* will produce identical harmonics, one can take each of the terms of the original major triad as fundamental, "such that new fundamental Sounds produce as many new Chords."[42] From the ratios of each of the three components of the major triad, then, Rameau derives all the other intervals.[43]

In his *Traité de l'harmonie* (1722), Rameau had already asserted the primacy of harmony over melody: "Music is ordinarily divided into Harmony & Melody, although the latter is only a part of the former."[44] In the *Génération harmonique*, Rameau establishes that the harmonic partials of the fundamental bass underlie and provide the basis for melody, thus incorporating melody into his new theory of the *corps sonore*: "To find the fundamental Bass of a given Tune [*Chant*] is to find not only the entire Harmony which this Tune is capable of sustaining, but also the principle from which it derives."[45] He asserts that "music is a Physico-mathematical Science: Sound constitutes its Physical basis, & the proportions [*rapports*] found between different Sounds constitute its Mathematical basis."[46] Thus, the bewildering array of chords (their inversions, as well as each of the consonances and dissonances

---

[39] *Ibid.*, 3:19.   [40] *Ibid.*, 3:28.   [41] *Ibid.*, 3:28.

[42] "De sorte qu'autant de nouveaux Sons fondamentaux, autant de nouvelles Harmonies" (*ibid.*, 3:35).

[43] Rameau identifies the progression of these ratios as being in "arithmetic proportion" and "harmonic proportion" on either side of the fundamental: "Table of the Triple and Subtriple progression (G flat = 729; D flat = 243; A flat = 81; E flat = 27; B flat = 9; F = 3; C = 1; G = $\frac{1}{3}$; D = $\frac{1}{9}$; A = $\frac{1}{27}$; E = $\frac{1}{81}$; B = $\frac{1}{243}$; F sharp = $\frac{1}{729}$)" (*ibid.*, 3:36). For an explanation of these proportions, see Christensen, *Rameau*, 307–308.

[44] Rameau, *Traité de l'harmonie*, 1.

[45] Rameau, *Complete Theoretical Writings*, 3:110–111.

[46] *Ibid.*, 3:29.

which make them up) and the voices (melodies) in a given composition are all derived from and have allotted functions within a
fundamental bass line. The whole system, by way of the *fondamental*, is
in turn derived from the nature of the *corps sonore*. It was the systematic and totalizing aspect of Rameau's theory that struck his contemporaries as so powerful and that led them to applaud Rameau's
system as a model of scientific elegance.

By defining the fundamental bass as "the Ear's sole Guide," Rameau
set melody's relationship to harmony as one of subordination:
harmony, like a compass, guides the wandering melodic line.[47] In his
Observations sur notre instinct pour la musique, Rameau expands on this
relationship and at the same time clarifies the origin of our sense of
music: "this sense guides us in all our musical Activities."[48] Rameau
argues that music is natural to us, that we have a musical instinct, and
maintains that he has discovered the guiding principle of this instinct
in harmony: "This principle is now known: it resides, as one cannot
deny, in the Harmony which results from the resonance of any *corps
sonore*."[49] To prove his point, Rameau invokes the common sense of
"an unexperienced man, who has never heard of Music": "if this man
began to sing a slightly low, but very clear and distinct Note, & if he
then let his voice continue quickly, without thinking of anything, not
even of the interval that he would sing, the action being purely
instinctual [*machinale*], he would sing a *Fifth* first, before any other
interval."[50] The *corps sonore* being the physical principle of musical
sound, the human voice will naturally and mechanically follow the
prescribed order of its resonance: first the fifth, then the third, and so
on until it forms the diatonic scale. Voice is led through melody by the
physical dictates of harmony, "the sole foundation of Music, & the
principle behind its greatest effects."[51] The unalterable physical laws of
the *corps sonore* are at the origin of both harmony and melody.

Beginning with the *Démonstration du principe de l'harmonie*, Rameau
widens the implication of his discoveries. Music, in the originating
form of the *corps sonore*, has suddenly become the origin and basis for
all the sciences: "it is in Music that nature appears to designate the
Physical principle of those first and purely Mathematical notions on
which all the Sciences are based; I mean, the Harmonic, Arithmetic,
and Geometric proportions from which follow progressions of the
same type, & which are revealed at the first instant of the resonance of
a *corps sonore*."[52] The natural resonance of the *corps sonore* provides the
mathematical foundation, not only for music, but also for geometry,

[47] "L'unique Boussole de l'Oreille" (*ibid.*, 3:9).
[48] "Ce sentiment qui nous meut dans toutes nos Opérations musicales" (*ibid.*, 3:259).
[49] *Ibid.*, 3:267.   [50] *Ibid.*, 3:269.   [51] *Ibid.*, 3:260.   [52] *Ibid.*, 3:157–158.

arithmetic, and the rest of the sciences.[53] As if he were attempting to outstrip the all-inclusive discourse of the *Encyclopédie*, from which he had been excluded or had excluded himself, to transform music into an autonomous and rival cyclopaedia, Rameau expands the scope of his theory of the *corps sonore* to include virtually every form of knowledge.[54] This position would offer one explanation for the incompatibility that both Rameau and the Encyclopedists perceived between the composer's theories and the larger project of the *Encyclopédie*, and for Rameau's antagonism toward the music articles it contained. What is at issue between Rameau's musical cyclopaedia – already at least partially in place by 1750 in the *Démonstration du principe de l'harmonie* – and the *Encyclopédie* is a fundamental, epistemological conflict. By situating music at the origin of all scientific knowledge, Rameau placed his system in contradiction with the "system of human knowledge" (which was in part borrowed from Bacon's tree of knowledge) that introduced the *Encyclopédie*, displaying and deriving all areas of knowledge from memory, reason, and imagination. Whereas for Rameau, the principles of science are derived from musical resonance, in the *Encyclopédie*'s system of human knowledge, music is a province of the imagination, not of reason – thus a kind of "poetry," understood in the largest sense of the term, and not directly related to philosophy or mathematics. The place allotted to music in the system of human knowledge is not an insignificant one, as d'Alembert's lavish attention to music and music theory in the "Discours préliminaire" testifies; yet it is a space of knowledge that is not essentially defined in terms of mathematics or geometry.

In the *Observations sur notre instinct pour la musique*, Rameau maintains his assertion of the *corps sonore* as the foundational principle for all the arts and sciences: "the Principle in question is not only the principle of all the Arts of taste, as a *Traité du Beau essentiel dans les Arts, appliqué principalement à l'Architecture* already confirms, it is also that of all the Sciences subject to calculation."[55] In the *Observations*, physical nature informs the multifarious artistic and scientific endeavors of civilization through the proportions of the *corps sonore*. In his

---

53 Kintzler notes the confusion that exists between mathematics and acoustics in Rameau's claims: "he believes that the object called the *corps sonore* acts like a mathematical object, that it has the properties of a mathematical object" (*Poétique de l'opéra français*, 422).

54 After the quarrel erupted between Rameau and the Encyclopedists, Rameau published a "Réponse de M. Rameau à MM. les éditeurs de l'Encyclopédie sur leur dernier avertissement" in 1757 claiming to have declined from the outset to undertake the music articles. See Thomas Christensen, "Diderot, Rameau and resonating strings: new evidence of an early collaboration," *Studies in Voltaire and the Eighteenth Century*, forthcoming.

55 Rameau, *Complete Theoretical Writings*, 3:265.

"Réflexions sur la théorie de la musique," d'Alembert maliciously described Rameau's claims to music as the master science: "[Rameau] ends up wanting to find all of geometry in musical proportions, the two sexes of animals in the major and minor modes, and finally the *Trinity* in the triple resonance of the *corps sonore*."[56] Despite the exaggeration clearly present in d'Alembert's characterization, the point is well taken. The single principle of resonance upon which Rameau's initial theory was based had become the principle for a vast array of human practices, from architecture to geometry; and this *esprit de système*, this confidence in systems, was precisely the element of Rameau's thought to which the Encyclopedists so fervently objected.

If Rameau's system conflicted with the genealogy of knowledge as it was presented in the *Encyclopédie*, it also violently clashed with the anthropology that Rousseau was developing through his examination of the origins of the arts and sciences. It would be a mistake, however, to see these theoretical positions as a separate domain, isolated from the context of personal and professional antagonisms that mark the period. It might be helpful, then, before examining the theoretical issues that separated Rameau and Rousseau, to situate the *Essai* within the context of the animosity between Rousseau and his (at that time) friends at the *Encyclopédie*, and Rameau.

There had been a great deal of low-level hostility between Rameau and Rousseau ever since the great composer had severely criticized Rousseau's opera *Les muses galantes* in 1745. Rousseau recalled the scene in the *Confessions*:

As soon as the overture began, Rameau, by his extravagant praises, intended to make it understood that the work could not be my own composition ... he addressed me with a brutality which gave universal offense, and declared that part of what he had just heard was the work of a consummate master of the art, while the rest was by an ignorant fellow, who did not even understand music ... Rameau declared that he saw in me only a contemptible plagiarist, without talent or taste.[57]

With the music articles he wrote for the *Encyclopédie*, Rousseau hoped to revenge himself on Rameau. He described his intentions in a letter to Madame de Warens, dated 27 January 1749: "I have those who have mistreated me exactly where I want them, and bile gives me strength, wit, and wisdom ... Everyone has his own Weapons; instead of writing songs against my Enemies, I am writing dictionary entries."[58] Reflecting on Rousseau's relationship to Rameau, M.-E.

[56] D'Alembert, *Œuvres et correspondances inédites*, 138.
[57] Rousseau, *Confessions* (London: J. M. Dent & Sons Ltd., 1931), 2:305–306.
[58] "Je tiens au cu et aux chausses des gens qui m'ont fait du mal et la bile me donne des forces de même de l'esprit et de la science ... Chacun a ses Armes; au lieu de faire des

Duchez interprets the musical doctrine that Rousseau would later elaborate as a desire to overcome what he saw as the obstacles that the music and musicians of his time had created for him.[59] Rousseau's letter to Madame de Warens does appear to voice this aspiration. In the *Lettre sur la musique française* (1753), although Rousseau neither directly attacks Rameau the composer, nor develops any general critique of Rameau's theories, he nonetheless criticizes Rameau's interpretation of Lully's opera *Armide* and claims that the French language is entirely incompatible with music – an unmistakable, if implicit, rejection of Rameau's operas: "the French have no music and will never have one."[60] In his *Erreurs sur la musique dans L'Encyclopédie*, Rameau reacts sharply, not only rejecting positions taken by Rousseau in his articles for the *Encyclopédie*, but also personally attacking Rousseau: "a bad ear is a great obstacle for anyone presuming to make himself a Legislator in Music"; "an ordinary individual who must be excited, animated by movement, because he is sensible only to the difference between high & low, is excusable; but a Composer or Musician, at least he who calls himself one, who wants to lay down the law [*dogmatiser*] . . ."[61] The exchange became more heated as Diderot and d'Alembert felt obliged to defend Rousseau and the integrity of their project in the foreword to the sixth volume of the *Encyclopédie*. One might read this animosity as the reaction of the preeminent French composer and music theorist of the Enlightenment to the *philosophes'* implicit claim to a kind of master discourse on music (not to mention all other arts and sciences). Seen in this light, Rameau's writings, from the mid-1750s on, are those of a man whose theories had been "usurped" and misconstrued by Rousseau and the Encyclopedic clan.[62] As d'Alembert's *Elemens de musique* maintained its scientific self-assurance, Rameau's later music theory desperately sought to reclaim its authority by expanding music theory to the level of metaphysics.

These theoretical stances and personal disagreements can be seen as the backdrop (and perhaps a starting point) for Rousseau's *Essai sur*

chansons à mes Ennemis, je leur fais des articles de Dictionnaires" (Rousseau, *Correspondance*, 2:113).

[59] Duchez, *Principe de la mélodie*, 57.

[60] Rousseau, *Ecrits sur la musique*, 322. On the political implications of Rousseau's words, see Wokler, "Rousseau on Rameau and revolution," 267; for an opposing view, see Duchez, *Principe de la mélodie*, 43–45.

[61] Rameau, *Complete Theoretical Writings*, 5:203, 5:210.

[62] James Doolittle takes this reasoning further by pointing out that Rameau had been refused admission to the Royal Academy of Sciences – "the ambition which Rameau treasured above all others" – whereas d'Alembert, half his age, had become a member *adjoint* at the age of 24 and *associé* four years later (Doolittle, "A would-be *Philosophe*," 235–237).

l'origine des langues. I will argue that by taking a detour through the origin of languages, Rousseau sought to gather enough evidence to prove that Rameau's theories were wrong – that melody is primary rather than secondary, and that the physical nature of the *corps sonore* can account for nothing more than the physical properties of music. In Rousseau's view, Rameau's theory of music entirely disregards the question of meaning, which would explain why it is so modern. Rousseau argues that the *corps sonore* cannot explain the relationship of music to society and culture. We have seen that Condillac's *Essai sur l'origine des connaissances humaines* depended on music for its discussions of the origin of language and knowledge: Condillac's desire to rebuild metaphysics led him into music theory. Rousseau uses a similar strategy in the *Essai sur l'origine des langues.* He launches his essay with considerations of the origin of language and of culture in order to defend and systematize a theory of music to which he would return repeatedly in other writings, and one that placed itself in radical opposition to that of Rameau. This passage into music theory is then integrated into the cultural and political considerations to which Rousseau returns in the last chapters of the *Essai.*

Music and the origin of culture

The first half of the *Essai* begins by establishing a series of differences in language – between gesture and voice, speech and writing, figurative and non-figurative language, needs and passions. Rousseau maintains that each pole represents a different stage in the development of cultures and their practices and that these practices retain the imprint of the natural and cultural conditions which produced them. At the very center of the *Essai*, two narratives locate in geographical terms the differences Rousseau has already established in the first part of the text. These chapters recount the story of the origin of southern languages born of "mild climates" and of the languages of the north, "sad daughters of necessity [which] reflect their harsh origins" (272–273).[63] In the second half of the *Essai*, devoted to music, yet another dichotomy supplements the series established earlier – that of melody and harmony. This dichotomy falls in line with the history and character of cultures that Rousseau has already described. The sections on language and on music share a chronology, beginning at the origin, proceeding through history, and ending with a glance at the current and, for Rousseau, largely unfortunate state of affairs. A chapter on "modern prosody" ends the introductory section on language, and "how music degenerated" concludes Rousseau's historico-cultural

---

[63] "Tristes filles de la necessité [qui] se sentent de leur dure origine" (*Essai*, 129).

analysis of music. After this final chapter on music, the *Essai* closes with a rapid discussion of the relationship between languages and government. Paul Fouquet saw the *Essai* as "a slightly confused and badly digested work."[64] Without seeking to disregard the inconsistencies in Rousseau's approach – as I have previously mentioned, these have been amply discussed by Derrida, among others – my purpose is to suggest a certain coherence in the unlikely combination of topics Rousseau chose to pursue. My claim is that the story of the origin of language and society presented in the *Essai*, in addition to being an argument in its own right and one that Rousseau will use to other ends in other contexts, serves here to explain the history and development of music, and to discredit Rameau's theory of the *corps sonore* which claimed to ground musical theory, practice, and reception in the physical properties of sound.

Whereas Condillac's *Essai sur l'origine des connaissances humaines* presented the history of knowledge as an uninterrupted progression, the very first chapter of the *Essai sur l'origine des langues* is already busy establishing differences – differences which separate human beings from animals and speech from gesture: "speech differentiates man from the other animals; language differentiates one nation from another" (240).[65] Language indicates two kinds of belonging: a general belonging to a larger group of beings – *Homo sapiens* – and a local belonging to geography and climate: "where a man is from is known only once he has spoken" (240). Or, perhaps more faithful to the tenor of Rousseau's words, one might say that language separates men from other animals and from each other: "speech differentiates [*distingue*]." Language is described here as a primitive form of social contract, which Rousseau will define later with this same paradoxical vocabulary of belonging and alienation; bound to a nation, one gives up one's belonging to humanity.[66] This linguistic difference between human beings, launching the argument of the *Essai*, was also the footing for the distinction between French and Italian music that Rousseau had already set down in the *Lettre sur la musique française*: "I have stated that every nation's music draws its principal character from the language that belongs to it."[67] We can begin to grasp, then, the degree to

---

[64] Fouquet, "J.-J. Rousseau," 117.
[65] "La parole distingue l'homme entre les animaux: le langage distingue les nations entre elles" (*Essai*, 27).
[66] The social contract is one in which "each one, uniting with all, nevertheless obeys only himself"; and yet it requires "the total alienation of each associate, with all his rights, to the whole community" (Rousseau, *On the Social Contract*, trans. Judith R. Masters [New York: St. Martin's Press, 1978], 53).
[67] "J'ai dit que toute musique nationale tire son principal caractère de la langue qui lui est propre" (Rousseau, *Ecrits sur la musique*, 264). With this passage on musical differences in the *Lettre sur la musique française*, as Derrida has noted, "the home

which many of Rousseau's theoretical writings – and certainly the *Lettre sur la musique française* and the *Contrat social* – are conceptually imbricated, resting on the premise of an original difference that is established here in the *Essai* and linked to the notion of perfectibility found in the second *Discours*.[68] On the one hand, speech (*la parole*) marks the distance which separates nature and culture: "conventional language belongs to man alone. That is why man makes progress in good as well as in evil, and why animals do not" (244). On the other hand, language distinguishes one culture from another. However, in addition to being a product of differences – a general difference in being (animals/human beings) and the local, climatic differences that define nations – language is also a point of fusion for the natural and the cultural: "since speech is the first social institution, it owes its form to natural causes alone" (240). Language exhibits differences between cultures, between human beings and animals, but at the same time reveals a hidden continuity between natural conditions and developing society.

Like Condillac, Rousseau believes that gestures came about through an instinctual desire to communicate our ideas to other human beings:

As soon as one man was recognized by another as a sentient, thinking Being, similar to himself, the desire or the need to communicate to him his sentiments and thoughts made him seek the means to do so. Such means can only be drawn from the senses, the only instruments by which one man can act upon another. Hence the institution of sensible signs to express thought. The inventors of language did not go through this [chain of] reasoning, but instinct suggested to them its conclusion [*conséquence*] (240).

Rousseau establishes that thought can only be communicated through the senses and that gesture is the natural expression of thought. Even though gesture and speech are "equally natural" according to the *Essai*, "the first is easier and less dependent on conventions. For more objects strike our eyes than our ears, and

[*logement*] of two origins, southern or northern, is already assured" (Derrida, *Of Grammatology*, 230).

[68] See Rousseau, *Œuvres*, 3:142. By inventing the homophone *différance*, Derrida suggests that traces of difference and deferring are always already in place where Western philosophy has tried to lay claim to an original fullness or presence. See Jacques Derrida, *Marges de la philosophie* (Paris: Editions de Minuit, 1972), 3–29. Habermas offers a sharp critique of Derrida's deconstruction by claiming that in his *différance*, Derrida merely replaces one origin with another, albeit a very differently constructed or de-constructed origin. From this standpoint, the process of deferral and difference merely repeats the eighteenth-century discourse on origins that grammatology supposedly supplanted: "Unabashedly, and in the style of *Ursprungsphilosophie*, Derrida falls back on this *Urschrift*" (Jürgen Habermas, *The Philosophical Discourse of Modernity*, trans. Frederick G. Lawrence [Cambridge: MIT Press, 1987], 179).

shapes exhibit greater variety than do sounds" (240). Rousseau states that gesture has a less conventional relationship to the objects which make up our physical environment and occupy our thoughts than does speech; to indicate things, we can easily touch or point to them. And since gesture conveys information by the same sensory path as do the objects of nature – that is, both are visual – there is an analogic relation between gestural signs and the objects they indicate. Using gestures, we simply figure the objects we desire or fear. Human beings thus adopt the forms of the natural world to "sign." These forms speak through the mediation of gesture: "how many things the girl who took such pleasure in tracing her Lover's shadow was telling him!" (241).[69] Gestures are "also more expressive and say more in less time" (240). Rousseau supports his claims with examples of the effectiveness of "visual argument" from ancient history: "Darius, waging war in Scythia, receives from the King of the Scythians a frog, a bird, a mouse, and five arrows. The Herald transmits his gift in silence and departs. This terrible harangue was understood, and Darius had no more urgent desire than to get back to his country as best he could" (241–242). The king's terrible harangue conveys information quickly and silently. If the eighteenth- or twentieth-century reader has to resort to a paraphrase of the message (which Voltaire provides in his *Essai sur les mœurs* – if Darius does not flee as fast as a bird or hide like a mouse, he will die by their arrows), it is a measure of the degree to which our mode of communication and understanding has changed over time.[70] Rousseau suggests that some traces remain of this "silent eloquence." Even speech, at its most eloquent, borrows from gesture: "the most eloquent discourses are ... those with the most images embedded in them" (242). For Rousseau, the sophisticated interplay of verbal images contained in modern languages must be considered the modern heir of the instinctual *ut pictura poesis* that already appears in primeval gesture.

The origin of speech is altogether different from that of gestural signs. Rousseau presents this origin using an example that appears eminently theatrical, even operatic, in its delimitation of a space of performance, on the one hand, and a space of reception on the other:

But when it is a question of moving the heart and enflaming the passions, things stand entirely differently. The successive impression made by discourse, striking with cumulative impact, arouses a very different emotion in you from that produced by the presence of the object itself, which you take in completely at one glance. Imagine a situation where you know perfectly well

---

[69] "Que celle qui traçoit avec tant de plaisir l'ombre de son Amant lui disoit de choses!" (*Essai*, 29).

[70] See Porset's notes to his edition of the *Essai*, 32.

that someone is in pain; you are not likely to be easily moved to tears at the sight of the afflicted person; but give him the time to tell you everything he feels and you will soon burst into tears (242–243).

In this passage, the visual effect of the object is shown to be vastly different from the impression created by discourse. Here, Rousseau opposes visual signs (the use of objects or gestures to convey information) to audible signs; yet, as Catherine Kintzler has pointed out, Rousseau does not simply oppose the visual to the audible. The difference he seeks to establish is between the gestural and the vocal.[71] Whereas gestures communicate ideas more clearly, vocal sounds, as in Condillac's *Essai*, are the privileged signs of passion: "pantomime alone, unaccompanied by discourse, will leave you almost unmoved; discourse unaccompanied by gesture will wring [*arrachera*] tears from you" (243). On the one hand, exact meaning is more accessible through the visible realm, since an object and its gestural sign are isomorphic. In other words, in Rousseau's view, gestures (like hieroglyphs) more closely resemble the objects they represent than do sounds: "visible signs make for more accurate imitation" (243). Both gestures and objects can be used as modes of visual argumentation. Emotions, however, are more easily aroused through vocal signs: "interest is aroused more effectively by sounds" (243). Looking further, we notice that underlying this dichotomous logic for which the gestural is to ideas as the vocal is to emotions, Rousseau has set up a more fundamental difference. The synchronic nature of visual signs is radically opposed to the diachronic nature of vocal sounds. With visible signs, meaning is instantaneously produced – *d'un coup d'œil* – at a glance. The sequential sounds of the voice, however, reproduce the passions whose very nature is movement and can only be captured in movement:

The passions have their gestures but also their accents; and these accents, which cause us to shudder, these accents to which one cannot close one's ear and which by way of it penetrate to the very depths of the heart, in spite of ourselves convey to it the [e]motions that wring them [from us], and cause us to feel what we hear (243).

As an expression of passion, the successive sounds of the voice also produce the same passion in the listener, "in spite of ourselves." It is possible for gestures to express the passions, but vocal sounds have access to a deeper region of the self. The *Essai* dramatizes the violence of the effect of verbal signs on the emotions: the vocal accents are drawn from the subject in passion, these sounds then "penetrate" the listener and "cause us to shudder." Rousseau at first appeared to

---

[71] Kintzler, *Poétique de l'opéra français*, 444.

privilege gesture, linking it to passionate and pre-linguistic communication in the example of the woman tracing the shadow of her lover. With the advent of language, Rousseau claims that vocal signs are more closely bonded with passion because they project the movement of passion.[72] Gestural signs do not have this profundity, working instantaneously, on the outside, at the surface, and at a distance. Whereas passionate sounds lead to engagement and identification with other beings, Rousseau characterizes the use of gesture as an abdication of speech to objects. Gestural signs "strike our eyes" rather than penetrating to the heart, and can "address arguments to the eyes" rather than "enflaming the passions" (240–241). Gestural language can be put to rational, political use: thus, "the Jews' Prophets and the Greeks' Lawgivers who frequently presented visible objects to the people, spoke to them better with these objects than they would have done with long discourses" (242). Whereas "to see" and "to understand" are for Rousseau direct and punctual in nature, leading to an essentially rational and indifferent understanding of objects which are external to the body, "to hear" and "to feel" profoundly connect one human being to another. Rousseau later continues the external/internal opposition by characterizing the visual as *parure*, as ornament or embellishment, in the opposition he establishes between colors and sounds in subsequent chapters (285).

Although Rousseau has not yet explicitly mentioned music, the difference between the instantaneity of visual signs and the successive nature of vocal ones will prove to be the same dichotomy which lies behind his stark opposition of harmony and melody. As Derrida has stressed, the description of these passionate accents is absolutely necessary for the discussion of music later in the *Essai*: "there is no music before language. Music is born of the voice and not of sound. No prelinguistic sonority can, according to Rousseau, open the time of music. In the beginning is the song."[73] The word Rousseau uses to describe primeval vocal sounds – *accens* – is a term with both linguistic and musical components. According to Du Marsais, *accent* designates both "the degree of elevation of the voice" – what we would generally

---

[72] Derrida has shown that Rousseau above all seeks to privilege immediate presence and that this desire reveals conceptual inconsistencies in his treatment of writing: "when the latter [presence] is *better represented* by the range of the voice and reduces dispersion, he praises living speech ... When the immediacy of presence is *better represented* by the proximity and rapidity of the gesture and the glance, he praises the most savage writing" (*Of Grammatology*, 237). Jean Starobinski nuances Derrida's position when he notes that the scene of the lover's drawing, asserting the superiority of gesture over words, specifically concerns a farewell. From that standpoint, the drawing is already produced by an anticipated absence, and not essentially the product of passionate communication (Rousseau, *Essai*, ed. Starobinski, 60n3).

[73] Derrida, *Of Grammatology*, 195.

call pitch – and "the quantity & the particular pronunciation of each word & each syllable" – what we, in English as in French, more commonly refer to as accent.[74] In his *Dictionnaire de musique*, Rousseau contends that "Dionysius Halicarnasseus rightly sees *Accent* in general as the seed of all Music".[75] As Belinda Cannone has suggested, the meaning of accent is somewhat equivocal, so that the expression "accent of the passions (is) both a metaphor for song and original language."[76] The original voice, insofar as it is an assemblage of accents, is impregnated with passion and movement, the constituent elements of both speech and song. From this standpoint, the *accent* to which Rousseau refers appears as a phantasmagoric entity whose qualities describe the superposition of speech and song in original voice.[77]

The second chapter of the *Essai* clarifies the distinction between gesture and speech which began to take form in chapter 1. At the beginning of the first chapter, Rousseau asserted that when one being is confronted with another, "the desire or the need to communicate to him his sentiments and thoughts made him seek the means to do so" (240). This statement is refined in the second chapter, desire being expressed by the voice and need by gesture: "it would seem, then, that the needs dictated the first gestures, and the passions wrung the first utterings [*voix*]" (245). Communication is of two radically different species: one expresses desire, the other need. These two "languages" – gestures and vocal sounds – differ in all respects: each has a separate origin – need vs. passion – and each conveys a different kind of information using distinct systems of signs. Here, proposing "to think about the origin of languages altogether differently from the way in which it has been thought about until now," Rousseau implicitly takes Condillac to task: "man did not begin by reasoning but by feeling. It is claimed that men invented speech in order to express their needs; that seems to me an untenable opinion. The natural effect of the first needs was to separate men, not to unite them" (245). Though Condillac had maintained the opposite in the *Essai sur l'origine des connaissances humaines*, Rousseau argues that vocal language is not the result of need. He goes as far as to claim that "if we had never had any but physical needs, we might very well never have spoken and [yet] have understood one another perfectly by means of the language of gesture alone" (243). Speech is not at all necessary, nor is speech the preferred expression of necessity; it belongs to an entirely different

---

[74] *Encyclopédie*, 1:66.   [75] Rousseau, *Dictionnaire de musique*, s.v. "Accent."

[76] Cannone, *Philosophies de la musique*, 52.

[77] In his *Traité de la formation méchanique des langues* (1765), Charles de Brosses ventured into a discussion of the musical accent, which he defines as "an intermediate category [*espèce*] between speech and song" (1:166).

order and as such has an origin radically distinct from that of gesture. Rousseau locates this origin in the passions which he also calls "moral needs" (245). Passions may be necessary to human beings, but these moral needs are wholly dissimilar in their effects to physical needs:

All the passions unite men, while the necessity to seek their subsistence forces them to flee one another. Not hunger, nor thirst, but love, hatred, pity, anger wrung their first utterings [*voix*] from them. Fruit does not shrink from our grasp, one can eat it without speaking; one stalks in silence the prey one means to devour; but in order to move a young heart, to repulse an unjust aggressor, nature dictates accents, cries, plaints: here [then] are the oldest invented words, and here is why the first languages were songlike and passionate before they were simple and methodical (245–246).

Whereas activities relating to need are silent and solitary, those connected to the passions are social, relating one human being to another. The voice, as the expression of these passions, is specifically human: an animal can be hungry or thirsty, but only a human being can feel love, hate, pity, or anger. Indeed, Rousseau claims that the innate languages of animals that "work and live together, such as Beavers, ants, bees ... are gestural and speak only to the eyes" (244). Gesture alone fulfills their common physical needs; yet common physical needs do not define a society. To human beings, nature supplies "accents, cries, plaints." This specifically human nature is, of course, not the external, physicality of the natural world, but rather an inner nature, "a faculty peculiar [*propre*] to man" (244). Made possible by the inner constitution of a common "humanity," vocal language can only take place as a social event.

In a recent article, Ian Hacking asserts that the French philosophical tradition (specifically identified as that of Condillac and the ideologues) conceived of language as effectively private: words represent ideas in the mind. Hacking argues that the move from private language to public language can occur only if words and ideas are considered identical; and he identifies the first public linguist as J. A. Hamann, born in 1730. For Hamann, "Language is essentially public and shared; it is prior to the individuation of one's self ... there is an 'I' only in linguistic communities."[78] Indeed, eighteenth-century theories of language in the French tradition do posit an isolated subject who then seeks to communicate with other isolated subjects. Rousseau nonetheless alters this view by asserting the concomitant emergence of language and society. It would be implausible, of course, to claim for Rousseau's *Essai* a theorization of the performativity and self-reference that marks linguistic theory today. Yet language is and can only be a shared and public event for Rousseau, however dependent it may be

[78] Hacking, "How, why, when, and where?," 86.

on "private" psychic structures regulating the passions. Referring to a pre-social state of nature in the second *Discours*, Rousseau even questions the need for any kind of conventional signs: "the first difficulty that arises is to imagine how languages could have become necessary; for Men having no relationships with one another and no need of any, one cannot conceive the necessity or the possiblity of this invention if it was not indispensable."[79] For Rousseau, vocal sounds are not so much expressions of ideas as they are moments of identification and social bonding. That is why Rousseau explains that theatrical declamation has such a great effect upon the audience: "only thus do the scenes of tragedy produce their effect" (243). Speech is not the reproduction of an inner "theater of ideas." Language requires not simply a private subjectivity that experiences passion, but rather relies on the sympathy of a "public" to constitute that passion as a relation. Hence, the importance of the notion of *pitié* for Rousseau's history of language and culture, and the description of the origin of language as an essentially theatrical moment.

At this point in our analysis, it is important to emphasize the degree to which Rousseau's representation of the origin differs from that of Condillac. The *Essai sur l'origine des connaissances humaines* rests on a teleology of single principles: for Condillac, all of culture and all of knowledge must be traced to sensations. The natural cry bridges the gap between the reflex and the signifier, between nature and culture. Condillac wants to emphasize the ability of empiricism to provide an alternative narrative to Cartesian or other essentialist metaphysics. Rousseau, on the contrary, begins his *Essai* by stressing that, although the senses are "the only instruments by which one man can act upon another," there is a specifically human faculty lying behind cultural practices such as language and music, and that recourse to sensationalism cannot fully account for this faculty: "for it is not so much the ear that conveys pleasure to the heart as the heart that conveys it to the ear" (284–285). Physical sensation cannot fully explain language and its social development. Whereas Condillac describes a material continuum of sensation which is displaced and transformed in various ways, Rousseau posits a history that is constantly and violently disrupted. The continuum that Rousseau seeks to establish is hidden away in passion from the semiotic and social upheavals the *Essai* describes. This position will be of fundamental importance for Rousseau's rejection of the theories introduced by Rameau. Rousseau objects to both Condillac's and Rameau's reliance on the physical. If an original sensation in Condillac operates in a similar way to the discovery of resonance in the *corps sonore* for Rameau, Rousseau sees

[79] Rousseau, *Discourse*, 153.

material sensation as carrying information but unable to move the passions and thus unable, in and of itself, to explain the existence of society and culture.

As part of its story of historical degradation, the *Essai*'s next step is to trace the pattern of differences separating gestures and need from speech and emotion, to the history of vocal language itself. The first languages, reflecting the civilizations they fostered, were inarticulate and passionate:

> The genius of the oriental languages, the oldest ones known to us, completely contradicts the didactic development they are imagined to have followed. These languages are in no way methodical or reasoned; they are lively and figurative. The speech of the first men is represented to us as [if they had been] Geometers' languages, whereas we can see that they were Poets' languages (245).

As the expression of sentiment, language is first poetic; only later in its history does it become rational and analytic. The first language begins for Rousseau, as for Condillac, with an inarticulate cry. Only later does the development of articulation lead to analysis and method: "simple sounds issue naturally from the throat, and the mouth is naturally more or less open; but the modifications of tongue and palate, by which we articulate, require attention and practice" (247). It is a simple affair to emit sound, to yell; but when it comes to articulating that sound, the complex arrangements of the tongue and the palate require skill: "all children must learn them, and some do not do so easily" (247). Vocalization is natural, articulation is studied. Vocal sounds even "issue naturally from the throat," as if of themselves, whereas articulated sounds, like Condillac's conventional signs, are the result of conscious choice: "we do not make them without intending to make them" (247). Hence, the primacy of vocal sound over articulation: "in all languages the liveliest exclamations are inarticulate; cries, moans are nothing but utterings [*voix*]" (49). Whereas Condillac points to certain inadequacies of early speech, Rousseau celebrates the infinitely rich resources of the first language:

> Articulations are few in number; sounds are numberless, and the accents placed on them can similarly be multiplied; all musical notes are so many accents; it is true that our speech has only three or four; but the Chinese have many more; on the other hand, they have fewer consonants. To this source of combinations, add that of meter or quantity, and you will have a greater variety not only of words, but of syllables, than the richest language needs (247).

As vocal accent, music makes it appearance on the side of inarticulate sound and thus falls neatly into the paradigm Rousseau has established. The first vocal language has a wealth of sonorous resources, is passionate, inarticulate, and musical – characteristics Rousseau projects onto the Chinese language. Geography and the history of civilizations are confounded in Rousseau's vision of the origins of language, endebted as it is to the accounts of explorers and missionaries. Geographic and temporal distance are conflated: as a language of the Far East, Chinese is identified with an early stage of linguistic development: the exotic stands in for the origin. At the opposite pole of history, at the apogee of modern European civilization, French speech must logically be the antithesis of this first language, lacking all of its primitive characteristics: "we have no idea of a sonorous and harmonious language" (255). While inaugurating an idealization of the Orient that would characterize European writing throughout the nineteenth century and into the twentieth, Rousseau reverses the characteristic linguistic arrogance of early modern French writers. If the original, musical language has an abundance of accents, then our speech is reduced to three or four. Likewise, if an accentuated language such as Chinese has few consonants, our language must be overrun by them.

The first language is connected with the physical and moral circumstances to which it responded, filled with the movement and passion that are foreign to gestural signs: "not only must all of the phrases [*tours*] of this language be in images, sentiments, figures of speech; but in its mechanical aspect it would have to answer to its primary aim and convey to the ear as well as to the understanding the almost inescapable impressions of passion seeking to communicate itself" (248). Language displays or assumes the shape of the passion it seeks to express, and conveys this passion (in)to the listener. As Rousseau describes it, the voice figures passion by shaping sound into images and figures. Rather than being based on the abstraction of words, this first language would be devoted to "euphony," "harmony," and "the beauty of sounds" (248). At this stage, before reason and abstraction work their way into language, the sonorities of the voice operate on two levels. For the benefit of the senses, there is a sensual play with the medium of sound, and at the same time the voice molds itself to "figure" that which it seeks to communicate. The relation of the signifier and the signified is marked by play and indifferentiation.

These passages clearly reveal the extent of Rousseau's cratylism: "you will find that Plato's *Cratylus* is not as ridiculous as it appears to be" (248). From this standpoint, it would be easy to show that what Rousseau designates as the expressions of the passionate voice – synonyms, expletives, augmentatives, diminutives, euphony, onomatopoeia – are just as conventional as the abstract words that, for Rousseau, make up the fabric of later languages. Seen from this perspective, we could claim that Rousseau was in contradiction with himself, or that Rousseau's text reveals larger inconsistencies in the logic of binary oppositions. However, my purpose in this chapter is not to deconstruct Rousseau; that task has been accomplished many times over. Instead, I want to examine his attempt to develop a theory of music, supported by an entire "anthropology" to which it will be integrated, and attacking Rameau's theory of the *corps sonore*. In order to accomplish this task, it is important to follow the logic of the *Essai* (without necessarily taking it at face value) so as to examine the links that Rousseau would like to establish between human nature, semiosis, socialization, and the development of culture. The *Essai* seeks to demonstrate that the first language and its expressions are natural by tracing them from an original human nature. Not that Rousseau assumes language to be natural in an absolute sense. For in his discussion of the formation of southern languages (as well as in the second *Discours*), he clearly indicates that "in the first times," there was no true speech at all, but only "a few inarticulate sounds" (260). Likewise, *la pitié*, which constitutes the very core of the emotions, at first lay dormant. The *Essai* reveals these emotions as the driving force behind language: "social attachments [*affections*] develop in us only with our knowledge. Pity, although natural to man's heart, would remain forever inactive without imagination to set it in motion" (261). *La pitié* – the socializing force of compassion – is activated in tandem with society and language. The ability to compare ideas (reflection) and to figure them (imagination) allows for the creation of a virtual space in which the subject exists, sympathetically, as the other. We create the bonds which are the foundation of society "by identifying with the suffering being": "it is not in ourselves but in him that we suffer" (261). Language is unquestionably the product of society, and society implies some measure of convention. Yet Rousseau attempts to differentiate those conventions (the first language, melody) which are aligned with the human nature of *la pitié* from those (writing, harmony) which he sees as distortions of it. The *Essai* separates certain features of speech from others, attributing to some – those of the first languages – the characteristics which can still be found in song and isolating others, as we shall see, by giving them qualities which distinguish them from song:

Since our natural utterings [*voix*] are inarticulate, words would have few articulations; a few interspersed consonants would eliminate the hiatus between vowels, and so suffice to make them smooth and easy to pronounce. On the other hand, its sounds would be extremely varied, and variety of accent would make the same utterings [*voix*] greater in number ... utterings [*voix*], sounds, accent, and quantity, which are by nature, would leave little to be done by articulations, which are by convention, men would sing rather than speak (248).

Closer to nature rather than to convention, smooth and easy to pronounce rather than marked by articulations, the sounds of the voice must have resembled song rather than speech. Diametrically opposed to the speech of the modern world, the first language would have been like song. Rousseau accomplishes this division by "reading" the origin of language into his experience of contemporary music while at the same time deriving a position from which to attack Rameau from original language and nascent society.

We have seen how the *Essai* sets the stage for the origin of language and examined the musical terms in which the first language is described. As a negation of eighteenth-century languages, primordial speech is situated outside of time. The origin obeys no chronology: it is, by definition, *u-chronique*. When Rousseau attempts to trace language from its prehistoric origins to the present day, he must introduce dichotomies that are historical in nature. The supposedly timeless values he had placed at the origin – energy, sonority, and pleasure – are slowly attenuated: "anyone who studies the history and progress of languages will see that as utterings [*voix*] grow increasingly monotone, consonants increase in number ... but these changes take place only gradually" (249). As the *Essai* progresses, language lapses into ever-increasing degrees of ruin: it gradually becomes unaccentuated, clearly articulated, and cold. But Rousseau must also find ways of planting absolute breaks and ruptures inside the apparent continuum of history, so that current language and music appear as radically estranged from the origin: thus, what is described at one point in the *Essai* as a gradual, natural development – "this progress seems entirely natural to me" (249) – is later revealed to be sudden *bouleversement*, revolution – "he who willed man to be sociable inclined the globe's axis at an angle to the axis of the universe by a touch of the finger" (266).[80] The impossible passage from outside history into historical time is reproduced within history as rupture and cataclysm. The *Essai*'s description of the origin and history of music will also conform to this pattern of breaks and ruptures inside the larger continuum of humanity.

As it moves through history, the original song-language undergoes drastic transformations. The *Essai* refers to the various languages of the globe, each at a different stage of development, to support the notion of an historical progress in the language of "humanity." But at the same time, Rousseau takes steps to ensure that the origin will remain unscathed by and protected from history: history is marked by both continual progression and radical discontinuity. Whereas our

---

[80] "Celui qui voulut que l'homme fut sociable toucha du doigt l'axe du globe et l'inclina sur l'axe de l'univers" (*Essai*, 109).

European languages have been swept away from their linguistic origins by progress, others appear to have remained closer to them. The culture of these non-European peoples is also closer to the primitive state described in the chapter on the formation of southern languages: due to their climate, "the needs that cause society to be born made themselves felt later" (266). In this chapter, Rousseau scatters references to contemporary travelers' accounts of the American Indians among his observations on "the first age" and "the age of the patriarchs" (264). Anticipating the claims of later anthropologists, civilization at the time of Moses and that of eighteenth-century native Americans are shown to be structurally comparable; although separated in time, both are examples of pastoral cultures (265). Rousseau compares the first language to a number of exotic tongues: "in some respects it would resemble Chinese, in others Greek, in still others Arabic" (248). The *vivacité* of oriental languages has been little diminished with time: they remain closer to the origin and thus more accentuated, varied, energetic, and replete with "cadence" and "fullness" (248). The qualities of the first languages are thus still present, safeguarded to some extent from European progress, in the not fully articulated, musical tones of the primitive languages of far-away cultures. Back in the familiar territory of Europe, however, languages are cold, clear, and reasoned: "Polish must be the most frigid of all languages" (259). That which is original and natural in language is equated with the exotic; and the exotic serves to protect the *Essai*'s conception of the origin as a haven which continues to influence certain cultures, far removed – geographically and hence conceptually – from the state of European culture in the 1750s. At the same time, far- and middle-eastern cultures can be said to harbor an original "truth" of the Occident, a logic that implicitly justified further European exploration and conquest.

Rousseau takes radical measures to protect his investment in an airtight and timeless origin, revealing that the present-day geographical difference is in fact an original difference within the notion of culture itself. Chapters 8 through 11 – the section of the *Essai* devoted to the birth of language – make it clear that what appeared to be a single origin of language is always already double.[81] The geographical locus of later languages which are simple and methodical is

---

[81] Here we encounter head-on what Derrida refers to as the logic of "supplementarity": unable to posit an actual zero degree of language or culture, Rousseau forever multiplies the breaks, the boundaries which separate an elusive "before" from an ever-encroaching "after." "It seems," notes Christie V. McDonald, "that with each step forward in the supplement the artificial substitution strangely moves closer to the origin as a kind of limit" ("Jacques Derrida's reading of Rousseau," 89). Supplementarity "accounts for the constant splintering of that unity of the origin – that is, the notion of presence to which Rousseau seems so ferociously to cling" (*ibid.*, 91).

separated from that of the first languages, "songlike and passionate": "mankind, born in the warm countries, spreads to the cold ones; there [mankind] increases, and eventually flows back into the warm countries" (260). In southern latitudes, language is the product of pleasure and passion. Rousseau nostalgically describes the language and society born under the kindly influence of the temperate climate of the south: "in a word, in mild climates, in fertile regions, it took all the liveliness of the agreeable passions to start men speaking. The first languages, daughters of pleasure rather than of need, long remained under the aegis of their father" (272). For northern peoples, however, in a perversion of the separation of need and linguistic expression that Rousseau established in the first chapters of the *Essai*, "their first word was not *love me* but *help me*" (274).[82] In accordance with this linguistic duality, Rousseau solidly places the de-centered origin of those methodical, geometric languages in Europe: "French, English, German are the private languages of men who help one another, who argue [*raisonnent*] with one another in a deliberate manner [*de sang-froid*]" (275). The series of drastic oppositions that Rousseau sets up is emblematically reduced to a minute morphological difference (*aimer*, to love, and *aider*, to help): all of history is prefigured in the difference between two consonants, one ("d") which strongly articulates, and one ("m") which glides gently between two vowels. The linguistic and musical revolution that has led to our present state of affairs is thus paradoxically exemplified by a virtually imperceptible alteration.[83]

The earlier dichotomies that we have examined are subsumed in the geographical distribution of languages among the northern and the southern. The northern *aider* is opposed to the southern *aimer*, as the reasoned languages of the former are opposed to the passionate speech of the latter: "southern languages must have been lively, resonant, accentuated, eloquent, and often obscure because of their vigor; northern languages must have been muted, crude, articulated, shrill, monotone and clear, through the addition of words rather than because of good construction" (274–275). Instead of the passionate speech of the south, the language of "the northern peoples" is directed by physical need; the heartfelt depth of southern speech is contrasted with the superficial and physical nature of northern gestures – "more in the arms than in the heart" (273); southern vowels and accents are

---

[82] "Le prémier mot ne fut pas chez eux, *aimez-moi*, mais, *aidez-moi*" (*Essai*, 131).

[83] This imperceptible alteration takes narrative form in chapter 9: "he who willed man to be sociable inclined the globe's axis ... by a touch of the finger ... With this slight motion I see the face of the earth change" (266). It can be shown that Rousseau offers "the imperceptible difference" as an emblem for most of the dichotomies presented in the *Essai* in order to illustrate that an almost invisible shift will later result in a catastrophic gap.

opposed to northern consonants and articulations, and so on. There is thus a "good," primary origin and a "bad," secondary origin, a malignant outgrowth of the first. The original language of gesture returns as the perversion of northern speech, unable to transcend physical need to reach the passions. The *Essai* protects the naturally energetic and passionate qualities by isolating them in the sonorous vocal sounds of southern speech, keeping all unfavorable attributes under quarantine in the separate and disqualified origin of northern languages. Otherness – in temporal, geographical, cultural, and linguistic terms – acts as the imaginary site of an authentic, timeless, and decidedly Edenic origin:

Here the first festivals took place; feet skipped with joy, an eager gesture no longer proved adequate, the voice accompanied it with passionate accents, pleasure and desire merged into one and made themselves felt together. Here, finally, was the true cradle of peoples, and from the pure crystal of the fountains sprang the first fires of love (271).

The *Essai* presents an unending series of ruptures following on the heels of the oppositions between the north and the south, between animals and humans, gesture and voice, and need and emotion. These ruptures are intended to clearly delimit (and thus preserve) the boundaries of the "true cradle of peoples"; they attempt to create a qualitative distinction between the origin and the moment which begins the progressive and inevitable surge towards the present state of affairs. To take yet another example (one that has been discussed at length by Derrida), Rousseau seeks to demonstrate that speech and writing do not simply differ through some kind of evolutionary development – writing being somehow born of speech and progress – but that they are the result of two entirely distinct needs: "the art of writing does not in any way depend on that of speaking" (251). As Starobinski has noted, for Rousseau, "history as a whole is divided into a *before* and an *after*."[84] Like the simple melody he recalls from his childhood in the *Confessions*, which "has obstinately resisted all my efforts to recall it," Rousseau's "before," which holds the secret of an original and passionate language, has become inaccessible to those who live within the civilized "after" of a modern society.[85]

Chapter 5 moves into the postlapsarian world, following the tide of history and progress through the development of writing. History tells the story of the inevitable infection of all languages – southern as well as northern – with the backwash [*reflux*] of the north. This *reflux* is identified as method, clarity, and reason:

---

[84] Jean Starobinski, *Jean-Jacques Rousseau: la transparence et l'obstacle* (Paris: Gallimard, 1971), 14.

[85] Rousseau, *Les Confessions*, ed. Voisine, 11.

Anyone who studies the history and progress of languages will see that as utterings [*voix*] grow increasingly monotone, consonants increase in number, and that as accents disappear and quantities are equalized, they are replaced by grammatical combinations and new articulations ... In proportion as needs increase, as [men's] dealings [with one another] grow more involved [*s'embrouillent*], as enlightenment spreads, the character of language changes (249).

Leaving its passionate origins, language "becomes more precise and less passionate; it substitutes ideas for sentiments; it no longer speaks to the heart but to the reason" (249). There is a direct correlation between the state of a culture, the kind of ideas expressed in its language, and the sonorous substance of the language itself. As needs multiply, so do linguistic articulations and consonants – the sounds best adapted to the expression of needs and ideas. At the same time, the passions are silenced and language cools off: "language becomes more exact and clear, but more sluggish, subdued [*sourde*], and cold" (249). Writing has a crucial role in fixing language: "it substitutes precision for expressiveness. One conveys one's sentiments in speaking, and one's ideas in writing" (253).[86] Language continues its movement away from passion and energy, towards clarity and monotony: "all this tends to confirm the following principle, that by a natural progress all lettered languages must change character and lose vigor as they gain in clarity" (258). For Rousseau, a purely natural process (which he cannot simply describe as a process at all, as we have seen, but rather as a series of "natural disasters") leads a rich and sonorous vocal language into the servility and silence of the written word – into the "mute sign"[87]: "since there is nothing left to say to the people but *give money*, it is said with posters on street corners" (294).[88] The loss of voice to which Rousseau refers has a definite political meaning: the representation that becomes possible with the written word is an alienated version of the original, passionate, and vocal expression of identification and sympathy with others. The abdication of speech to writing has its analogue in the emergence of political representation and proxy with which Rousseau prognosticates the end of the State: "is it necessary to march to battle? They pay troops and stay at home. Is it necessary to attend the council? They name deputies and stay home."[89] The zero degree of civilization – the natural and silent state before society in which "men [are] scattered over the face of the earth"

---

[86] See Derrida's analysis of the place of writing in Rousseau, in *De la grammatologie*, 379–445.

[87] Derrida, *Of Grammatology*, 233.

[88] Rousseau connects money with the ultimate perversion of the sign: "give money and you will soon have chains" (*On the Social Contract*, 102).

[89] Rousseau, *On the Social Contract*, 101–102.

(260) – thus joins the frozen and likewise silent state of modern societies: "societies have assumed their final forms" (294). Our languages, now separated from the (musical) voice, no longer resonate. Rousseau claims that "among the ancients it was easy to be heard by the people in a public square"; our languages can no longer be heard on the public square and thus no longer fulfill a social function (294). Since the social fabric has ruptured, rulers take advantage of this situation to maintain authoritarian control: "subjects must be kept scattered" (294). The silence of gesture, at first valorized, has returned again as the deplorable silence of writing and as the paradoxical condition of social isolation. Speech, music, and a dynamic society flourish in the utopian space between these two poles.

Music has already made its appearance in the *Essai* in the form of original language: that is, Rousseau has hypothesized and reconstructed the first language as a kind of song. One feature of texts on the origins of language, as we have already seen for Condillac's *Essai sur l'origine des connaissances humaines*, is the connection they establish between contemporary musical practices and a hypothetical, original language. The contemporary music Rousseau has in mind is of course not the French opera, with its various trills, appoggiaturas – *fredons, cadences, ports-de-voix* – "and other superfluous ornaments."[90] As he pieces together a model of original language, Rousseau finds it more appropriate to refer to the ostensibly less artful songs of simpler folk who, for one reason or another, have been spared the onslaught of Western civilization. Just as Rameau had in his *Observations sur notre instinct pour la musique*, Rousseau defers to "a person with a true but untrained ear" (281); to "the ear of a Carib" (283); and to "the songs of American savages" (289). In its most basic forms, European music seems to have transcended, or at least momentarily bypassed, the

---

[90] Rousseau, *Ecrits sur la musique*, 263. In Condillac's discussion of the speech and declamation of the ancients, which, he claimed, retained many of the qualities of the first language, he criticizes Dacier's commentary of Aristotle because "Monsr. Dacier forms an idea of the Greek pronunciation from that of the French, and of the music of the ancient tragedies from that of the modern opera's" (Condillac, *Essay*, 187). Dubos, he claims, makes a similar mistake: "I am much mistaken, or this writer had not a very clear idea of what constitutes the vocal music [of the ancients]. He seems to judge of it only from that of our operas. Having mentioned that Quintilian complained of some Barristers [*orateurs*] for pleading in the same manner as they recited on the stage, is it to be imagined, adds he, that those orators sang as we sing at our operas? I answer, that the succession of the tones which constitute a song may still be much more simple than that of our operas; nor is it at all necessary they should have the same transitions, the same strained cadences [*ports de voix cadencés*], and continued quavers [*tremblemens soutenus*]" (Condillac, *Essai*, 193n). The ancients spoke not in the intricately modulated recitatives of eighteenth-century French opera, but rather in the kind of primitive solfège Condillac describes in part 2, chapter 5, of his *Essai*.

114

continual degradation that the *Essai* portrays: "all musical notes are so many accents" (247). Even if our speech no longer exhibits these accents, they are nonetheless still intact in the most basic forms of music. It is important to note that Rousseau defines music as, or restricts it to, vocal melody. At every point in the *Essai* where music is shown to stray from vocal melody and passionate accent, it is also represented as moving away from the musicality that is at the origin of the emotional and social bond between sentient beings: that is, it has become something other than music. For Rousseau, when we listen to melody we hear an echo of the origin. Rousseau's description of his preferred forms of eighteenth-century music in the *Dictionnaire de musique* and the *Lettre sur la musique française* – monodic song, for example, or Italian recitative with its *vivacité* and its ability to "reproduce all the inflections with which the most vehement passions animate discourse" – bears a close resemblance to the hypothetical original language described in the *Essai*.[91] By projecting selected characteristics of eighteenth-century music into the distant past while singling out others such as harmony and counterpoint as later, non-musical additions, Rousseau is able to reconstruct an original, sonorous, and musical language out of valorized elements of eighteenth-century music. He is also prepared to tell a story about the subsequent degradation of music, language, and nations: "now, I maintain that any language in which it is not possible to make oneself understood by the people assembled is a servile language; it is impossible for a people to remain free and speak that language" (295). In the *Lettre sur la musique française*, he had come to the conclusion that French music, following the language, was a degenerate form: "I believe that I have shown that there is neither measure nor melody in French music because the language is not capable of it."[92] Language and music are tied to the cultural and political conditions under which they came to be and the historical changes they have undergone. More is at stake here than Rousseau's "personal" musical preferences. As I pointed out in the first chapter, the linking of music and language is the mark of a paradigm, of an episteme. Rousseau is one of many writers who view music, and particularly song, as a kind of language. Charles Batteux, for example, makes the relationship quite clear when he suggests that music speaks to the listener: "music speaks to me in tones."[93] For Rousseau, the energy and urgency of melody bring to language precisely those qualities of movement and passion with which he described the first language. As Saint Preux explains to Julie in *La Nouvelle Héloïse*, these are the marks of the aria and recitative of Italian opera:

91 Rousseau, *Ecrits sur la musique*, 310.   92 *Ibid.*, 322.
93 Batteux, *Les Beaux arts*, 262.

How strangely I had been mistaken in my judgement of the productions of this charming art [of music] ... I did not perceive, in the accents of melody applied to those of language, the powerful and secret link between passions and sounds; I did not see that the imitation of the various tones with which emotions animate the speaking voice in turn give the ability to move hearts to the singing voice, and that the energetic painting of the movements of the soul of he who makes himself understood, is what makes the real charm of those who listen to him.[94]

This passage bears a striking resemblance to many of those we have seen in the *Essai* which likewise describe the "powerful and secret" link between passions and sounds. This link is conspicuously absent from Rousseau's depiction of the monotonous language and music of eighteenth-century France, marked by the dislocation and alienation of northern origins.

There is another, more "technical" way to account for the fact that Rousseau describes the first language as a musical language. As in Condillac's *Essai sur l'origine des connaissances humaines*, the *Essai sur l'origine des langues* appears to have borrowed a technical and descriptive vocabulary from music theory that Rousseau, along with other writers of the period, found to be particularly apt for the depiction of a hypothetical original state of language. Together with a loosely defined empiricism, Rameau's discoveries and earlier music theory provided a theoretical foundation and a vocabulary, neither of which were bound by the book of Genesis or the accounts of the divine implantation of language derived from it. Having no "science" of language that would adequately fit with a narrative of origins, eighteenth-century writers borrowed from the precise, technical conceptual vocabulary of music theory in order to represent the first vocal sounds. Describing Greek speech and song, for example, Rousseau referred to "intervals smaller than consonances and simpler than commas" (290). This borrowing is perhaps not surprising since both eighteenth-century music theory and these hypothetical accounts of the first speech considered the same object: the human voice. Most useful for Rousseau was a general musical vocabulary (words such as "tone," "rhythm," "cadence," and "melody"), adapted to describe the contours of original speech. This borrowing was by no means limited to the particular cases of Condillac and Rousseau. In his treatise on the arts, the *Réflexions critiques sur la poésie et sur la peinture*, Jean-Baptiste Dubos offered composers a theory of musical imitation which looks much like Rousseau's description of original voice: "the Musician [*Musicien*] imitates the tones, the accents, the sighs, the inflections of the voice, and all the sounds with whose help nature itself expresses its

---

[94] Rousseau, *Œuvres*, 2:131–132.

emotions and passions."[95] I am not suggesting that Rousseau borrowed from Dubos, but rather that since music and language were considered to be intimately related (both being expressions of the passions), eighteenth-century reflections on the origin of language in part shared a conceptual framework with music theory and criticism. Rousseau's nostalgic look at hypothetical, original music and language crosses paths with Dubos' utopian musical aesthetics. Both deplored the state of contemporary French music because it is "so laden down with rubbish that one hardly recognizes a trace of natural expression."[96] Rousseau's representation of the origin and Dubos' commentary have a similar relation to the present: both constitute a glance towards what the present might have been or towards what the future might be. The nostalgia for origins, coming from a reflection on the present state of affairs, thus joins a utopian striving for the perfection of musical expression.

The importance of Rameau's publications for the musings of both Condillac and Rousseau on the origin of language cannot be overemphasized. If music enters into the description of original language, it is in many respects due to the influence of Rameau's new theory and its methodology. On the one hand, Condillac's discussion of Greek and Latin, as well as his chapter on the origin of music, lean heavily on the concepts found in Rameau's *Génération harmonique*. On the other, I intend to demonstrate that the *Essai sur l'origine des langues* can, in some measure, be shown to be a "product" of Rameau's theory – produced, that is, by a desire to provide an alternative to the origin of music posited by Rameau and to disprove his most fundamental assertions. In the music articles he wrote for the *Encyclopédie*, Rousseau had already challenged many of the conclusions Rameau drew from his principle of the *corps sonore*. In the *Essai*, once an account of the origin and history of language was in place, Rousseau drew from it a narrative of the origin and development of music which would support his other writings on language and culture and, at the same time, invalidate Rameau's system by attacking it at the foundation – the *corps sonore*. Rameau had held that it was natural for human beings to emit vocal sounds, and that the act of singing was based on and best understood through the harmonies generated by the physics of resonance – "this principle is Nature itself."[97] Although Rousseau would certainly not disagree with the first part of Rameau's statement – that music is natural to human beings – he dismissed the explanation of music founded on a principle of physical resonance. Whereas Condillac constructed his story of the original language through the

---

[95] Dubos, *Réflexions critiques*, 1:634–635.   [96] *Ibid.*, 1:663.
[97] Rameau, *Complete Theoretical Writings*, 3:259.

117

conceptual support of Rameau's theories, Rousseau used his own fictional account to disprove them. In the *Essai*, after having discussed the origin and decadence of language, Rousseau prepares to attack Rameau in chapter 12 by describing the origin of music.

The chapters on music were written to fully concur with the chapters on language: they retell the same story of origins from a slightly different standpoint. From the perspective of later chapters, the *Essai*'s valorization of the vocal (as melody) and the condemnation of the instrumental (as closely associated with harmony) point to a double origin. Similarly, from the point of view of genealogy, the division of northern and southern language forces a split in the origin of music: "together with the first utterings [*voix*], the first articulations or the first sounds were formed, depending on the kind of passion that dictated either of them" (276). As north is opposed to south, so articulation is opposed to vocal sound. The origin that Rousseau attributes to music thus patterns itself after the differences established earlier between the harsh languages of the north, which, determined by "superficial" physical need, appear to have developed *in reverse* ("in the case of languages burdened with useless consonants, writing even seems to have preceded speech"), and the deep and lyrical languages of the south (259): "anger wrests [from us] threatening cries which the tongue and the palate articulate; but the voice of tenderness is gentler: it is modulated by the glottis and becomes a sound" (276). It is not only the needs of the north and the passions of the south that differ; passion, too, splits in this passage. There is anger, on the one hand, and tenderness on the other. Earlier, Rousseau had amputated the ugly speech found in northern climates from the beautiful language of southern origin; now with respect to music he attempts to dissociate the renegade, bilious articulations of the north (a kind of anti-music) from the tender and truly musical sounds of southern speech. The *Essai*'s desire to disassociate completely these two types of voice is so strong that the impatient anger of Europeans ("excited [*emportés*] men who get angry") and the warm intonations of the people of southern climates are shown to stem from two entirely different bodily organs (275): the tongue and the palate produce articulations while vocal sound is modified by the glottis in the deeper regions of the vocal tract. Music is split from the very beginning: Rousseau claims that the modulated voice exists naturally as sound, whereas articulations (produced by the tongue and palate) are the labored product of convention and experience: "utterings [*voix*], sounds, accent, and quantity, which are by nature, would leave little to be done by articulations, which are by convention" (248).

Articulation and its effects on music having been set aside for a subsequent chapter, the *Essai* goes on to detail what it imagines to be the "proper" (understood as the essential belonging as well as the correct version of) origin of music. Modulations in vocal sound are directly produced by variations in emotions: "its accents . . . are more or less frequent, its inflections more or less acute depending on the sentiment that accompanies it" (276). Passion produces and is expressed in vocal melody. At the origin of music, as Rousseau describes it, the voice generates a scale of rhythms and pitches (more or less frequent accents and more or less acute inflections) which reproduce different shades of emotion. At the origin of music, the voice moves with and is driven by the passions: "thus cadence and sounds are born together with syllables: passion rouses all of the [vocal] organs to speech and adorns the voice with their full brilliance; thus verse, song, speech have a common origin" (276). The passions speak not only in the voice but also through the body. Likewise, the body speaks for the passions. However, the musical voice appears to be the privileged and natural expression of the passionate body, as it was for Condillac. Indeed, Rousseau had pointed out earlier that "simple sounds issue naturally from the throat" (247). The *Essai* joins song and speech – both comprised of vocal sounds – through their common link to the passions. Music, like speech, is thus the product of something which is particular to human nature – a specifically human faculty that reaches out to other beings: "in order to move a young heart, to repulse an unjust aggressor, nature dictates accents, cries, plaints: here [then] are the oldest invented words, and here is why the first languages were songlike and passionate" (245–246).

The origin of music, as Rousseau describes it, stems directly from the formation of southern languages, the subject of chapter 9. In that chapter, Rousseau placed the origin of society and language at the wells and springs where young men (coming "to water their herds") and women (fetching "water for the household") would necessarily give voice to the emotions they felt upon first meeting each other. The first language, "the first ties between families," and "the first festivals" all came into existence simultaneously at these local wells (271). Once Rousseau has begun his discussion of the origin of music (from chapter 12 on), he refers back to these propitious meetings to explain that the first words were as much sung as they were spoken. The origin of music is presented as an operatic scene of the meeting of the sexes whose melodic language acts as a natural recitative:

Around the fountains which I have mentioned, the first speeches were the first songs: the periodic and measured recurrences of rhythm, the melodious inflections of accents, caused poetry and music to be born together with language; or rather, all this was nothing other than language itself in those happy climates and those happy ages when the only pressing needs that required another's collaboration were needs born of the heart (276).[98]

Here in the south, at the origin proper, love urges on the first social gatherings, the first song-speech, and the first poetic eloquence. The *Essai* describes love's preferred expression – "the voice of tenderness" – as a kind of vocal music (276). Through the natural order of musical "accents" and "melodic inflections," the body expresses itself freely and sexuality is open and unhindered: "pleasure and desire merged into one and made themselves felt together" (271). Rousseau's syntax basks in the undifferentiated, circular plenitude that characterizes the first melodic language he describes: "at first there was no music other than melody, nor any other melody than the varied sound of speech; accents made up the song, quantities made up measure, and people spoke as much by sonorities and rhythm as by articulations and sounds" (276). The first social acts ("the first festivals"), "the first fires of love," and the rhythmic intonations of the first melodies all coincide. Following Lacanian theories of language, Rosalind Coward and John Ellis have asserted that the formation of language, of society, and the construction of the self are all coeval: "thus the submission of the subject to the signifier (language) in order to master his dependency in needs through the acquisition of a separated signifying place in language means submission to the cultural order by which human sexuality is regulated."[99] From a psychoanalytic perspective, Rousseau is describing an inaugural (and final) moment of plenitude in which the musical accents of language are made to express a state of being free from the troubles of work, repressed sexuality, and social constraint. Rousseau uses music to represent this liminal, pre-linguistic state that is nonetheless inhabited by unrepressed signification and social practices. If the scene Rousseau chooses to describe the first music appears operatic, it is because opera is made to commemorate both an original communion and its loss.[100] In the *Essai*, music becomes this liminal moment.

[98] "Autour des fontaines dont j'ai parlé les prémiers discours furent les prémiéres chansons: les retours périodiques et mesurés du rhytme, les infléxions mélodieuses des accens firent naitre la poesie et la musique avec la langue, ou plustôt tout cela n'étoit que la langue même pour ces heureux climats et ces heureux tems où les seuls besoins pressans qui demandoient le concours d'autrui étoient ceux que le cœur faisoit naitre" (*Essai*, 139–141).
[99] Coward and Ellis, *Language and Materialism*, 117.
[100] Herbert Lindenberger notes that opera has a tendency "to raise actions to a mythical level" and that opera is "usually set in times and places far removed from the worlds of the audiences for whom composers write" (*Opera, the Extravagant Art* [Ithaca: Cornell University Press, 1984], 51). From this standpoint, the operatic scene is an ideal one for Rousseau's description of a mythical origin.

For Rousseau, then, music plays a determining role in the events which lead humans from solitude to society and culture. Although he doesn't yet mention Rameau by name, Rousseau's origin of music is strikingly different from that of the famous composer. Song is directly linked, on the one hand, to the passions that define subjectivity, and, on the other hand, to the social and sexual bonds (detailed in chapter 9) created by acts of musical expression and reception. The emergence of desire, the move away from the unmediated pleasure of self-sufficient solitude, and the "speaking" of melodies are all inextricably linked. After suggesting that the first melodic speech set up an original social contract, Rousseau solicits the reader's concurrence: "in view of the way in which the earliest societies united, was it surprising that the first stories were set in verse and that the first laws were sung?" (277). Just as there is no music without society and culture, Rousseau claims that there can be no society or culture without music. Rousseau intends this linkage as part of a comprehensive and rigorous argument, not in the way it is often articulated in concert program notes where we read about the intimate connection between Bach's compositions and his "world view." Rousseau states that music is both an original and an originating element of the social fabric. If there are languages that are constitutive of freedom, as Rousseau claims in the last chapter of the *Essai*, what does it mean for him to assert here that the first laws were sung? Against Rameau, the *Essai* places musical practices squarely within cultural contexts. By claiming that the first laws were sung, Rousseau asserts that music signifies, and that as a signifying practice – as the signifying practice that activates social bonding – music has an affinity to the law. This tie between music and the law (that Rousseau claims has since been broken) will return again in the last chapter on government.

The first primordial melody is immediately authenticated through its association with all of the favorable qualities of temperate climates and their cultures. But what of articulation, the unfortunate and secondary by-product of the true origin which Rousseau quickly dismissed as undesirable, in music as in language? As the course of history separates music from language, these stillborn articulations soon return, cultivated by the studied movements of the tongue and palate. Soon the sonorous quality of the speaking voice becomes enveloped in articulation, the melodic nature of the singing voice is overrun by the hard consonants of the men of the north, and harmony is invented as a desperate attempt to give a kind of *éclat* (meaning a sparkle or brilliance, but also a raucous outburst) to these ugly sounds (291). The development of reason, grammar, and philosophy fixes language, making the voice monotonous with consonants and encouraging the addition of "grammatical combinations" and "new

121

articulations" (249). Concurrently, music underwent a similar change. As spoken articulations were the preferred vocal expressions of the northern tribes and their physical needs, harmony was likewise an invention of these same "barbarians" from the north, who hoped to compensate for "the coarseness of their speech" with the brilliance of chords and counterpoint (291). Harmony began to flourish and "the calculation of intervals replaced delicacy of inflection" (290). Just as language abounded in consonants, music was laden with consonances. In order to compensate for an irretrievable loss of sonority, there was an attempt to stress "vowel sounds in order to cover up the profusion and the harshness of their consonants" (291). Rousseau claims that contemporary language and music are the result of this continual decline. Far from the idyllic origin, "we have no idea of a sonorous and harmonious language" (255) and, not surprisingly, "for us music [has] lost all of its vigor" (293). According to the *Essai*, this end state of affairs is the inevitable result of progress: yet original melody was extinguished by the arrival of harmony from elsewhere. This "elsewhere" could be understood as the repressed "other" within, since, as I have argued, Rousseau's use of binary oppositions causes the origin to split in two from the very beginning. If original gestures are banished to the north, projected away from the valorized southern origin, harmony and articulation also figure as the other of melody, likewise excluded from the "the voice of tenderness" (276). Harmony is the result of an attempt to compensate for the multiplication of articulations in language and thus is centered on a primal loss of "musicality" as Rousseau defines it. In this story of origins, the values that Rameau attached to melody and harmony have been inverted. In the *Essai*, contrary to the implications Rameau derives from the *corps sonore*, melody has primary status and harmony is relegated to a secondary and degraded existence.

But despite the degeneration of music, which, like the degradation of language, revealed for Rousseau the degree to which eighteenth-century culture had become estranged from its origins (the scenes of chapter 9), the *Essai* contends that melody had never entirely severed its link to the origin. The original bonds between melody, language, emotions, sexuality, and society – whence music's "primitive energy" – are all latent, Rousseau claims, in the music of the present day. According to Rousseau, it is for this reason that melody – which eighteenth-century French music theory, in all its forms, opposes to harmony – continues to deeply affect its listeners (288). In certain passages, Rousseau appears to refer to a timeless "music," conflating the original scenes he describes in the *Essai* and the experiences of the eighteenth-century spectator who is sensitive to musical expression:

By imitating the inflections of the voice, melody expresses plaints, cries of suffering or of joy, threats, moans; all the vocal signs of the passions fall within its province. It imitates the accents of [various] languages as well as the idiomatic expressions [*les tours affectés dans chaque idiome*] commonly associated in each one of them with given movements of the soul; it not only imitates, it speaks; and its language, though inarticulate, is lively, ardent, passionate, and a hundred times more vigorous than speech itself. This is where musical imitation acquires its power, and song its hold on sensitive hearts (282).

Melody has always been tied to language and culture; it is for this reason that music continues to affect listeners. And if music had always been in part a cultural construct, then eighteenth-century music was *a fortiori* far from "natural." Rousseau reveals his position quite explicitly in the discussion of the "false analogy" between painting and music: "nature by itself engenders few sounds and, short of believing in the harmony of the heavenly spheres, living beings are needed to produce it. Painting is thus seen to be closer to nature, while music is more closely related to human art" (287).[101] Just as he did not consider language to be natural in any absolute sense – he had described man's original silence and solitude in the second *Discours* – Rousseau viewed music as an indispensable component of socialization and the advent of culture. Catherine Kintzler has seen Rousseau as condemning all forms of cultural mediation, calling him a "theorist of transparency."[102] I find this reading unconvincing, given the treatment of music in the *Essai* where Rousseau does not hold melody to be a natural form, if "natural" is understood as free from all convention. On the contrary, music is located at the heart of primeval acculturation. Melody expresses the passions through the imitation of vocal inflections and accents; and these accents are closely tied, not to a nature out there in the world, but to the constitution of the human being as a participant in cultural structures and exchanges which ultimately revolve, Rousseau claims, around the emotions that first determined them. Those vocalizations which, at the origin, were predisposed for emotive display (being the "direct" expression of the passions of the soul), continue to affect listeners when they are resurrected within the context of eighteenth-century musical practices. What were once the natural sounds of the passions – the "plaints," "the cries of suffering or of joy, threats, moans" – must now be re-created through the artifice of musical composition: as Batteux explains, music is "the artificial

---

[101] Far from being a mark of Rousseau's intellectual idiosyncrasy, this comment is in perfect accord with most eighteenth-century judgements on the arts. In the "Discours préliminaire" to the *Encyclopédie*, d'Alembert notes that in painting and sculpture, "the imitation comes closest to the objects that it represents" (1:xj).

[102] Kintzler, *Poétique de l'opéra*, 28.

123

portrait of human passions" (Batteux 15).[103] Melody serves in the *Essai*
as a meeting place for nature and culture, revealing the art of the
composer at the same time as the natural accents and inflections of the
passions. Rousseau insists that nature's voice must be cultivated: "in
every imitation, some sort of discourse must always complement
[*supplée à*] the voice of nature" (282). The "discourse" to which
Rousseau refers is the fruit of the composer's art. The composer must
first reproduce and shape the unhewn sounds of human passions, and
then integrate them into the conventional "discourse" of melody.
Music consists in "the use & arrangement of the various accents of the
voice," as Le Pileur d'Apligny noted;[104] it can then become "a kind of
discourse," as d'Alembert argued in the "Discours préliminaire."[105]
Like many writers before him (and after him), Rousseau is pleading
the case for a musical "rhetoric": using its imitation of the passionate
sounds of the human voice, music is able to construct a discourse, a
musical "oration." Batteux enjoins the composer to imitate the orator:
"since the sounds of Music & the Gestures of Dance have a meaning,
just as the words do in Poetry, the expression of Music & of Dance
must have the same natural qualities as oratorical Elocution."[106]
Rousseau, however, says little about this musical rhetoric, being
content to insist that the composer do more than simply imitate
sounds: "objects have to speak ... for it is not enough for him merely to
imitate, he must do so in a way that both moves and pleases; without
that, his dreary imitation is nothing and, by failing to arouse anyone's
interest, it fails to make any impression."[107] However, Rousseau makes
an anthropological claim beyond the musical mimesis advocated by
writers such as Batteux. The *Essai* suggests that the rhetorical quality of
the musical discourse must be the calculated result of the composer's
art. At the same time, Rousseau indicates that music is able to transcend its own mimetic artifice by adopting those sounds which human
beings naturally use to express suffering and joy: "[melody] not only
imitates, it speaks" (282). Melody has the power (the "energy," the

[103] Batteux, *Les Beaux arts*, 15. The problematic alliance between nature and artifice in
eighteenth-century aesthetic formulations is nowhere more evident than in *Les Beaux
arts réduits à un même principe*. Batteux defines musical tones as coming from "nature's
dictionary," a peculiar yet revealing epithet which represents music as a natural
language: "speech expresses passion only by way of the ideas to which the emotions
are linked, & as if by reflection. Tone and Gesture go directly to the heart without any
detour. In a word, Speech is a conventional language ... Tones are like the Dictionary
of simple Nature" (*Les Beaux arts*, 254–255). Although he would concur with Batteux's
linking of music and passion, Rousseau articulates a somewhat different view of the
natural and cultural conditions of musical expression.
[104] Le Pileur d'Apligny, *Traité sur la musique et sur les moyens d'en perfectionner l'expression*
(Paris: Demonville, 1779), 3.
[105] *Encyclopédie*, 1:xij.   [106] Batteux, *Les Beaux arts*, 270.   [107] *Ibid.*, 282–283.

"force") to the authentic "passionate accent" behind the artificial mask of the imitation: "This is where song [acquires its] hold on sensitive hearts" (282). If Rousseau brings up the issue of a musical rhetoric, it is because the very possibility of this discourse is the consequence of an anthropological continuity with the original, passionate conditions of human interaction.

In addition to inflecting a standard account of musical mimesis with "anthropology," Rousseau used the traditional view of the arts to overturn the contemporary aesthetic hierarchy which rested upon it. According to seventeenth- and eighteenth-century theories of the arts, music was endowed with the least efficacious powers of artistic representation, whereas painting stood at the summit of the aesthetic hierarchy.[108] This order is presented quite clearly in d'Alembert's discussion of the imitative arts in the "Discours préliminaire" to the *Encyclopédie*:

Painting and sculpture ought to be placed at the head of that knowledge which consists of imitation, because it is in those arts above all that imitation best approximates the objects represented and speaks most directly to the senses ... Poetry, which comes after Painting and Sculpture, and which imitates merely by means of words disposed according to a harmony agreeable to the ear, speaks to the imagination rather than to the senses ... Finally, music, which speaks simultaneously to the imagination and to the senses, holds the last place in the order of imitation – not that its imitation is less perfect in the objects which it attempts to represent, but because until now it has apparently been restricted to a smaller number of images. This should be attributed less to its nature than to the lack of sufficient inventiveness and resourcefulness in most of those who cultivate it.[109]

In the *Essai*, Rousseau reverses this hierarchy, placing musical imitations above those created by the palette and the brush. Although this aesthetic shift would require a lengthy commentary in itself, there are two factors contributing to music's superiority which concern us here: first, the very nature of melody links it to the original vocalizations and passions which accompanied the formation of society; second, through imitation the composer re-creates these passionate sounds, integrating them into a contemporary musical discourse while nonetheless retelling a timeless story of human passion. Isolated from the text, neither of these stances would have been particularly original; yet Rousseau interpreted them in such a way as to reverse the standard hierarchy of the arts:

---

[108] It is because of this hierarchy that one finds so many metaphors of painting in eighteenth-century reflections on music. Music is described as the "portrait" of the passions; its imitations "paint" the passions. Rousseau attacks this metaphor in the chapter entitled "Fausse analogie entre les couleurs et les sons."

[109] D'Alembert, *Preliminary Discourse*, 37–38; *Encyclopédie*, 1:xj–xij.

Music is also felt to [involve our] interest more than does painting, precisely because it brings man closer to man and always gives us some idea about our own kind [*semblables*]. Painting is often dead and inanimate ... One of the great advantages the musician enjoys is that he can paint things that cannot be heard, whereas the Painter cannot represent things that cannot be seen; and the greatest wonder of an art that acts solely through movement is that it can fashion it even into an image of repose (287).

This aesthetic reversal is in keeping with the *Essai*'s position on Rameau. In direct opposition to Rameau's "materialist" theory of the *corps sonore*, where music is derived from the acoustical properties of sound, Rousseau stresses the connection between sound and psyche. Music's moral resonance can only be awakened through the imitation of vocal sounds – the cries of suffering or of joy – which, by definition in Rousseau's *Essai*, have an original link to the passions:

As long as sounds continue to be considered exclusively in terms of the excitation they trigger in our nerves, the true principles of music and of its power over men's hearts will remain elusive. In a melody, sounds act on us not only as sounds but as signs of our affections, of our sentiments; that is how they arouse in us the [e]motions [*mouvemens*] which they express and the image of which we recognize in them (283).

The *Essai* contends that the physics of sound does not provide a satisfactory explanation for the origin of music, nor for the pleasure and meaning we continue to derive from it: "for it is not so much the ear that conveys pleasure to the heart as the heart that conveys it to the ear" (284–285).[110] Rameau claimed that the entire range of musical practice and theory was based on the acoustic phenomenon of harmonic overtones – the octave, perfect twelfth, and major seventeenth (assuming octave identity, the octave, perfect fifth, and major third) – that can be heard above a single fundamental tone. For the author of the *Essai*, Rameau's theory of the *corps sonore* does not take into account that which is specifically human in music: "sounds proclaim movement; the voice proclaims a sentient being" (171). Melodic strains affect the listener not as a series of pitches that can be derived through specific ratios from the *corps sonore* – as vibrations reaching the ear – but as signs, "signs of our affections, of our sentiments." Recalling the

[110] It is significant that Rousseau revised the *Encyclopédie* entry "Musique" for his *Dictionnaire de musique*. In the *Encyclopédie*, one passage refers to the "true source of the pleasure of the ear" (10:898); in the *Dictionnaire*, a succession of tones makes a strong impression "on the ear and on the soul" (s.v. "Musique"). In the *Dictionnaire*, there is also an extensive interpolation on the difference between music which is "natural" and that which is "imitative." The first is "limited to the physical alone"; the second "expresses all the passions." These changes reflect conceptions that are developed in the *Essai* and indicate a desire to formulate a coherent theory of music, constructed in opposition to Rameau.

differences Rousseau established in the first chapter of the *Essai* between gesture and voice, it becomes evident that the intimate link between melody and our "affections" – so important for music – is prefigured in the voice's original connection to the passions. Indeed, it is explicitly stated in Rousseau's definition of melody that the connection between tones and emotions is properly semiotic. Different from the other two types of signs – accidental signs and conventional signs – that d'Alembert defines in the article "Signe (métaphys.)" of the *Encyclopédie*, the vocal sounds of the passions are natural signs that are inherent to the human constitution: "the natural signs or cries that nature has established for the feelings of joy, fear, suffering, and so on."[111] Rousseau's above description of melody perfectly matches the *Encyclopédie*'s definition of natural sign. For Rousseau, the sounds of melody "arouse in us the [e]motions [*mouvemens*] which they express"; similarly, in d'Alembert's definition of sign, "the sign contains two ideas, the first of the thing that represents, the other of the thing that is represented; & its nature consists in arousing the second by the first."[112] The musical sign simultaneously represents and excites passion.

The origin thus continues to exert an influence over our musical practices, and over the spectator, through the inalienable bond between vocal sound and emotion. Vocal accents – "these accents to which one cannot close one's ear" – not gestures or articulations, move the passions (243). The description of music and affect has slipped from the past into the present. Rousseau imagines a contemporary audience ("these accents, which cause *us* to shudder . . . cause *us* to feel what we hear") whose members experience the operatic scenes representing and reenacting fundamental passions (243; emphasis added). Rousseau appears less concerned with the workings of dramatic mimesis or plots than he is with the musical expression of particular emotions and the affective state in which music places its audience. Whereas in the traditional theater the action is of greater interest, in the lyric theater the sonorous expression of the passions takes precedence over the plot. Batteux noted the preeminence of emotion in the lyric theater: "the action will be only a kind of canvas meant to carry, sustain, bring forth, link, the various passions that the Artist [the musician] wants to express."[113] Music derives its meaning from the passions it represents, which are brought together in sequence and contextualized in the dramatic plot. Yet, given the context of Rousseau's reflection on music in the *Essai*, melody is deemed important not so much for its musical expression of the theatrical action, but rather because it draws on an archaic link to the origin, because it is

---

[111] *Encyclopédie*, 15:188.   [112] *Ibid.*   [113] Batteux, *Les Beaux arts*, 258–259.

seen as the catalyst for an original social bond. Independently of the plot itself, melody is represented as having a certain meaning which it gleans from the prestige accorded to the vocal origins of humanity. As Derrida points out, the voice evokes an original presence which is then projected into the social act of speaking to another being: "Conversation is, then, a communication between two absolute origins that, if one may venture the formula, auto-affect reciprocally, repeating as immediate echo the auto-affection produced by the other."[114] Derrida depicts Rousseau's social bond as an echoed self-presence. I want to insist, however, on melody in the *Essai* as the site of an anthropological reflection on the social bond. Rousseau's text constantly represents, not isolated, pre-social presence and self-sufficiency, but a valorized form of society which takes form as an inversion of the present. The link between music and the law to which I drew attention earlier is revealed again through the primordial role of vocal accent as the instigator of the social bond. If the first laws were sung, it reveals that music is already a form of social observance. In Rousseau's text, the emergence of music coincides with the appearence of the signifier and with the development of subjectivity and desire through a fortuitous encounter with another being. Rather than self-presence, the continual splitting of the origin that Rousseau describes in the *Essai* mirrors the heterogeneity and contradictions within the subject whose coming into being he seeks to link to the emergence of the signifier in music. The marking of differences – as much a characteristic of Rousseau's writing as it is a quality of what he describes – reveals the importance of *semiosis* for the development of the social being. This emergence is necessarily marked by the law and the appearance of the signifier.[115] From the standpoint of my reading of the *Essai*, it would be possible to argue that "music" is this signifier. If Rousseau's descriptions of original moments seem at times operatic, it is because in the *Essai* these moments constantly shift into the present, to (operatic) scenes of commemoration where the original social bond is recalled and re-enacted in the present, through musical representation. Through melody, the listener re-experiences the emotional link to other beings which was once the intersubjective force that brought dispersed individuals into society; and at the same time, she/he re-encounters the cultural order that defines the terms of the social bond. The bonds between vocal expression and the passions that issue from the origin of society are summoned in music through the particular kind of

---

[114] Derrida, *Of Grammatology*, 166. "Le colloque est donc une communication entre deux origines absolues qui, si l'on peut risquer cette formule, s'auto-affectent réciproquement, répétant en écho immédiat l'auto-affection produite par l'autre" (*De la grammatologie*, 236).

[115] See Coward and Ellis, *Language and Materialism*, 117.

imitation that Rousseau describes: "by imitating the inflections of the voice, melody expresses plaints, cries of suffering or of joy" (282). If music both represents and arouses passion, then every melody constitutes in some measure a commemoration (representation) and re-enactment (arousal) of an original and authentic social cont(r)act: "as soon as vocal sounds strike your ear, they herald a being like yourself; they are, so to speak, the organs of the soul, and if they also depict solitude, they tell you that you are not alone in it" (287). Music may indicate the solitary confines of emotion; yet, by virtue of its primordial, semiotic link to social *affections*, music already figures the emergence of subjectivity through the contact of the other. Vocal melody commemorates these mythic events as the origin of the social order.

While Rousseau asserts that the bond between society and its inaugural "accents" is present in all civilizations, he suggests, echoing Montesquieu, that different natural causes such as climate have created differences in the speech and song of each culture. Rousseau thus answers the question he had posed in the very first paragraph of the *Essai*: "where a man is from is known only once he has spoken ... what causes this [particular] language to be the language of his country and not of another?" (240). In the chapters on northern and southern languages, Rousseau sought to demonstrate that although vocal accents go as deep as the origin, they remain bound by and define the particular society which brought them into existence. While assuming the universality of passion, Rousseau stresses the cultural differences indigenous to the various kinds of music scattered throughout the globe: "melody ... imitates the accents of [various] languages as well as the idiomatic expressions commonly associated in each one of them with given movements of the soul" (282). It is not surprising, then, to find that Rousseau places a great deal of emphasis on the geographical and temporal variation of language and music: "an Italian requires Italian tunes, a Turk would require Turkish tunes. One is affected only by accents that are familiar" (284). The "nation" stands less for actual geographico-political boundaries, than it does for a larger set of affective, cultural, and political concerns and ideals. The differences Rousseau remarks in the musics of the world are not merely the result of different national styles, but even affect the physical properties of music that Rameau considered to be universal: those peoples who do not use stringed instruments "have inflections in their songs which we call false because they do not fit into our system and we have no notations for them. This has been observed in the songs of American savages" (289). The original difference that opposed northern and southern cultures gives way to a myriad of differences between "peoples," defined as a linguistic and cultural entity. Rousseau contends that to base an understanding of music on

129

European practices is to misunderstand the function of music. While defining music as a culturally bound expression of human passion, Rousseau takes advantage of the opportunity to take a passing jab at the French tradition and, indirectly, at Rameau's claims to universalism: "Bernier's Cantatas are said to have cured a French musician of the fever; they would have given one to a musician of any other nation" (284).

Music is essentially vocal for Rousseau, because the vocal reveals the original and constitutive ties between language, music, and culture. However, vocality itself is not enough, as is clear from his joke about Bernier's cantatas. In the revisions of the *Encyclopédie* article "Musique" that Rousseau included in his *Dictionnaire de musique*, much of contemporary European vocal music is rejected as simply "natural." In these forms, Rousseau argues, the voice acts as if it were merely one musical instrument among other musical instruments: "limited to the physical qualities of sounds alone, acting only upon the senses . . . Such is the music of chansons, hymns, canticles, of all those songs that are only combinations of melodic sounds, and in general all music that is merely harmonious."[116] The equivalence that Rousseau attributes in this passage to "melodic" and "harmonious" could lead to confusion; but what is singled out and rejected as merely physical are all forms of music (vocal or otherwise, purely instrumental music being disqualified from the start) that foreground the pure pleasure of sense impressions. The term "melodic" refers here to one type of music – a pure play of tones lacking any linguistic accent. Rousseau's description of the other type of music, the "imitative," highlights the vocal accent: "the second [kind of music], through lively, accentuated, and, as it were, speaking inflections, expresses all the passions." An operatic form – and, Rousseau adds, "that of ancient poems" – this music is "truly lyrical and theatrical."[117] At the same time, it recalls the original, accented vocalizations which activated social consciousness in the *Essai*.

Towards the end of the entry on "Musique" in the *Dictionnaire*, Rousseau gives the example of a tune ("the well-known *Rans-des-Vaches*") that, while having absolutely no effect on other peoples, supposedly had such devastating effects on the Swiss that "it was forbidden on pain of death to play it among their troops because it made those who heard it burst into tears, desert, or die." The *Rans-des-Vaches* triggered the personal and collective memories of the Swiss soldiers, "reminding them of their country, their former pleasures, their youth, & all their ways of life." Rousseau's example serves as a modern counterpart to and revival of the tales of the prodigious effects

---

[116] Rousseau, *Dictionnaire de musique*, s.v. "Musique."   [117] *Ibid.*

of Greek music as *pharmakon*. The narcotic effect of this Swiss tune brought soldiers to tears and even led to death; this effect was also extremely pleasurable. Through the example of the *Rans-des-Vaches*, Rousseau claims an undeniable link between a given culture and specific forms of musical expression – for Rousseau, melody. It also suggests that the link between music and cultural memory is so strong that it risks disrupting the soldiers' self-possession by inviting an impossible return to local origins and youthful pleasures that is nonetheless irresistible. Here, the link between music and society is shown to be a complex and ambiguous one. If music can unite a group through a common bond, if it can marshal the troops to war, it can also have the opposite effect, leading to desertion and to the disintegration of the collective.

The *Essai*'s description of harmony and its treatment of the *corps sonore* confront Rameau's theories head-on. For Rousseau, the antithesis of the human accent of the voice is the inert physicality of the *corps sonore*. Rousseau concedes, however, that sounds are by nature beautiful to the human ear: "the beauty of sounds is by nature; their effect is entirely physical; it is due to the interaction of the different particles of air set in motion by the *corps sonore* and by all of its constituent parts [*aliquotes*] ... all of these taken together, produce a pleasant sensation" (280–281). Yet he insists that the physical nature of sound – its various relations and proportions – cannot explain the meaning that sound can acquire in music. Nor do all forms of music (as in the hymns of the *Dictionnaire* which are said to give merely physical stimulation) move beyond pleasure to *volupté*:

everyone in the universe will take pleasure in listening to beautiful sounds; but unless this pleasure is enlivened by familiar melodic inflections it will not be [totally] delightful [*délicieux*], it will not become utter pleasure [*volupté*]. The songs which, to us, are the most beautiful will only moderately affect an ear completely unaccustomed to them; it is a language for which one has to have the Dictionary (281).

Melody is inextricably linked to custom and convention.[118] The cultural context provides the "dictionary" in which musical expressions find meaning. Rousseau establishes an analogy between music and painting, between melody and *dessein* (meaning shape, contour, but also design) on the one hand, and harmony and color on the other.

[118] Rousseau's opposition between nature and artifice is more elusive than it may appear at first glance. I take issue with Kintzler's claim that harmony is rejected by Rousseau because "it is a mere artifice" (*Poétique de l'opéra français*, 464). As I have argued, melody is praised by Rousseau precisely because of certain "artificial" qualities.

Just as the overall shape and contour make sense of the colors of a painting, it is melody that fashions a cultural "discourse" out of the "vocal signs of the passions," shaping sound into musical expression: "melody does in music exactly what drawing does in painting; it indicates the lines and shapes, of which the chords and sounds are but the colors" (278–279).[119] Rousseau contends that if we are searching to understand the origin and purpose of music, rather than looking to the physical properties of resonance, as had Rameau, it is more useful to think of music as semiotically tied to the "moral needs" which link human beings to each other in a common culture and a common language: "we attribute both too much and too little power to sensations; we do not realize that often they affect us not only as sensations but as signs or images, and that their moral effects also have moral causes" (278). Rousseau seeks to describe melody as the representational, and thus active, element in music which gives shape to an essentially indifferent harmonic structure. Saturated with the collective memories of a culture and its language, melody brings significance to what the *Essai* depicts as purely "physical" sound.

Rameau appears in Rousseau's text disguised as "some famous artist" in the short allegory of painting included in the chapter on melody, where Rousseau imagines a country in which aesthetic pleasure is based on the various possible combinations of colors rather than on the shaping of *dessein*. In the allegory, Rameau is attacked for his materialist attachment to the merely physical, for his unwillingness to place emphasis on that which is rooted in culture, on the representational act which shapes sensation:

Finally they might perhaps by dint of progress get to the experiment with the prism. Straightway some famous artist would be sure to erect a fancy system on the basis of it. Gentlemen, he would say to them, if we are to philosophize properly we must go back to the physical causes. Here you have the resolution of light, the primary colors, their relationships, their proportions, the true principles of the pleasure you derive from painting ... I have shown you the great, the true principle of the art. What am I saying, of the art? Of all the arts, Gentlemen, of all the Sciences. The analysis of colors, the measurement of prismatic refractions provide you with the only precise relations to be found in nature, and the rule for all relations (279–280).[120]

[119] "La mélodie fait précisément dans la musique ce que fait le dessein dans la peinture; c'est elle qui marque les traits et les figures dont les accords et les sons ne sont que les couleurs" (*Essai*, 149).

[120] Cf. Batteux, *Les Beaux arts*: "let us conclude that if the music which was the most accurately calculated in its tones, the most geometrical in its chords had no meaning, then one could only compare it to a Prism, which presents the most beautiful shades, & yet does not make a painting" (269). Catherine Kintzler has noted the divergences that exist in the comparisons of the visual and musical arts found in Batteux, Rousseau, and Dubos. She concludes that Batteux and Dubos are primarily con-

Although this passage attacks sensationalism in general and the inflated claims that issue from its principles, it is primarily a denunciation of the theory of the *corps sonore*. In "the experiment with the prism," "the primary colors," "their relationships," and the pretension of optics to explain all the arts and sciences, Rousseau parodies the *corps sonore*, the three elementary sounds it produces, the ratios which describe these three sounds $(1, \frac{1}{3}, \frac{1}{5})$, and the ambitious claims Rameau made in his *Démonstration* – that music holds the master key to all the arts and sciences. The *Essai's* comparison of pictorial *dessein* and melody, both of which "give ... life and soul" respectively to "dead" colors ("painting is often dead and inanimate") and to the lifeless sounds of physical resonance, ends with a denunciation of Rameau and his theory (278, 287): "what would we say about a painter so lacking in sense and taste that he would reason in this way, stupidly limiting the pleasure painting gives us to the physical aspects of his art? What would we say about a musician who, filled with similar prejudices, believed that harmony alone is the source of the great effects of music?" (280). Though Rousseau had earlier insisted upon the distinction between the eyes and the ears, the analogy between painting and music allows him to make a point about the difference between physical sound, and the forms it takes in the hands of the composer. Rousseau has argued all along that melody, with its ability to imitate vocal inflections, can mold the physical nature of sound into the passionate accents of the human subject. Harmony, whose structures Rameau derived from the principle of physical resonance, cannot define music for Rousseau, except in the most meaningless of ways: "music is not the art of combining sounds in ways pleasing to the ear" (280). Music, in this negative formulation, is implicitly equated with vocal accent: harmonic sounds do not make "music" in Rousseau's view. Because of its origin in the resonance of objects, harmony has no access to the emotions and is condemned to remain in physical nature as inanimate sound, as noise.

To reinforce the distinction between melody and harmony, Rousseau abruptly alters the terms of his argument. Beginning with an analogy that opposes contour and color, on the one hand, to melody and harmony, on the other, Rousseau now sets up an opposition

cerned with an aesthetic of the object, where the debate is focused around the object as appropriately or inappropriately treated, whereas Rousseau is concerned with a moral distinction (*Poétique de l'opéra français*, 496–497). Batteux, for example, referred to the arts as creating "portraits" of the passions, a kind of representation that Rousseau condemns in an introductory variant to the *Confessions*. In the place of the shallow "portrait" and the "character," Rousseau suggests that the writer represent the contradictory and unexpected moves of his "secret affections" (*Les Confessions*, ed. Voisine, 797).

between painting and music in a chapter devoted to the mistaken analogy between colors and sounds. Rousseau's first task is to expose the "false analogy between colors and sounds" that the père Castel, whose ocular harpsichord supposedly produced bands of color when the keys were depressed, instead of sounds, was guilty of advancing: "what a gross misunderstanding of how nature operates it was, not to see that the effect of colors is due to their permanence and that of sounds to their succession" (285).[121] Rousseau reasserts the distinction between the instantaneous meaning produced by gesture – "which you take in completely at one glance" – and the diachronic nature of speech – "the successive impression made by discourse" – bringing it into the domain of music (242). As in speech, he argues, the sounds of song are heard "successively and one after the other" (285). Once the aesthetic difference between colors and sounds is established, Rousseau moves to distinguish melody from harmony within this argument by identifying the "economy" of musical harmony with that of painting: "thus every sense has its own proper realm. The realm of music is time, that of painting is space. To multiply the number of sounds heard all at once, or to present colors one after the other, is to alter their economy, it is to substitute the eye for the ear, and the ear for the eye" (286). The discursive nature of melodic sounds announces life and movement: "sounds [of melody] proclaim movement; the voice proclaims a sentient being" (285). To change melody into harmony by multiplying the number of simultaneous tones is to instigate semiotic perversion, to attempt to use the eyes to hear and the ears to see. The synchronic nature of colors and of harmony is further degraded as "lifeless." Devoid of movement and life, color is "the ornament [*parure*] of inanimate beings"; equally inert, because it can signify nothing ("of what is harmony the sign?"), harmony exists only as the materiality of concomitant vibrations in the *corps sonore* (285).

Drawing support from earlier chapters, the fundamental difference between melody and harmony is prefigured in the distinction between the needs expressed by the languages of the north and the passions of southern speech: "what a difference there is between the touching

[121] Castel states that the immutable laws of harmony direct both the pleasures of the eye and those of the ear: "you see, Sir, how Painters & Organ makers, Dyers & Luthiers, surely without having communicated their intentions to each other, and without having consulted each other, have the same aim, drawn in no doubt by the same nature which dictates to the eyes of the former the same laws of harmony that it dictates to the ears of the latter." He goes on to explain the analogical basis for his ocular "music" in the following terms: "for if blue is the base, red is the fifth, yellow the third: this is surely demonstrated by the number of 6 semitones or intermediary chromatic nuances between blue & red like between C & G" (Louis-Bertrand Castel, "Suite et troisième partie des nouvelles Expériences d'optique & d'Acoustique," *Journal de Trévoux*, vol. 35 [1735; Geneva: Slatkine, 1968], 458–459).

inflections that issue from movements of the soul, and the cries wrested by physical needs" (273). The *Essai* had already established that articulation and gesture are tied to physical need – "more in the arms than in the heart" – whereas language and music (as melody) are based in emotion (273). So it comes as no surprise that since harmony is derived from the physical nature of the *corps sonore*, the passions are inaccessible to chords and counterpoint. "These crude men from the North" are precisely those who attempted to compensate for their rough, nasal language ("the Emperor Julian compared the speech of the Gauls to the croaking of frogs"!) with the invention of polyphony (291). The bleak existence of the northern peoples is later matched by the "meaningless" harmonies they produce. The *Essai* seeks to promote a music which would be in keeping with the fundamentally human aspect of the passions; and these passions are linked exclusively to the sounds of melody. Considered to be a later addition and thus severed from the passionate origin of melody, harmony is banished to the meaningless calculation of intervals that filled contemporary musical treatises: "even after a thousand years spent reckoning the relations of sounds and the laws of harmony, how can that art ever be turned into an art of imitation? What would be the principle of this supposed imitation, of what is harmony the sign, and what have chords in common with our passions?" (281). Rousseau rejects "embellishment [*remplissage*] and chords," "proportions and figures," because "one can discover in them no *sort* of link with human nature."[122] Having no connection to the origin of human contact and passion, harmony cannot have the same meaning: "it is not surprising that when the natural proportions are altered, natural pleasure disappears" (281). Rousseau noted earlier that sounds are naturally pleasant to the human ear. However, with no mimetic relationship to emotion, harmony remains only noise. Moreover, Rousseau even refuses harmony the ability to imitate physical nature:

By itself, harmony is not even adequate to express what would seem to fall entirely within its province. Thunder, murmuring waters, winds, storms are but poorly rendered by simple chords. Do what you may, mere noise says nothing to the mind; objects have to speak in order to make themselves heard; in every imitation, some sort of discourse must always complement [*supplée à*] the voice of nature. A composer [*musicien*] who tries to render noise with noise errs ... teach him that he must render noise with song, that if he wished to make frogs croak, he would have to make them sing (282–283).

With yet another jab at Rameau – and at an entire tradition of representing natural sounds in operatic composition – whose comic opera *Platée* included a chorus of frogs, Rousseau claims that it is not

---

[122] Quoted in Duchez, "Principe de la mélodie," 77.

enough to reproduce the sounds of natural objects in the musical composition: these objects must be made to "speak."[123] The physicality of sound must be transformed into rhetoric; thus, "a composer [*musicien*] who tries to render noise with noise errs." The *Essai* asserts that in order to reach the spectator, music must give life to the material objects of its representation through a mimetic supplement. It is not a question of reproducing sounds; rather, an additional effort is required of the composer. In a paradoxical twist of common sense, the elaborate constructions of harmony become physical nature in the *Essai*, and simple melody is represented as a complex and "supplemental" discourse. If it is to reflect the presence of living beings, nature must be animated with "some sort of discourse."

There are other elements from the first half of the *Essai*, in addition to the opposition of reason and emotion, of the physical and the moral, that Rousseau methodically exploits in order to elaborate his distinction between melody and harmony. The *Essai*'s theory of music works in tandem with the positions set forth in the chapters on language in order to sketch out an integral theory of the origins and development of culture and its signifying practices. The exoticism, for example, that Rousseau invokes to describe the beneficial qualities of the first language – "in some respects it would resemble Chinese, in others ... Arabic" – reappears in the chapters devoted to music (248). But this time, the simplicity and "irregularities" of Chinese and Arabic reappear in a different guise, as the innocent and rustic melodies of uncultivated voices closer to home:

Rustic ears perceive our consonances as mere noise ... M. Rameau contends that comparatively simple trebles [*dessus*] naturally suggest their basses, and that a person with a true but untrained ear will naturally sing this bass. That is a musician's prejudice, contradicted by all experience. A person who has never heard either bass or harmony will not only fail to find them on his own, he will even dislike them if he should hear them, and he will very much prefer a simple unison (281).

In this context, Rousseau's attack is directed less against Western music per se, as it is against the conclusions Rameau drew from his theory of the fundamental bass. Rousseau insists that the uneducated ear prefers the melodic accompaniment of monody ("a simple unison") to the fundamental bass suggested by the *corps sonore*. Formal

[123] In his *Lettre à M. Grimm, au sujet des remarques ajoutées à sa Lettre sur Omphale*, published the year before the *Lettre sur la musique française*, Rousseau praises *Platée* as "the masterpiece of Mr. Rameau, and the most excellent piece of music which has been heard up until now in our theater." However, Rousseau undercuts this praise by making an implicit comparison between French comic opera [*le genre bouffon*], if it exists at all in France, he cautions, and the Italian genre: "a fat goose does not fly like a swallow" (Rousseau, *Ecrits sur la musique*, 434).

music theory does not coincide with the musical experience of the uncultivated, of those who have not already been indoctrinated into the particular practices of Western "art" music. This passage reappears in the *Dictionnaire de musique* and, in this context, the natural disposition toward melody among "rustics" – uneducated Europeans – is explicitly linked to the same disposition exhibited by the peoples of distant lands:

> When one considers that, of all the peoples of the earth, who all have Music & Song, Europeans are the only ones who have a *harmony*, chords, & who find this mixture agreeable ... that oriental languages, so sonorous, so musical; that Greek ears, so delicate, so sensitive, cultivated with so much Art, have never guided these sensual and passionate peoples towards our *Harmony*.[124]

Dismissing Rameau's theory, the *Dictionnaire* characterizes modern European music as eccentric while the musics of other cultures reveal an unblemished, original sonority. Because Western theory serves insidiously to account for Western musical practices, the displacement that Rousseau effectuates shows it to be both narrow and "barbaric" – foreign to the original conditions of the musical experience. Chabanon, a follower of Rameau in his insistence on the physical, universal, and non-discursive basis of music, repeats Mersenne's earlier conviction of a universal music: "I have written down a few songs of the American Savages from the testimony of an Officer who lived a long time among them. These airs sound exactly like ours ... the same turns, the same implicit harmonic rules."[125] Chabanon concludes that "one could send an Opera to Canada: it would be sung in Québec just as in Paris."[126] In the *Essai*, Rousseau claims the exact opposite, that the melodic inflections of "the songs of American savages" do not follow the consonances dictated by Western harmony: "[they] have inflections in their songs which we call false because they do not fit into our system and we have no notation for them" (289).[127] The types of music preferred

---

[124] Rousseau, *Dictionnaire de musique*, s.v. "Harmonie."

[125] "J'ai noté quelques chansons des Sauvages d'Amérique, d'après un Officier qui avoit vécu long-temps parmi eux. Ces airs ressemblent absolument aux nôtres ... c'est le même tour de chant, c'est la même règle d'harmonie sous-entendue" (Chabanon, *De la musique*, 102).

[126] *Ibid.*, 103.

[127] Rousseau clearly criticizes the ethnocentric and universalist judgements of his contemporaries: "the great failing of Europeans is always to philosophize about the origin of things in the light of what happens right around them" (259–260). He has similar doubts about the Chinese, Persian, and indigenous American songs that are transcribed in the *Dictionnaire de musique*: "I have also transcribed in the Plate a Chinese Air taken from Father du Halde, a Persian Air taken from the Chevalier Chardin, & two Songs of American Savages taken from Father Mersenne. One will find in all of these pieces a Modulation in conformity with our Music which could lead some to admire the excellence & universality of our rules, and others to suspect

by the uncultivated man ("a person with a true but untrained ear") and the American native are versions of accented melody, both equally foreign to the musical practices of Western civilization: the first, because it does not follow the fundamental bass, which, for Rameau, always grounds musical practice; the second, because the inflections of the voice cannot be notated using Western notation, and thus likewise cannot obey the fundamental bass. As he had in the chapters on language, Rousseau safeguards that which is original and authentic in music (passionate accents, song) by praising these qualities in the musics of cultures which are characterized by the absence of modern European scales and musical practices.

Using the form of "anthropological fiction" – that is, the description of the origin of culture and its signifying practices (which Derrida refers to as an "archeo-teleology") – Rousseau has constructed a foundation for his theoretical preference for melody and distaste for harmony.[128] Melody, inseparable in Rousseau's anthropology, if not in eighteenth-century musical practice, from language, is directly traceable to the origin of *semiosis* and of culture. In Derridian terms, melody – as the voice of the origin – has "all the rights constituted by our logos."[129] The development of melody is closely linked to that of culture and community. The later arrival of harmony is characterized as perverse and inhuman: "what have chords in common with our passions?" (281). Rousseau's *Essai* tells the story of a loss. The development of languages through philosophy and reason eclipsed the passions upon which original vocal sounds had been based. Similarly, harmony, with its calculated use of the physical proportions of the *corps sonore* in the form of chords, divorced music from the realm of the passions and thus from (its origin in) meaning. Rousseau's rejection of harmony as abject calculation and proportion, alien to human concerns, thus echoes his earlier refusal to consider the first language as a language "of Geometers": "man did not begin by reasoning but by feeling" (245). Whereas melody is linked to the energy of southern speech, harmony is associated with northern clarity – a product of the repressive work and physical needs of colder climates. By adopting harmony, music has lost touch with the origin of culture. Harmony is characterized by Rousseau as a return to pure sensation and, as such, can have no possible meaningful relationship to the moral realm of the human passions: "the pleasure of Harmony is only a pleasure of pure sensation, & the rapture [*jouissance*] of the senses is always brief, satiety & boredom following closely behind it; but the pleasure of Melody &

the intelligence or honesty of those who have transmitted these Airs to us" (Rousseau, *Dictionnaire de musique*, s.v. "Musique").
128 Derrida, *Of Grammatology*, 198.   129 *Ibid.*, 243.

of Song is an engaging, emotional pleasure which speaks to the heart."[130] Harmony, although the product of the sophisticated techniques of musical composition (Rousseau attacks it on this ground as well, notably in the *Lettre sur la musique française*), is reduced to the level of meaningless, masturbatory sensation: pure "rapture of the senses."[131] Melody, following Rousseau's metaphor, owes its erotic enticements to the circumstances of its southern origin. The climactic movement of this passage from the *Dictionnaire*, culminating in "an engaging, emotional pleasure which speaks to the heart," closely resembles the language with which Rousseau describes the sexual and linguistic utopia of the meridional climates in the *Essai*: "here the first meetings between the sexes took place ... Here the first festivals took place; feet skipped with joy, an eager gesture no longer proved adequate, the voice accompanied it with passionate accents, pleasure and desire merged into one and made themselves felt together" (271). Whereas the last chapter of the *Essai* offers only bleak presages of the future of music, here Rousseau exuberantly describes the timelessness of a social utopia in an overtly theatrical scene. Rousseau asserts that musical imitations surpass all other forms of expression (including speech), endowed with the unique ability to stimulate the passions in such as way as to re-create precisely the presence that is missing in the lifeless forms of painting – the warm presence of emotion:[132]

the musician's art consists in substituting for the imperceptible image of the object, that of the [e]motions [*mouvemens*] which that object's presence excites in the beholder's heart. It will not only churn up the sea, fan the flames of a conflagration, cause rivers to run, rain to fall, and streams to swell, but will also depict the desolation of dreadful deserts, darken the walls of a subterranean dungeon ... It will not represent these things directly, but it will excite in the soul the very same sentiments which one experiences upon seeing them (287–288).

---

[130] Rousseau, *Dictionnaire de musique*, s.v. "Unité de mélodie."

[131] The association of harmony and "reason" (as opposed to *sentiment*) also appears in the *Lettre sur la musique française*, where he suggests that composers have concocted "a learned music" filled with the material excess of "trills ... and other superfluous ornaments" instead of retaining the sentimentally satisfying and simpler music of "pleasant melodies" (Rousseau, *Ecrits sur la musique*, 262–263).

[132] In the fragment which Duchez has entitled "Principe de la mélodie," Rousseau compares melody and speech: "it seems that just as speech is the art of transmitting ideas, melody is the art of transmitting emotions [*sentimens*], and yet Mr. Rameau wants to rob it of everything that acts as their language and which he cannot give to harmony" (quoted in Duchez, "Principe de la mélodie," 68). Rousseau singles out melody as the only musical form capable of maintaining a viable link with the passions. Although speech originally shared this access, it has now been infected by the clarity and reason of writing: "when we say everything as it would get written, all we do is to read as we speak" (*Essay*, 254).

Rousseau introduces a *topos* echoed by other mid to late eighteenth-century aesthetic theorists such as Lessing and Moses Mendelssohn.[133] Music should no longer imitate the sounds of natural objects, of storms and torrents. Rather than directly reproducing the objects of the external world, music goes beyond the traditional doctrine of imitation to represent the passionate movements of the human subject in the presence of these objects and in so doing, excites the same emotions in the listener: "these accents to which one cannot close one's ear and which by way of it penetrate to the very depths of the heart, in spite of ourselves convey to it the [e]motions [*mouvemens*] that wring them [from us], and cause us to feel what we hear" (243). Restoring the intersubjective links that established the first societies, Rousseau's aesthetic seeks to bring human beings together through their involuntary response to melodic sounds: "music ... brings man closer to man and always gives us some idea about our own kind [*semblables*]" (287). By virtue of its essential semiotic ability and in conjunction with theatrical representation, music conveys the feigned emotions of the stage into the "heart" of the spectator. Rousseau also claims that music is also the only art to transcend the ordinary confines of its medium (that is, sound): "the greatest wonder of an art that acts solely through movement is that it can fashion it even into an image of repose. Sleep, the quiet of night, solitude, and silence itself have a place in the spectacles [*tableaux*] of music" (287). The sensory confusion which musical sounds produce is no longer considered to be a perversion, as it was in the comparison of harmony and color; on the contrary, it becomes an inconceivable "wonder": "through an almost inconceivable achievement, it appears to put the eye in the ear, & the greatest marvel of an Art that acts only through movement is to be able to form even the image of repose".[134] Through its ability to go beyond traditional representation by creating not an image but an impression or a feeling, music produces the most captivating of artistic illusions: sound creates the impression of silence.[135]

---

[133] The similarities between Rousseau's views and those of Lessing and Moses Mendelssohn are quite striking on this point. For Lessing and Mendelssohn, "Painting is referentially highly mimetic because it shares physical properties (color, contour) with its original. Precisely for this reason, though, its mimetic efficacy is reduced, for painting brings something of the physical nature of the original with it ... The ideal medium for an effective mimesis would be one which is immaterial" (David E. Wellbery, *Lessing's Laocoon: Semiotics and Aesthetics in the Age of Reason* [Cambridge: Cambridge University Press, 1984], 67–68).

[134] Rousseau, *Dictionnaire de musique*, s.v. "Imitation."

[135] Michel Murat relates the notion of perfectibility (from the second *Discours* and alluded to in the first chapter of the *Essai*) to music's ability to transcend the normal limitations of sound through imitation: "at a more general level, the power of music is homologous to the 'perfectibility' that the second *Discourse* had defined as the

The *Essai* constructs a speculative fiction of the origin of language and culture which provides the rationale for an alternative music theory, opposed to that of Rameau. This music theory, in no way a mere appendage to the *Essai*, is also an integral element of the larger context of Rousseau's "anthropology." At the same time that he raises the issue of the origin of language and music to construct a refutation of Rameau's theory, Rousseau elaborates and exploits reflections on harmony and melody in order to address larger questions concerning aesthetics, signs and signification, and the development of culture. If harmony, according to the differences carefully set in place in the *Essai*, leads to the aesthetic mutilation of eyes in the place of ears and to the ultimate substitution of sensation for sentiment, vocal melody is seen as a way in which human beings, who existed naturally as isolated individuals, could establish communication and community. Melody, insofar as it is considered a part of language, is a crucial element in the social contract.

Given Rousseau's desire to fuse his reflections on the origins and ends of culture with political and social issues, the apparently awkward transition from the penultimate chapter on the "degeneration" of music, to the hasty final chapter on the relationship between languages and governments, becomes somewhat clearer. Earlier, Rousseau had recounted the loss of spontaneous accent to the refined articulations of writing. In the penultimate chapter, music is separated from speech and falls prey to the overwrought harmonic rules with which the men of the north were obliged to compensate for the ugly articulations of their voice. This degradation of music is directly related to changes in the linguistic, cultural, intellectual, and political climate that occurred in the north: "as language became perfected, melody imperceptibly lost some of its former vigor [*énergie*] by imposing new rules on itself" (290). Likewise, language exhibits a loss – of energy, of its musical qualities, of its passion: "the study of philosophy and the progress of reasoning, having perfected grammar, deprived language of the lively and passionate tone that had originally made it so song-like" (290). Soon, disastrous political and social consequences seem to issue from the changes in music and language: "soon servitude added its influence to that of philosophy. Greece in chains lost the fire that warms only free souls, and she never recovered for the praise of her tyrants the tone in which she had sung her Heroes" (291). As part of the same movement through which harmony engulfs melody and philosophy consumes language, social and political freedom are lost to servitude. Music is seen by Rousseau, not as a natural science whose

specific difference between man and animals: this 'veritable virtuality' consists in the fact that man, contrary to animals, *is not* determined by his 'organization'" (Murat, "Jean-Jacques Rousseau," 161).

laws are consummated in the physical resonance of the *corps sonore*, but rather as a cultural form which is intimately linked to the revolutions of society. Just as there are "some languages [which] are conducive to liberty," Rousseau suggests there is a music which goes hand in hand with freedom: this music takes the form of accented melody (294). Rousseau represents the advent of harmony as the result of a process which also brings oppression and corruption into the world. If speech and music have regressed into incomprehensible noise, perhaps it is not surprising that modern governments and despots have lost all significant contact with their subjects ("there is nothing left to say to the people"). Our conversations have become an aimless cacophony: social interaction has been reduced to "the buzz of the Sultan's Council Chamber" (294).[136] Similarly, Rousseau asserts that the complicated harmonies of eighteenth-century (French) music can no longer have any claim to meaning: "do what you may, mere noise says nothing to the mind" (282). For Rousseau, the hidden catastrophe is that music (in the degenerate form of harmony and counterpoint) having drifted from its origins and lost its original energy, has largely lost its ability to connect with the passions: "by abandoning the accents of speech and adhering exclusively to the rules of harmony, music becomes noisier ... It has already ceased to speak" (288). Music has given up communication and communion for the privacy of pure sensation. The *Essai's* reflections on music, language, and culture thus end with baleful predictions of a long silence.

Rousseau's dismissal of sensation, of harmony, and of Rameau also led to other concerns that are present only in broad outline in the final chapters. The *Essai* placed great emphasis on the inherent representational quality of the vocal accent; yet this representation is of interest to Rousseau only insofar as it leads to an affective state in the listener and to the formation of a bond between two or more beings. If operatic frogs must speak for Rousseau, it is not because noise falls outside a neo-classical concept of reason; but because the voice that originally brought human beings together, the voice that is representation of desire, is the subject of opera. Whereas Batteux was concerned with the way in which music could fit the bill of mimesis, the focus of the verbal paradigm in Rousseau has shifted from representation as reproduction to representation as a form of communion. If Rousseau is interested in music as discourse, it is not primarily because that discourse represents something; rather, it is because music leads the listener to a self-consciousness that is defined as the awareness of the presence of another being.

[136] "Le bourdonement des Divans" (*Essai*, 199).

5

Sensible sounds: music and theories of the passions

By examining the place of music in "ideology" – by which I mean both Condillac's study of the development and structure of knowledge, preparing Destutt de Tracy's coinage of the term, and at the same time the more recent sense of a systematic cultural network of meanings – I have sought to understand the place of music within specific discourses in the eighteenth century while attempting to rekindle an interest in "musicology" as cultural discourse. Having discussed the texts of Condillac and Rousseau in some detail, I will now broaden the scope of my analysis. I want to shift the focus of my inquiry from the primordial semiotic bond between the voice and passion at the origin of society to the connection between music and passion in the eighteenth-century present. A relation to the present was always implicit in Condillac's *Essai sur l'origine des connaissances humaines* and Rousseau's *Essai sur l'origine des langues*. The importance of these essays, as I have suggested, is not so much in what they tell about an original state, as in their effort to seat an anthropological discourse in the present. This discourse comes into particular focus, I argue, in medical texts and in writings on musical theater. In both these areas, music filled an epistemological gap by providing a way to discuss and represent the relationship between observable behavior and external forces, on the one hand, and inner passions on the other. I will argue, as I did in the chapter on Rousseau's *Essai*, that if the discussion of origins was finally intended as an understanding of the present, then the essays of Condillac and Rousseau can be seen not so much as framing historical debates, but rather as inventing an eighteenth-century anthropology, which is understood in the particular texts I will examine as the medical or dramatic "science of man."

The notion of music as original signifier appears in a number of eighteenth-century treatises on the passions of the soul which can be considered a mixed breed of medical and philosophical treatises. Writers influenced by Descartes had long been committed to the study of the relations between body and soul, and many eighteenth-century

143

writers benefited from earlier work in this area.[1] The Cartesian treatment of the body sought to limit and temper the malevolent effects of the body on thought through the control mechanisms of the will. For many eighteenth-century writers, it was increasingly difficult to distinguish between the body and the soul, the soul itself remaining always hidden and inaccessible. In his *Traité des animaux*, for example, Condillac asserts that "I feel my soul in my body; all my sensations seem to me simply to be the permutations of a single substance."[2] The body for some writers tended to displace the soul entirely, exhibiting a mechanism that obeyed the logic of a purely material world.

Because they sought to represent the actions and reactions of bodies on the stage, writers on the lyric theater had a stake in concerns similar to those of the doctors and philosophers. However, opera theorists were more interested in the passions expressed in the body as signs of moral force or weakness which could be exploited for aesthetic purposes; medicine, of necessity, was concerned with tracing the harmful effects of passion in order to prevent the consequences of emotional and physical "deregulation." Both medical discourse and theories of the lyric theater drew attention to the voice as a bodily site of passionate expression to be studied and controlled, or aesthetically exploited. The extended argument of this chapter traces the effects of music discussed in the medico-philosophical discourse of treatises on the passions to descriptions of the lyric voice elaborated in theories of musical drama. The latter, I argue, become an aesthetic laboratory – a theoretical testing ground, different from that of medicine – for conceptions of the passions.[3]

---

[1] The story of Descartes' reception by eighteenth-century writers is quite complicated. Aram Vartanian has shown that those eighteenth-century writers who so forcefully rejected Cartesian metaphysics (Diderot and La Mettrie, for example) were also those who were most indebted to a conception of and an approach to the physical world which had been introduced by Descartes. See Aram Vartanian, *Diderot and Descartes: A Study of Scientific Naturalism in the Enlightenment* (Princeton: Princeton University Press, 1953).

[2] Condillac, *Traité des animaux*, in *Œuvres complètes* (1821–22; Geneva: Slatkine, 1970), 3:343.

[3] I do not intend to suggest an epistemological hierarchy, in which lyric drama merely borrowed or embodied a concept of passion that was already fully developed in medicine. As Anne C. Vila has argued in her study of sensibility in the eighteenth century, "one should not consider the matrix of *sensibilité* as 'internal' to any one, supposedly dominant field of knowledge; for this is a matrix that, amoeba-like, spread over and encompassed the discourses of multiple fields, along with their reciprocal resonances and mutual permeations" (Anne C. Vila, "The sensible body: medicine and literature in eighteenth century France" [Ph.D. dissertation, The Johns Hopkins University, 1990], 13). In a thought-provoking article, Vila has examined the clinical language in Diderot's *La Religieuse* to argue that he transforms the novel of sensibility into an "experimental" genre that fully engages a philosophico-medical discourse.

In Rousseau's *Essai sur l'origine des langues*, as in Condillac's *Essai sur l'origine des connaissances humaines*, music was valorized through the privileged and primordial bond between voice and emotion. As I noted in the previous chapter, this connection is also put forth by many eighteenth-century tracts on the arts. Le Pileur d'Apligny, whose treatise on music offered composers the means to perfect musical expression, began his argument by returning to the origin of music to describe the first passionate, musical expressions. The link between voice and passion was not seen as the exclusive property of a distant and lost origin, but continued to figure as the most valuable (or as the most dangerous, as Bossuet had complained) attribute of contemporary music. Rousseau claimed in the *Essai* that music evokes the "plaints," "cries of suffering or joy," or "moans [*gémissemens*]" that remain the universal signs of passionate engagement.[4] The assertion of an active bond between music and passion would go virtually unchallenged until about 1780, when the notion of musical expression was dismissed as an illusion (*chimère*) by Boyé. However, if Boyé rejects the relationship between music and emotion, he nonetheless concedes that music has a certain "character" which is conveyed to the listener: "it is naïve in Romances, gay in Allemands."[5] The question of music as expressive (of something), then, is one that bridges the gap between the scenes of original social bonding, described by Bourdelot, Blainville, Condillac, and Rousseau, and the debates that surrounded eighteenth-century music and aesthetics.[6] The notion of an original bond joining vocal sounds and human emotions conferred another dimension of meaning and authenticity upon operatic representations

---

Vila also links the clinical role of the *médecin-philosophe* (Bordeu) to the description of the actor in Diderot's writings. See "Sensible diagnostics in Diderot's *La Religieuse*," *MLN* 105 (1990), 774–799.

[4] Rousseau, *Essay*, 282.

[5] Boyé, *L'Expression musicale mise au rang des chimères* (Amsterdam: Esprit, 1779), 11. Boyé wonders how music could ever imitate the passions if "the passions never manifest themselves in singing" (*L'Expression musicale*, 5). Even so, the contest Boyé staged was less over the relationship of music to passion, which continued to be important for virtually every writer (with a very few notable exceptions such as Boyé), than it was over an aesthetic framework and hierarchy in which music was seen as a secondary or subservient art. Chabanon, while rejecting opera as servile in its dependence on words, nonetheless refers to all music as a "universal language" (*De la musique*, 129).

[6] Since the term "aesthetics" was coined by Alexander Gottlieb Baumgarten in 1735 (but only fully developed in his *Aesthetica* of 1750), my usage here might be considered slightly anachronistic. In the article "Esthétique" in the supplement to the *Encyclopédie*, Sulzer acknowledges that Baumgarten "is the first to have ventured to create, on philosophical principles, the general science of the fine arts, to which he gave the name *aesthetics*." However, Sulzer finds the first traces of modern aesthetics in Dubos' 1719 treatise, *Réflexions sur la poésie et sur la peinture* (*Supplément à l'Encyclopédie*, 2:872–873).

of the passions. Opera, by virtue of the fact that it was rhetoric *in musica*, was given an origin and a purpose in its representation of the human subject as lyric voice. With the continued focus on reception in writings on music through the end of the eighteenth century and into the nineteenth, as Mark Evan Bonds has shown, purely instrumental music adopted some of the same rhetorical concerns that are found in treatises on the lyric theater. Giving his daughter advice on her *toucher* (touch, technique) at the harpsichord in the *Leçons de clavecin*, Diderot, for example, insisted that she must "speak to the soul and to the ear, and know the origins of song and of melody whose true model is in the depths of the heart."[7] In its concern with rhetoric and affect, instrumental music covered much of the same territory as writings on opera. I will return to Diderot's *Leçons de clavecin* later in this chapter to illustrate the point of common concern between theorists of the lyric theater and those who describe the "discourse" of instrumental music.

In an effort to contextualize the question of music and passion, I will examine briefly the history of the perceived relationship between musical theater and its effects on the human constitution. Since this history is long and involved, and has been amply documented in recent books by Belinda Cannone and Catherine Kintzler, among others, I will give only a brief account, referring the reader to other studies where appropriate. The present chapter has two central aims, both of which concern the relationship of music to the physical and emotional experience of the spectator. First, following a brief introduction to the debates on opera and passion, I will discuss the presence of music and its relation to affect in mid to late eighteenth-century medical discourse. My second aim will be to reveal the continuities between medical discourse at mid-century and the musical concern with communicative affect. Here, I will focus on the aesthetic purposes attributed to music through its ability to conflate physical and moral response.

Because of the emphasis it placed on sensual arousal and on implausible events (*invraisemblance*), French opera raised the suspicion of many theorists. Opera had its defenders, of course; in his *Théâtre lyrique*, Antoine-Louis Le Brun countered the arguments against operatic spectacle by remarking that it was "a spectacle that amuses, & refreshes the mind."[8] However, most defenses of opera in the early eighteenth century, like that of Le Brun, were informal and left open to attack for lack of unified theoretical underpinning. Whereas Houdar de la Motte would later consider opera a model for all theater, the

---

[7] Denis Diderot, *Œuvres complètes*, ed. Varloot, 19:353.

[8] Antoine-Louis Le Brun, *Théâtre Lyrique*, in François Lesure, ed., *Textes sur Lully et l'opéra français*, (Geneva: Minkoff, 1987), 21.

question in 1673 – the year of Lully's first *tragédie en musique, Cadmus et Hermione* – was whether opera was really theater at all. Kintzler notes that opera initially established itself in an area from which almost all other theater had withdrawn.[9] The influence and importance of French classical tragedy and theory, however, had created an aesthetic climate in which opera was judged first and foremost, as Kintzler has shown, by criteria drawn from poetics, constantly being compared (most often unfavorably) with the plays of Racine and Corneille.[10] In the "system of human knowledge," reworked from Bacon by the editors of the *Encyclopédie* as one of the organizing systems of their dictionary, opera is categorized as belonging to the *belles-lettres*, not as a subcategory of music.

Arguments against the lyric theater centered on both the objects and means of operatic representation. In Jaucourt's tidy and rather prudish *Encyclopédie* article "Opéra," the tensions that had surrounded opera over the previous seventy-five years – its violations of the dramatic idiom and its hybrid nature – are succinctly presented. Jaucourt holds that opera is an unprecedented spectacle and has no clear generic status. Saint-Evremond's well-known denunciation of opera is cited: "a *chimerical assemblage of poetry & music*, in which the poet and the composer torture each other."[11] In the lyric theater, moreover, the concept of mimesis is stretched to its limits to include the supernatural (*le merveilleux*). According to Grimm's article "Poème Lyrique," it is the *merveilleux* that defines opera as a genre:

The tragic poet takes his subjects from history; the lyric poet sought his in the epic; & after having exhausted all of ancient mythology & all of modern wizardry [*sorcellerie*]; after having put on stage all possible divinities; after having given every imaginable thing form and figure, he created yet more fantastic beings, & giving them a supernatural power & magic, he made them the principal mechanism of his *poem*. Thus, it is the visible *merveilleux* that is the soul of French opera.[12]

Though not opposed to operatic drama per se, Grimm recycled the arguments that earlier theorists had directed at traditional French opera to put forward his bid for a new definition of the lyric theater. Grimm argued that the lyric theater, having exhausted the resources of mythology and the epic, went too far beyond the normal limits of representation ("he created yet more beings"). Aside from the

---

[9] Kintzler, *Poétique de l'opéra français*, 232. [10] *Ibid.*, 18.

[11] "Saint-Evremond appelle l'*opéra* un *chimérique assemblage de poésie & de musique*, dans lequel le poëte & le musicien se donnent mutuellement la torture ... Il est certain que le spectacle que nous nommons *opéra*, n'a jamais été connu des anciens, & qu'il n'est, à proprement parler, ni comédie, ni tragédie" (*Encyclopédie*, 11:494).

[12] *Encyclopédie*, 12:828.

extravagance of the supernatural, Grimm protests the excessively visual aspect of French opera. If this objection to the visible returns frequently in criticisms of the lyric theater, it is because the visible was a touchy subject within neo-classical codes of *bienséance*, or propriety. The visible makes available to the direct gaze of the spectator what should be sublimated in poetic discourse. Boileau had explicitly mentioned the need to exclude certain objects from sight: "That which should not be seen, let a narrative expose it: / The eyes, upon seeing, would grasp the thing better; / Yet there are objects that judicious art / Must offer to the ear and draw away from the eyes."[13] If there are certain objects that should be heard and not seen, it is because the interest and enjoyment of drama should lie in the *intrigue* – the plot, conveyed by the measured discourse of the alexandrines – and not in sensual pleasures of the eyes. In "Poème Lyrique," Grimm noted that this was precisely where opera had trangressed neo-classical norms: "that which the discretion of the epic poet reveals only to our imagination, the lyric poet has undertaken in France to represent to our eyes."[14] From this standpoint, opera was not only the representation of monstrous objects (those drawn from the supernatural). The mimetic act itself was montrous in the lyric theater. The gap that opera opened up in this discourse on the arts is repeatedly evoked in metaphors of monstrous births and deviation from nature: in opera, "one moves away from nature";[15] opera is a "monster," a "freak" [*avorton*];[16] and as Grimm noted, "a false genre in which nothing recalls nature."[17]

For critics like Saint-Evremond and Bossuet, opera is at the same time lacking and excessive: it fails because the poetic focus of dramatic mimesis is lost – opera "loses the spirit of representation" – and because it overcompensates for this lack with the spectacular.[18] Because there is little "real" mimetic value to opera, the spectator gives him- or herself over to its special scenic and musical effects. Whereas classical tragedy sublimates passion in measured discourse, in opera the sensual seduction of the ears and the eyes releases and encourages affective disorder: "while one is enchanted by the sweetness of the melody, or stunned by the spectacle's supernatural effects, the emotions insinuate themselves without our notice ... one soon becomes a secret actor in the tragedy, playing out one's own

---

[13] Nicolas Boileau, *Œuvres* (Paris: Garnier-Flammarion, 1969), 1:99.

[14] *Encyclopédie*, 12:828.

[15] Gabriel Bonnot, abbé de Mably, *Lettres à Madame la Marquise de P... sur l'opéra* (Paris: Didot, 1741), 16.

[16] *Ibid.*, 3, 39.   [17] *Encyclopédie*, 12:829.

[18] Saint-Evremond, *Sur l'opéra*, in Lesure, ed., *Textes sur Lully*, 85.

passion."[19] The risk is that the disorderly passions feigned by the actors will be assumed by the spectators: the imaginary passions of the stage become real through the spectator's desire and identification. This moral objection could apply, and was applied, to traditional theater as well; yet opera was singled out by its critics because it was the spectacle which, by far, placed the most emphasis on the seduction of the senses. Referring to Lully's operas, Bossuet suggested that the music was an unsuspected carrier of harmful passions: "its airs, so repeated in society, serve only to insinuate the most treacherous [*décevantes*] passions."[20] In addition to the visual extravagance of opera, the lyric had a corrupting effect even outside of the theater, able to mask dangerous passion with enchanting music.

If sensation was rejected in the arguments of Bossuet and Saint Evremond in favor of the reason and self-possession which sensation supposedly blocked or effaced, then the rehabilitation of sensation through the notion of *sensibilité* would have important consequences for the theorization of lyric theater. In the place of a metaphysical bond between the object and our representations of that object, guaranteed by the existence of God, as Crousaz had asserted in his *Traité du beau* (1724), a new series of connections were formed, based on the increasing importance given to sensibility.[21] I want to draw attention to the epistemological links between the paradigm shift that revalorized sensation, on the one hand, and changes in the conception of the role of music in theater, on the other. By examining the ways in which a number of treatises on the passions defined vocal sounds as signs of affect, it will be possible to see how opera might have been understood as a lyrical study of the human soul, rather than rejected as "bad mimesis." In other words, I want to suggest that the reconceptualization of the lyric theater was in some measure dependent on the conceptual matrix of sensibility.

If it was a question of "speaking to the soul" or learning the "language of the soul," then eighteenth-century conceptions of the soul and the mechanism of the passions were necessarily implicit in theories of musical representation. Aristotle's *De Anima* had proposed to elucidate the complex interrelations between the body and its

---

[19] Jacques Bénigne Bossuet, *Maximes et réflexions sur la comédie*, in *Œuvres* (Bar-le-Duc: Guérin, 1863), 8:73–74.

[20] *Ibid.*, 8:73. Almost identical arguments have been made against music in recent years and, in some cases, musicians have gone to court for "insinuating passions," as Bossuet expressed it. See Robert Walser, *Running with the Devil: Power, Gender, and Madness in Heavy Metal Music* (Hanover: Wesleyan University Press / University Press of New England, 1993), 137–171.

[21] J. P. de Crousaz, *Traité du beau* (Amsterdam: L'Honoré & Chatelain, 1724), 1:175.

sensations, and the activities of the soul. For Aristotle, the soul was the "form" and active principle of the essentially passive matter of the body. The passions of the soul were considered to be inseparable from the body;[22] as the principle of movement, desire, for example, was necessary for human activity.[23] Descartes rejected Aristotle's vitalism. His treatise on *Les Passions de l'âme* asserted that the soul did not form the principle or potentiality behind the body's functions: thought alone belonged to the soul whereas warmth and movement depended entirely on the independent mechanism of the body.[24] Resulting from the union of the body and the soul, the passions were a mixed breed of perceptions (*confuses et obscures*) and, for this reason, deserved to be regarded with suspicion.[25] For Descartes, as Anthony Levi has noted, the soul and the body were locked in combat despite their temporary union: "one is master of one's passions in so far as one can successfully halt the flow of spirits which sustains them, and in so far as one can resist consenting to those actions which are solicited from the soul by the body in passion."[26] Descartes asserted that it was possible to stop the harmful passions by representing to oneself objects that were usually associated with salutary passions.[27] Though *Les Passions de l'âme* was ground-breaking in many ways, Descartes was not alone in his suspicion of passion. Other philosophers, some opposed to Cartesian metaphysics, also considered the passions a potentially dangerous influence requiring strict control. Pascal, for example, likens uncontrolled passions to poison: "for when the passions dominate, they are vices; then, they give their sustenance to the soul, and the soul feeds on this and poisons itself."[28]

Many eighteenth-century writers emphasized the centrality and usefulness of the passions rather than their danger. The passions were considered to be as essential to being as movement was to the physical universe. Helvétius made precisely this claim in *De l'esprit* (1758): "the passions are to the moral what movement is to the physical: it creates, destroys, conserves, animates everything, and without it all is dead. They likewise give life to the moral world."[29] If the physical universe –

---

[22] Aristotle, *De Anima*, trans. R. D. Hicks (1907; Hildesheim: Georg Olms, 1990), 403a.

[23] *Ibid.*, 433a.   [24] Descartes, *Les Passions de l'âme*, 157.   [25] *Ibid.*, 172.

[26] Anthony Levi, *French Moralists: The Theory of the Passions 1585 to 1649* (Oxford: Clarendon Press, 1964), 272.

[27] Descartes, *Les Passions de l'âme*, 182.

[28] "Car, quand les passions sont les maîtresses, elles sont vices, et alors elles donnent à l'âme de leur aliment, et l'âme s'en nourrit et s'en empoisonne" (Blaise Pascal, *Pensées* [Paris: Garnier, 1964], 200).

[29] Claude-Adrien Helvétius, *De l'esprit* (Paris: Fayard, 1988), 268. As Aram Vartanian has pointed out, although eighteenth-century philosophy generally rejected Cartesian metaphysics – the notion of innate ideas and the essential distinction between the body and the soul – Diderot and La Mettrie owed a great deal to Descartes' efforts in

made of matter in motion, as Descartes had asserted – would be entirely inert without the activity of its "vortices," similarly, as Helvétius claims, human beings would be lifeless without the energy of the passions: "one becomes stupid as soon as one ceases to be passionate."[30] But whereas Descartes had asserted that thought was the primary function of the soul and warmth and movement functions of the body, eighteenth-century thinkers dismantled the *cogito*, contending that the human mind was much closer to the body that Descartes had allowed and that the human organism as a whole was governed by sensibility and the complex transformations of sensation: "my Mind [*Ame*] continually reveals not thought, which is accidental to it, whatever the Cartesians may say about it, but rather activity & sensibility."[31] Likewise, d'Holbach suggested that the movements of passion define humanity.[32] For La Mettrie, the passions of the soul – indeed, the soul itself – were nothing but an endless permutation of feeling: "the emotions [*sentimens*] of the soul belong to it specifically as modifications of itself ... the soul is deprived of itself when it is deprived of sensations."[33] From this standpoint, there can be no essential difference between sensations and thought, the latter being only a highly processed and organized form of the former.

With a larger role accorded to sensation in the economy of the subject, interest shifted from the unknowable inner workings of the soul to the observable, corporeal expression of the passions. In his article on "Passion (Peint.)," Jaucourt notes that "such is the structure of our mechanism, that when the soul is stirred by a *passion*, the body shares its effects."[34] In *Les Passions de l'âme*, Descartes had already listed the passions and described their effects on the body. Yet, whereas Descartes' treatise led to the proper management and containment of the passions by a rational soul, eighteenth-century theorists were more interested in the expression of the passions, with the

physics and his emphasis on the scientific study of the human organism: "Cartesian physiology had proposed ... to explore the phenomena of sensibility, sensation, and the various states of the 'soul' as so many modifications of the organism defined as a machine. It was in the practical application of this method to questions of psychology that the striking originality of the *Traité des passions de l'âme* consisted ... From the standpoint of the *Traité des passions*, it fell within the jurisdiction of physiology and biology to clarify ultimately the workings of the soul – a point that the author of *L'Homme machine* was emphatically to echo at the same time that he attached his materialism to Cartesian precedents" (Vartanian, *Diderot and Descartes*, 214).

[30] Helvétius, *De l'esprit*, 283.

[31] Julien Offroy de La Mettrie, *Histoire naturelle de l'âme* (Oxford: n.p., 1747), 82–83.

[32] Jean Ehrard, *L'Idée de nature en France dans la première moitié du XVIIIe siècle* (Paris: SEVPEN, 1963), 1:383.

[33] La Mettrie, *Histoire naturelle de l'âme*, 133–134.

[34] "Telle est la structure de notre machine, que quand l'âme est affectée d'une *passion*, le corps en partage l'impression" (*Encyclopédie*, 12:150).

possible aesthetic and moral uses of emotion. Accordingly, in its articles on the passions, the *Encyclopédie* devotes lengthy passages to the rhetorical, poetic, and pictorial aspects of the passions – the practical aesthetic uses of the passions, related in many ways to medical semiology. For the eighteenth-century *médecins-philosophes*, diagnosis consisted "in the delicate art of tapping the resonances created by sensibility in the body" by the doctor-genius, as Anne Vila has argued.[35] Similarly, as theorists of the lyric theater would suggest, the energy of the passions should be tapped through aesthetic means to create sympathetic resonances in a healthy social body.

In the *Art poétique*, Boileau had asserted that "each passion speaks a different language."[36] The *Encyclopédie* sought to describe the natural "language" of the impassioned body: "since these inner movements are generally too violent & impetuous not to burst out, they appear only with sounds that characterize them & distinguish them. In this way, expression, which is the painting of thought, is also appropriate for & proportioned to *passion* which thought can only translate."[37] Passions reveal themselves as eruptions of vocal sound which, since they "characterize" and "distinguish" the passions, can be used in an aesthetic symptomatology. The theater sought to cultivate what was considered the more direct expression of passion in vocal sound; ordinary language, as the articulation of rational thought, was situated at a distance from passion as its "translation." Although extreme passions were considered dangerous because of the disorder they entailed, excessive passion was also the mark of an intense sensibility and valorized as such. This excess was frequently taken as the model for narrative, dramatic, and pictorial representations of passion. La Mettrie described the affective "body language" which he claimed was better suited to the strong primacy of the passions than were the conventional expressions of ordinary speech:

Conventional language, by which I mean speech, is not the sign which best expresses impassioned states. There is another one common to man & animals that manifests them with greater certitude: I am speaking of affective language, such as plaints, cries, caresses, flight, sighs, song, & in a word all the expressions of suffering, of sadness ... of anger, of pleasure, of joy.[38]

The musical use of the voice is mentioned here, along with other vocal sounds and rudimentary gestures, as a fundamentally affective

---

[35] Vila, "Sensible diagnostics," 779.   [36] Boileau, *Œuvres*, 1:101.

[37] "Comme pour l'ordinaire ces mouvemens intérieurs [les passions] sont trop violens & trop impétueux pour n'éclater pas au dehors, ils n'y paroissent qu'avec des sons qui les caractérisent & qui les distinguent. Ainsi l'expression, qui est la peinture de la pensée, est aussi convenable & proportionnée à la passion dont la pensée n'est que l'interprète" (*Encyclopédie*, s.v. "Passions, en poésie," 12:148–149).

[38] La Mettrie, *Histoire naturelle de l'âme*, 25–26.

element of language. Condillac and Rousseau had made precisely the same claim and had placed this "natural" language at the origin of all conventional languages. In the *Entretiens sur le fils naturel*, Diderot proposed the reintroduction of these affective gestures into the theater as pantomime. Indeed, judging also from La Mettrie's treatise on the soul, eighteenth-century writers wanted to see the natural language of cries, gesture, and song as another language existing in the present alongside conventional language, but reserved for the expression of elementary human passion. Grimm, too, in his article "Poème Lyrique" in the *Encyclopédie*, asserted that "every living being is inspired by the sentiment of its existence to cry out at certain moments with more or less melodious sounds [*accens*]."[39] For Maupertuis, gestures and especially vocal sounds, which are "more apt to move someone" than are gestures, remained bound to the most intimate confines of being: "the first language, this natural language of gestures and cries, is always ready to manifest itself when a passion returns us to the state we were in when we needed it."[40]

Having been attacked as false and artificial, the language of the lyric theater – its representation of passionate gestures and cries – was always implicitly justified in the eighteenth century by this rhetoric of origins. Music was the first language, but "it is also a language that we continue to understand."[41] Le Pileur d'Apligny, for example, in his treatise devoted to music and to "the means of perfecting its expression," sought to authorize his undertaking with a reference to the original (and, as he later asserted, pre-linguistic) link between music and the passions:

The use & arrangement of the various accents of the voice, & consequently Song or Music, owe their origins to the sensations that the first men felt upon seeing the marvels of the universe, & to the first passions that they felt. To express them, they only needed to follow Nature, which endowed us with a preference & a singular sensibility for harmony and rhythm [*cadence*].[42]

The passionate experience of existence – which takes place as an intersubjective encounter for Rousseau, and as a private feeling of being in the universe for Le Pileur – and the origin of musical sounds are brought together through a double logic. Music is the expression of the passions aroused by the first sense experiences. Yet at the same time, the semiotic connection between music and emotion already exists for "man" who is predisposed, through his "sensibility," to "harmony and rhythm." If the object of music is to perfect the expression of the passions, as Le Pileur's title claims, then the composer must

---

[39] *Encyclopédie*, 12:823.   [40] Quoted in Porset, ed., *Varia linguistica*, 94–95.
[41] Jacques Lacombe, *Le Spectacle des beaux-arts* (Paris: Hardy, 1758), 248.
[42] Le Pileur d'Apligny, *Traité sur la musique*, 3.

base his art on the original imbrication of emotion and vocal sound. The origin of music and its close link with emotion is the key to its future development: if musical composition was to be better understood and improved, it was necessary to understand the original conditions that determined the human production of, and reaction to, vocal sound.

In 1751, the doctor Jean Baptiste Joseph Lallemant published his *Essai sur le méchanisme des passions en général* – a curious blend of reflections on medicine and music. A brief examination of his essay will help to clarify how and why eighteenth-century theorists found it useful to articulate their conceptions of music in terms of its origins in passionate, physiological response. Lallemant notes that there are many possible views of the passions: the metaphysician examines the passions of the soul, "disregarding what they may have in common with the body"; the moral philosopher, "scrupulous observer of all that can influence morals, conduct, & virtue," will judge the passions from the perspective of moral conduct.[43] Lallemant suggests that the medical doctor takes a more interesting and neglected view of "the physical [*méchaniques*] causes & effects" of the passions. The study of the body is important because, "sooner or later the body gets involved [*s'intrigue*] in the affairs of the heart."[44] The author asserts that, while treating the medical aspect of the passions, he seeks to address a larger public since the subject concerns everyone. It is from this standpoint that he examines the effects of musical and theatrical representations on the passions.

Lallemant claims that we not only experience and express our own emotions, but are also affected by the emotions of others: "through a hidden [*secret*] impulse independent of the will, it happens that we are naturally given over to the passions whose effects we see in others."[45] Lallemant transposes this understanding of affect into the aesthetic domain: "we are all without exception, necessarily & regularly subject to the Passions & each man seeks himself, as it were, & likes to find himself in the various portraits that can be made of them."[46] Passions are necessary to life; they can only be pleasurable. This pleasure comes from the recognition that occurs as the spectator sees him- or herself in the various representations that can be made of passion. The portrayal of passion leads to a pleasurable form of self-knowledge. Lallemant thus echoes Aristotle's conception of drama (that is, of mimesis) as leading the spectator through a process of self-recognition. The sym-

---

[43] Jean Baptiste Joseph Lallemant, *Essai sur le méchanisme des passions en général* (Paris: Le Prieur, 1751), i–ij.
[44] *Ibid.*, 41–42.   [45] *Ibid.*, 6.   [46] *Ibid.*, vij–viij.

pathy with the afflictions of others that occurs in real life is mirrored in the reaction of the spectator.

One might be tempted to see a resemblance between this economy of sympathy and Rousseau's notion of compassion (*la pitié*). In both the *Essai sur l'origine des langues* and the second *Discours*, the innate mechanism of *la pitié* inaugurates human society by allowing the subject to find him- or herself in the other, in the representation of the passions of another being: "pity, although natural to man's heart, would remain forever inactive without imagination to set it in motion. How do we let ourselves be moved to pity? By transporting ourselves outside ourselves; by identifying with the suffering being."[47] Society is based on acts of identification triggered by compassion which also define the subject as an individual: one is made conscious of one's humanity – of being in and belonging to a community – through the other's pain. The vocal sounds of the passions serve as fuel for this social bonding by making passion perceptible. Though Rousseau and Lallemant both emphasize the place of representation in the definition of self, Rousseau's description of passionate identification takes place as a living, social theatrics, whereas Lallemant locates this identification in a contemplation of "portraits." Whereas Rousseau draws a distinction between the false theatrics of the stage and the healthy theatrics of compassion at the origin of society, Lallemant sees no interest in marking a strong difference between the spectator's experience in the portrait gallery or at the theater, and the relationship of compassion and identification between two human beings. From Lallemant's standpoint, the aesthetic and social contexts are interchangeable in their potential effect on passion within *l'œconomie animale* – the system of internal and external actions and reactions that define the existence of living beings. Whereas Rousseau is suspicious of the amorality of sensation, Lallemant's position speaks to a growing confidence in the moral effects of the arts.

After describing at some length the biological mechanism by which sensations make an impression on the soul through the *corps calleux* – the physical site of mediation between the body and the soul, located in the brain – Lallemant explains that the passions are particularly affected by music, and, conversely, also find their preferred expression in music: "music, which in its origin was intended to express & to excite only joy, has since become a general expression, & the shared spark of all the passions."[48] Lallemant refers to the contributions of Rameau, specifically to the *Traité de l'harmonie* and the *Nouveau système de musique théorique*, in supporting his position on music and affect. Yet similarly to Rousseau, Lallemant gives preference to vocal melody in

[47] Rousseau, *Essay*, 261.   [48] Lallemant, *Essai*, 9.

the expression of the passions: "melody acts on the Passions in two ways: either by expressing the movement that it inspires, or by the simple impression that rhythm makes on the ear."[49] As melody, the voice can represent the movements of the passions. Its rhythms can also move the soul in a purely mechanical fashion. Melody and, for different reasons, liquor, are termed "immediate occasional causes" of passion, having a close and privileged access to the soul. Instrumental music, however, along with other external sensations – the impressions of fever, of the air, and so on – are "remote accidental causes" in relation to the passions: "one must admit that in general the sound of instruments has a much more limited power on the soul than does song."[50] In the case of instrumental music, no representation takes place, only a physical reaction of cause and effect. Showing his Aristotelian inclinations, Lallement has offered a choice between mimesis and mechanics. Whereas instrumental music moves the soul through its effect on the senses, melody triggers a process by which the subject experiences passion through a more complex kind of sympathetic response: in melody, the spectator hears and responds to the passion of another voice. A better understanding of these acts of representation could lead to a better grasp of the effects of sensibility on the constitution of individuals and on the social body. If musical sound can be considered to be part of the "animal economy" through its effect on the passions of the subject, by extension music must also act upon society in some way. However, Lallemant does not indicate what the relationship might be between individual passions and collective ones, other than to indicate that the passions have "something contagious about them" and that in this way music is like oratory.[51]

The medical doctor, like the theorist of the lyric theater, is interested in passion as a case of the extreme. Lallemant focuses on the perpetual agitation he sees in the "fibers" that transmit sensation: he does not indicate what an unaffected state of being might be. The body is always affected by the input it receives in the form of sensation; likewise, the body continually exhibits feedback from sensation in the form of gestural or vocal response. In its focus on the outward signs of passion, Lallemant's treatise briefly coincides with that of La Mettrie, despite the ideological differences that oppose the latter's materialism to the former's odd blend of Cartesian and scholastic influences, and recent medical theory. Rather than seeking to know the essence of the passions, Lallemant urges the study of the various signs with which the body expresses the movements of the soul. In other words, he follows the general move away from ontology toward semiology.

Lallemant was not the only writer to relate medicine and music.

---

[49] *Ibid.*, 14.   [50] *Ibid.*, 18.   [51] *Ibid.*, 7.

Pierre Estève wrote on what he saw as the "mechanical" relations between music and the soul in his *Nouvelle découverte du principe de l'harmonie* (1752); Béthisy de Mézières, the author of the simplistic but enthusiastic *Effets de l'air sur le corps humain* (1760), examined the effects of music on the body and the soul; and in 1777, Mirabeau published a pamphlet, *Le Lecteur y mettra le titre*, describing the effects of music on the human organism and urging medicine to take music seriously: "it seems certain to me that music can be of real use in the art of healing. The knowledge of the animal economy, of the action of the fibers, of nerve fluids, of the influence of changes in the air & above all that of the passions on the human mechanism [*machine*], makes this opinion very probable."[52] In his article, "Tarentule," written for the *Encyclopédie*, Jaucourt noted the interest some scientists had taken in the curative effects of music. The article mentions a presentation to the Académie des Sciences in 1702 by Etienne-François Geoffroy, who claimed to have witnessed a musical cure for tarantula bite.[53] According-ing to Geoffroy, the victim was made to listen to and to danse along with a brisk air for several days, after which time the effects of the poison completely disappeared. Though this cure is rejected by Jaucourt as a myth [*un roman*], the possible effects of music on the human constitution appear in various articles throughout the *Encyclopédie*. In another article, "Musique, effects de la," probably by Dr. Ménuret de Chambaud, the history of the relations between medicine and music is summarized and suggestions are put forth for the medici-nal use of music. Ménuret de Chambaud argues that "the action of *Music* on men is so strong, & above all so palpable [*sensible*], that it appears absolutely superfluous to assemble evidence in order to verify the possibility."[54] We can observe the action of music on inanimate objects, on animals, and on human beings from the perspective of both medical and moral considerations.[55] Leaving aside metaphysical ques-tions, the author remarks on the power of music to affect the body: "if the human mechanism is now considered to be endowed with an exquisite sensibility, what action would music not borrow from that?"[56] Though knowledge of music and a particularly acute sensibi-lity contribute to the intensity of the experience, it is not necessary to be a connoisseur to feel its effects: "it is enough to be sensible."[57] The

---

[52] Honoré Gabriel Riquetti, comte de Mirabeau, *Le Lecteur y mettra le titre* (London: n.p., 1777), 23.

[53] *Encyclopédie*, 15:905–907. See Albert Cohen, *Music in the French Royal Academy of Sciences* (Princeton: Princeton University Press, 1981), 21. Dozens of texts from the period, both musical and medical, mention music as a possible cure for tarantula bite. The rapid dance called the tarantella supposedly got its name from the spider whose poison it was reputed to counteract.

[54] *Encyclopédie*, 10:903.   [55] *Ibid.*, 10:904.   [56] *Ibid.*, 10:907.   [57] *Ibid.*

article concludes with some suggestions for the appropriate prescription of music for specific medical problems, so as to "calm the furors of a frenetic, to charm away, as it were, the sharp pains that torment a person with gout, one will dispel the ills of a melancholic, hypochondriac ..."[58]

Diderot, too, affirms music's exceptional ability to affect the listener and remarks on the medical properties of music.[59] In the article "Ame" from the *Encyclopédie*, Diderot gives a number of examples which demonstrate the soul's existence in, and dependence on, the well-being of the body. One of these examples tells of a famous musician who was cured of a life-threatening fever by a strong dose of music:

> Mr. Dodart relates this item after having verified it. He does not claim that it can be used as an example or rule; but it is rather curious to note how in a man for whom *Music* had become, as it were, the soul through a long & continuous practice, musical concerts little by little returned his spirits to their natural course. It is not likely that a Painter could be cured in the same way by paintings; Painting does not have the same power over the spirits, & it would not carry the same impression to the *soul*.[60]

Though Diderot's principle aim in this article is to provide a convincing materialist description of the soul, the musical example leads him into aesthetics. The article "Ame" ends here with a comparison of the relative influence of painting and music on the soul. Despite his effort to minimize the exemplary value of this particular anecdote, Diderot's other writings of this period (particularly his "Lettre à Mademoiselle de la Chaux," and the *Lettre sur les sourds et muets*) demonstrate that he is deeply interested in the connection between music and sensibility as an aesthetic, as well as physiological, question.

In this brief survey of texts, I think we can begin to distinguish a way of thinking about music, a conceptual framework that emphasized the physiological link between sound and emotion in the human organism, in the "animal economy." This conceptual framework extends from medico-philosophical writings on the passions to theories of musical expression. In order to affect the listener, the lyric

---

[58] *Ibid.*, 10:908.

[59] Diderot's *Le Rêve de d'Alembert* adopts the metaphor of the harpsichord to describe the relationship between the fibers, sensation, and memory. More than thirty years earlier, in his *Essai historique et philosophique sur le goût*, Cartaud de la Vilate used the metaphor of the harpsichord ("we are like harpsichords that resonate ...") to describe the "resonance" of the body when exposed to certain sensations (quoted in Cannone, *Philosophies de la musique*, 35). Condillac, too, adopted the harpsichord metaphor to describe sensibility as a kind of resonance. See Condillac, *La Logique*, 162–179. See also Marie-Hélène Huet, *Monstrous Imagination* (Cambridge: Harvard University Press, 1993), 285n16.

[60] *Encyclopédie*, 1:343.

theater depended upon an understanding of the physiological and emotional resonance of musical structures. Laurent Garcin, for example, in his *Traité du mélodrame*, insisted that a thorough knowledge of the human soul and its passions was absolutely indispensable to the musician: "he who has studied neither nature nor man, he who is unaware of the hidden relations that link actions to an agent, resolutions to the will, external movements to internal passions, will never be a Musician or Composer [*Musicien*] for the mind, nor for the heart."[61] It is likely that the lyric theater invented, to some extent, its own affective symptomatology together with the musical resources with which it sought to calm and excite the passions, independently of medical discourse. The point I want to make, however, is not that writers on musical issues and medical theorists had identical views or agreed on a system of "music therapy," but that they both saw a direct relationship between music and the passions. When critics began to call for a new opera that would leave behind the supernatural gods and heroes which had previously dominated the lyric stage, they emphasized the musical expression of the various passions to which Garcin referred.[62] The guiding principle of the lyric spectacle would no longer to be located in spectacular *deus ex machina* of earlier opera, but in the representation of passion. Music thus provided an avenue for the exploration of the human character.

The question of musical representation – its objects and processes – was much debated in the eighteenth century. In his 1755 *L'Art du chant,*

---

[61] Laurent Garcin, *Traité du mélodrame* (Paris: Vallat-la-Chapelle, 1772), 243.

[62] One should not imagine that the *merveilleux* disappeared from the stage after 1750. Operatic practice was, of course, much more heterogeneous and fluid than were theoretical positions. Seventeenth-century operas were musically and scenically reshaped to conform to changing tastes (as eighteenth- and nineteenth-century operas are today). From its première in 1686, Lully's *Armide*, for example, was performed intermittently until 1766 (Lois Rosow, "How eighteenth-century Parisians heard Lully's operas: the case of *Armide*'s fourth act," in *Jean-Baptiste Lully and the Music of the French Baroque: Essays in Honor of James R. Anthony*, ed. John Hajdn Heyer [Cambridge: Cambridge University Press, 1989], 217). As Lois Rosow points out, the eighteenth-century *Armide*s were thoroughly altered to conform to current musical norms: "from the mid-1750s to the mid-1770s, numerous operas by Lully and his successors were edited for presentation at the Opéra, and it is clear both from surviving musical sources and from contemporaneous descriptions that these were major reworkings, involving copious adjustments of the original music as well as the addition of many new instrumental pieces and songs" (Rosow, 228). Many of these changes evoke the *opera buffa*, the genre praised by those (such as Diderot and Rousseau) who clamored for an entirely new kind of opera (Rosow, 231). Hence, one might venture to say that the eighteenth century attempted to rewrite the seventeenth-century French musical tradition according to changing notions of operatic representation.

Berard notes two kinds of representation: "Cicero says that Music aims to depict the passions of the human heart & the movements that take place in the Physical World".[63] An extreme example of the second kind of representation can be found in the description of a gallstone operation – "Le Tableau de l'opération de la taille" – that Marin Marais wrote for his fifth book of viol pieces. However, music as a depiction of objects or actions was frequently ridiculed as discussion of musical representation increasingly emphasized passion after the mid-century. According to the anonymous author of *Sentiment d'un harmoniphile, sur différens ouvrages de musique*, "poetry sketches for Music the passions that it is to paint."[64] Similarly, Chastellux insists that music must "express all the passions & all the sentiments that the Poet has developed."[65] Music finds the emotional states that it is to express in the poetry of the lyric theater. Rousseau uses this definition of musical representation to take a stand against the old *tragédie en musique*. Referring to the supernatural plots of these operas, he argues that it is ridiculous to try to represent things that never existed nor could ever exist, "when any man can judge for himself if the Artist has succeeded in making the passions speak their language": "the Gods were driven from the Stage when we discovered how to represent men there."[66] The object of operatic representation had undergone a transformation: "everyone began to tire of all the showiness of wizardry, of the idiotic ruckus of the machines, & of fantastical images of things that have never been seen."[67] Leaving behind the supernatural effects and mythological heroes which, according to Rousseau, had nothing to do with the actions and emotions of sentient beings, the lyric theater aimed more specifically at the "language" of human passion. Accordingly, as Grimm argued in his article on the "Poème lyrique," the spectator should be "touched" rather than "dazzled": "a God can amaze, he can appear grand & formidable; but can he arouse concern? How will he manage to touch me?"[68] The focal point of lyric expression had moved from Parnassus to a theater of sensibility.

For the opera, as for other kinds of theater, the key to the study of

---

[63] Jean Antoine Berard, *L'Art du chant* (1755; New York: Broude Brothers, 1967), 25.

[64] *Sentiment d'un harmoniphile, sur différens ouvrages de musique* (Amsterdam, Paris: Jombert, Duchesne, Lambert, n.d.), 54.

[65] François-Jean de Chastellux, *Essai sur l'union de la poésie et de la musique* (A La Haye, et se trouve à Paris: chez Merlin, 1765), 21.

[66] Rousseau, *Dictionnaire*, s.v. "Opéra."

[67] "[L'on commençait] à se dégoûter de tout le clinquant de la féerie, du puérile fracas des machines, & de la fantasque image des choses qu'on n'a jamais vues" (*ibid.*).

[68] *Encyclopédie*, 12:829.

emotional response was the *caractère*.[69] J. G. Sulzer's definition of the notion of character in the supplement to the *Encyclopédie* merits quoting at length. For Sulzer, the character is an aesthetic abstraction drawn from the collected actions and responses of the human subject:

it is the *characters* of the dramatis personae that form the essential part of the poem. If they are well portrayed, they allow us to read into the hearts of men, to anticipate the impression of exterior objects on them, to predict their emotions, their resolutions, & to know clearly the mechanisms [*ressorts*] that make them act. *Characters* are literally [*proprement*] the soul's portrait, the real object, of which the body's portrait is only a shadow. The poet who can sketch moral *characters* with exactitude & with force teaches us to understand men &, at the same time, to know ourselves well. But the effect of well-drawn *characters* on the faculties of our soul is not limited to this understanding. For just as we share the sorrow of afflicted persons, we also feel all the other emotions when they are vividly expressed & true to life. Any strong represen-tation of the soul's state causes us to feel whatever is occurring in it as appreciably [*sensiblement*] as if it were happening in ourselves. In this way, the thoughts & emotions of others become in some measure modifications of our own being.[70]

La Mettrie claimed that since the essence of the soul could not be known, one could at least study the physical traces it left through its activities and its *sensibilité*.[71] Regarding this empirical scrutiny of the soul by way of the body, Sulzer makes a strong epistemological claim for the fine arts. Through the actor's representation – through the "character" – it is possible to have a practical understanding of what makes men tick (*les ressorts*). What had been the subject of the treatises on passion – that is, the outward expression of the obscure workings of the soul and the influence of external objects on the soul – found an effective representation in the theatrical character. Sulzer argues that it is possible to represent on stage the relation between the physical actions of bodies and the effects that these actions have on the human organism. The inscrutable human soul becomes "legible" through the signifying system of the character. And by understanding men through their characters, Sulzer claims, one is also led to greater self-knowledge. Unlike the rational knowledge of metaphysics, however, the understanding to which Sulzer refers is sensorial and participatory. As in Rousseau's mechanism of compassion, in Sulzer's

[69] See Jane R. Stevens, "The Meanings and uses of *Caractère* in eighteenth-century France," *French Musical Thought, 1600–1800*, ed. Georgia Cowart (Ann Arbor: UMI Press, 1989), 23–52.
[70] *Supplément à l'Encyclopédie*, 2:230. Sulzer's articles on aesthetics appearing in the supplement to the *Encyclopédie* were excerpted and translated from his *Allgemeine Theorie der schönen Künste* (1771–74).
[71] La Mettrie, *Histoire naturelle de l'âme*, 82.

view passions are sympathetic.[72] Just as we sympathize with the real suffering of others, as spectators, we vicariously feel the emotions of the dramatic characters. The staged passions become part of the spectator's experience, "modifications of our own being." Sulzer claims that the actual experience of emotion, by way of theatrical representation, will lead to a greater understanding of the human constitution. As the spectator experiences the thoughts and feelings that are played out on stage, these theatrical representations "teach us to understand men, & at the same time to know ourselves well."

Sulzer's notion of character reveals the triangular structure of mimesis linking representation, emotion, and self-knowledge. In *The Poetics*, Aristotle defined mimesis as a cognitive process, and asserted that "men have an instinct for representation."[73] Following Aristotle in this respect, rather than rejecting mimesis as a dangerous fiction, Sulzer saw it as a heuristic mechanism that exposed and analyzed passionate response. Through the sympathetic resonances it generated, opera would bring the spectator toward greater self-knowledge. Bossuet's charge against opera was reversed: instead of leading to moral corruption, the experience of emotion on the part of the spectator led to an "engaged" understanding of the passions and their effects on the body and the mind.

In the lyric theater, music had become the salient feature of this mimetic structure. Though Chastellux duly noted that the music of an opera was based on the poetry, he nonetheless claims that "one cannot deny that Music is the principal object of an opera."[74] With music as the focal point of lyric theater, Enlightenment discourse on opera noticeably veered away from the classical emphasis on the dramatic poem – its adherence to or violation of *vraisemblance* and *bienséances* – and its disregard for the music, whose "indistinct noise," for Saint-Evremond, allowed no place for "the mind which ... lets itself wander into reverie, or is unhappy in its uselessness."[75] Although it would reappear in the debate opposing *Piccinistes* and *Gluckistes*, Saint-Evremond's opposition between "the ear" and "the mind" was temporarily set aside, just as eighteenth-century epistemology erased the essential difference that Descartes had posited between body and soul. The emphasis on the poetry is diminished, and, as Chastellux

---

72 Rousseau rejected the notion of portraiture and characterology as artificial in the *Confessions*, and attacked the theater as a space of isolation in the *Lettre à d'Alembert*; yet his notion of *la pitié*, at the origin of community, is nonetheless eminently theatrical.

73 Aristotle, *The Poetics*, trans. W. Hamilton Fyfe (Cambridge: Harvard University Press, 1927), 1448b6–9.

74 Chastellux, *Essai*, 21.

75 Saint-Evremond, *Sur l'opéra*, in Lesure, ed., *Textes sur Lully et l'opéra français*, 80–81.

notes, even the "beautiful effects" of instrumental harmony, ostensibly destined only for the pleasure of the ear, cultivated a rhetoric: "the animated orchestra takes on the voice of the passions; it reveals to the listener their indeterminate course, he follows them in their wanderings, & its moving yet inarticulate sounds are the only language that can make them understood."[76] The fact that instrumental music produced "inarticulate" sound, unlike song, made it the preferred language of the passions, inarticulate sound corresponding to the indeterminateness of passion. Chastellux's praise of instrumental music over vocal music is unusual; yet it is indicative of the growing emphasis theorists placed on music as expressive in its own right, as cultivating a "voice" that moves beyond the articulate voice of poetry in the expression of passion. Through an expanded conception of rhetoric and a reconsideration of the role of sensation in knowledge, the meaning (*logos*) of music and the pleasure of the senses were not seen as mutually exclusive. Referring to "German symphonic composers," Chastellux observed that in their compositions "the instruments shine each in turn: they provoke & respond to each other, quarrel & make up. It is a lively & continuous conversation."[77] Mark Evan Bonds has shown the importance of rhetoric as the "central metaphor in accounts of [musical] form" from the late eighteenth century into the nineteenth century, when concepts of persuasion and eloquence were linked to instrumental music.[78] As it was for vocal music, passion was the focus of this musical rhetoric: Johann Nikolaus Forkel, for example, called music an *Empfindungssprache*, a language of emotion.[79]

The object of musical theater thus coincided with that of the regular theater by representing the passions which define the *caractère*: "the characters of the dramatis personae are for the composer nothing more than the emotions that they most often feel."[80] What Bossuet had found so dangerous in music – its emotional sway – is precisely what appealed to Sulzer: "music has incomparably more means than

---

[76] Chastellux, *Essai*, 49, 89.

[77] *Ibid.*, 49. In his "Fragment sur la musique en général et sur la nôtre en particulier," d'Alembert disagreed with Chastellux's confidence in instrumental music: "this language is such that, in and of itself, it can arouse at the best only a rather vague feeling when it is not joined to anything else." Like Chastellux, though, d'Alembert insists on the importance of "discourse" against pure virtuosity in instrumental music: "it is not to witness feats of virtuosity that one goes to hear music at the Concert Spirituel; it is a discourse to which one wants to listen" (d'Alembert, *Œuvres et correspondances inédites*, 182).

[78] Bonds, *Wordless Rhetoric*, 9.   [79] *Ibid.*, 67.

[80] "Les caractères des personnages ne sont pour le compositeur que les sentimens qu'ils éprouvent le plus souvent" (Bernard Germain Etienne de Lacépède, *La Poétique de la musique* [Paris: Serpenti, 1797], 1:165).

163

ordinary language of modifying & varying its expressions."[81] Rather than destroying *vraisemblance*, as opera's critics maintained, Rémond de Saint-Mard suggests that music could enhance representation through its extensive resources in passion: "there is in Music some sort of [*je ne sçais quelle*] Analogy with our passions, a certain force for portraying them that words alone will never attain."[82] In his *Encyclopédie* article "Poème Lyrique," Grimm's description of music as both sensual and representational draws attention to the direct effect it was considered to have on the sensible body: "a universal language immediately striking our [sense] organs & our imagination, is also by its nature the language of feeling & of the passions." He concludes that "musical drama must therefore make a much greater impression than ordinary tragedy & comedy."[83] Chastellux agrees that, as the language of the passions, music can express nuances in passion that the poet alone cannot.[84] He offers the example of Armide's hesitation as she readies to strike Renaud: "indeed, the Poet can have her say *strike; what makes me hesitate?* But only the composer can develop, make sensible that which makes her hesitate."[85] Only music can exhibit and embody the impenetrable mechanisms of the passions: "but what is extremely important is that every engaging situation, every expression of pathos, all the terrible or agreeable images be regarded by the Poet as the true domain of the Music."[86]

In order to "perfect the expression of the passions portrayed by the Poet," music makes them "sensible & present to the mind of the Spectators."[87] Lacépède concurs, and asserts that music constitutes the driving force behind the spectacle of the lyric theater through its

---

[81] *Supplément à l'Encyclopédie*, s.v. "Accent (Art de la Parole), 1:107. Restif de la Bretonne, not surprisingly, disagrees with Sulzer: "opera being a Spectacle as extravagant as it is useless to morals, dangerous in itself, because of its songs, its morals & above all because of its Actresses; a spectacle which can only excite the rage of all those ardent passions that, when controlled, make for the happiness & the virtue of the wise man: it must be tolerated only insofar as it is appropriate for displaying the taste of the Nation" (Nicolas-Edme Restif de la Bretonne, *La Mimographe* [1770; Geneva: Slatkine, 1980], 150). For Restif, opera is worthwhile principally because it can serve as a political and economic stratagem to attract foreigners and their money to France.

[82] Rémond de Saint-Mard, *Reflexions sur l'opéra* (The Hague: Neaulme, 1741), 10.

[83] *Encyclopédie*, s.v. "Poème Lyrique," 12:824.

[84] It is interesting to note that Stanley Sadie's definition of operatic music in the *New Grove* is almost identical to that of Chastellux: "music can strengthen, subtilize, or inflect any words that are uttered on stage. It can also carry hints about words or feelings that are left unexpressed" (*The New Grove Dictionary of Music and Musicians*, s.v. "Opera"). This coincidence may be interpreted as pointing to the modernity of Chastellux's opinions; and I suspect that it may also be seen as indicating how little our conception of the function of music in opera has changed.

[85] Chastellux, *Essai*, 24.   [86] *Ibid.*, 85–86.

[87] Le Pileur d'Apligny, *Traité sur la musique*, 107–108.

extraordinary ability to trigger the spectator's sensibility: "the power of Music appears almost limitless, when one only considers the ease with which it makes us feel the principal sensations aroused by the objects of artistic imitation, compelling us, by this means, to consider them as if they were present."[88] Music's privileged status as a signifier of passion derives from its ability to affect the body. Lacépède claims that music "activates" the representation set up by the other arts of the lyric theater – dance, poetry, architecture – through its unique link to the spectator's passions through sensation. The precise mechanism of this influence remains unexplained. Nonetheless, writers sought to make music the cornerstone of a theater of the Enlightenment through a confidence in the ability of music to rouse the affections, echoing the eighteenth-century fascination with accounts of the music of antiquity and its supposedly miraculous curative effects. Unlike Rousseau, Diderot praises the moral effect of the theatrical spectacle in the *Discours sur la poésie dramatique*: "O what good would befall men if all the imitative arts together were to consider a common object and were to unite one day with the laws so as to make us love virtue and hate vice!"[89] By reproducing the accents of passion, as Laurent Garcin claimed, music would allow theater to probe the mechanism and effects of passion: "the Theater has been for all time & will probably always be, as long as it endures, the living stage of all the mechanisms that incite humankind to act; it is a mirror in which man can learn to know himself."[90] While providing insight into the human character and its affections by representing "the present [*actuelle*] physiognomy of the soul," as Garcin argued, musical theater could offer models of virtuous action and self-knowledge – a laboratory for the moral education of the spectator through the lyrical "analysis" of the affections of the soul.[91]

It is not surprising, then, that music figures as a kind of knowledge in the "system of human knowledge" of the *Encyclopédie*. "Speaking simultaneously to the imagination and to the senses," as d'Alembert claimed in the "Discours préliminaire," music was ideally suited for the representation of the passions. D'Alembert categorized music as one of the "forms of knowledge consisting in imitation": the mimetic arts (pictorial, poetic, and musical), together with philosophy and history, thus figured as a type of "understanding."[92] If music was placed last in d'Alembert's classification, Diderot, like Rousseau, reversed the order in his letter to Mademoiselle de La Chaux: here,

[88] Lacépède, *La Poétique de la musique*, 1:55.
[89] Denis Diderot, *Œuvres complètes*, ed. Roger Lewinter (Paris: Club Français du Livre, 1969–73), 3:418.
[90] Garcin, *Traité du mélodrame*, 97.   [91] *Ibid.*, 242.   [92] *Encyclopédie*, 1:xij.

"music speaks most strongly to the soul."[93] Though he maintained the traditional aesthetic hierarchy, d'Alembert recognized the need to study the question further. While placing music last in the order of knowledge, he devoted more space to music than to architecture, painting, sculpture, and poetry combined, and called for more research into the largely unknown but promising field of musical representation:

music, which speaks simultaneously to the imagination and to the senses, holds the last place in the order of imitation – not that its imitation is less perfect in the objects which it attempts to represent, but because until now it has apparently been restricted to a smaller number of images. This should be attributed less to its nature than to the lack of sufficient inventiveness and resourcefulness in most of those who cultivate it.[94]

This conception of music as a largely unexplored and perhaps crucial area of knowledge underwrote, as I have argued, eighteenth-century explorations of the origin of signs and knowledge, and pre-dictions of a forceful new lyric theater. Yet in the *Encyclopédie*, rather than being conceived of within the framework of traditional epistemo-logy and ontology, the kind of cognition produced by the imagination and the senses is set aside from philosophy as a parallel, but separate, species of knowledge. The kind of sensate cognition which Diderot attributed to music, and which Sulzer described in the *Encyclopédie* article "Caractère," matches Baumgarten's inaugural definition of aes-thetics as, among other things, a subalternate epistemology (*gnoseo-logia inferior*), and as *ars pulchre cogitandi* (the art of beautiful think-ing).[95] Jeffrey Barnouw points out that in the eighteenth century, aesthetics was not concerned with art appreciation as it is customarily understood today; instead, it sought to define a particular field of knowledge:

If aesthetics at its early stages referred at all to appreciating works of art or the beauty of nature, this was not the core of its concern but only a secondary non-essential application. What it was really about ... was the analysis, nurture and refinement of feeling, as a principal element of knowledge and of motivation or character.[96]

Barnouw's assertion is supported by Sulzer's definition of aesthetics in the supplement to the *Encyclopédie* as "the science of emotion [*sentimens*]."[97] Much of Sulzer's aesthetics was committed to normative categories and hierarchies of the beautiful. However, by stressing the

---

[93] Diderot, *Œuvres complètes*, ed. Varloot, 4:207.
[94] D'Alembert, *Preliminary Discourse*, 38; *Encyclopédie*, 1:xij.
[95] Jeffrey Barnouw, "Feeling in Enlightenment aesthetics," *Studies in Eighteenth-Century Culture* 18 (1988), 324.
[96] *Ibid.*, 323–324.   [97] *Supplément à l'Encyclopédie*, s.v. "Esthétique," 2:872.

significance of sensibility in knowledge, eighteenth-century aesthetics as a whole supported the emergence of an epistemology based on bodily experience rather than metaphysical categories. By examining treatises on the passions in conjunction with theories of musical representation, I have sought to suggest the possibility of an interdisciplinary reading of the connection between music and emotion. The fact that Ménuret de Chambaud wrote a lengthy article on the effects of music on the human constitution places music within eighteenth-century reflections on sensibility in general and medical thought in particular. Writings on the role of music in the lyric theater shared the interest in sensibility elaborated in medical texts. Because of its foregrounding of musical expression, the lyric theater provided opportunities to represent pathos, to expose it, study it, and tap its resonances.

Diderot's *Leçons de clavecin* offers an opportunity to explore, within the confines of a particular text, the rhetorical paradigm and its theatrical presuppositions as it inflects the understanding of music without words. Diderot's text reveals an effort to trace the connections between music, interpretation, and reception, in the domain of purely instrumental music. Written in 1771 with Bemetzrieder, whom Diderot had retained for his daughter Angélique's harpsichord instruction, the *Leçons de clavecin* provides an example of how music's exclusive focus (even that of instrumental music) is that of the impassioned "image," of the "engaging situation."[98] Diderot's text addresses many of the questions I have explored in this chapter: it raises the issues of mimesis, of the musical exploration of character, of the relationship between the performance and the spectator/listener, and of the sensitivity to and transmission of affect. In the passage I have chosen from the *Leçons de clavecin*, an excerpt from the continuation of the twelfth dialogue ("troisième suite du douzième dialogue"), the instructor seeks to demonstrate to his student that music is something other than a simple concatenation of sounds. The text merits quoting at some length. In the first section of the dialogue, the instructor asks the student to follow a certain harmonic progression as he dictates it to her, without touching the keys of the instrument:

> The Instructor Gather your thoughts, sit down at the harpsichord, and try to follow me by ear. Starting from C, played twice andante, move on to F major; return to C; go to G major; and return again to C

[98] Chastellux, *Essai*, 24. The *Leçons de clavecin* has scarcely been touched upon by commentators. See Robert Niklaus, "Diderot and the *Leçons de clavecin et principes d'harmonie* par Bemetzrieder," *Modern Miscellany* (Manchester: Manchester University Press, 1969), 180–194. See also Béatrice Didier, "Aspects de la pédagogie musical chez Diderot," *Colloque international Diderot*, ed. Anne-Marie Chouillet (Paris: Aux Amateurs de Livres, 1985), 309–319; and Downing A. Thomas, "Musicology and

> ... Less purposefully this time, proceed to G sharp minor; then to G sharp or A flat major; to F minor; to F major and then to C where you will stop for a moment after having played the last four chords only once in the indicated tempo. Now, gather up speed. Move in fifths through the major keys all the way to F sharp ... When you arrive back in C major, surprised but weary, play this chord again slowly three times ... When you reach D flat minor, break off this languorous pace. Surprise the ear twice with D flat major, come in quickly the first time but linger a bit on the second. Then slip gently into F minor and return again to C ... Did you understand?
> The Student   I think so.[99]

If one were to examine the passage closely, what might appear at first glance to be a purely musical progression is already given a certain amount of narrative direction, even before the instructor's subsequent "translation" of it. First of all, rather than write out his progression in musical notation, the instructor prefers to "tell" it in natural language scattered with the appropriate solfège syllables. From the very beginning, this choice forces the issue of musical rhetoric (which is indeed the subject of this part of the lesson), integrating the musical example with the temporal and linguistic framework of narrative. Secondly, the narrator inflects the musical vocabulary with metaphors and adjectives evoking emotional or physical response: "less purposefully this time, proceed to G sharp minor"; "now, gather up speed"; "when you arrive back in C major, surprised but weary." Next, the instructor "translates" the passage, integrating the narrative fragments into a full-blown story. From the initial, partially hidden plot sketch, more complete images and narratives emerge from the musical example the instructor has improvised:

> The Instructor   Did I use anything but the simplest musical tricks?
> The Student   No.
> The Instructor   And yet if you have a little imagination, if you have feeling, if sounds move you, if you were born with a heart, if you are naturally enthusiastic and can convey this enthusiasm to others, then what will have occurred to you? You will have seen a man who wakes up in the middle of a labyrinth. He searches left and right for a way out. For a moment, he thinks he has come to the end of his wandering. He stops short; then slowly and with trepidation he follows the path, treacherous perhaps, that opens before him. Now he is lost once again. He runs, rests, runs again. He climbs, he climbs. He glances around and recognizes the very spot where he awoke. Overcome with worry and distress, his laments echo throughout the

---

hieroglyphics: questions of representation in Diderot," *The Eighteenth Century: Theory and Interpretation*, 35.1 (1994), 64–77.

[99] Diderot, *Œuvres complètes*, ed. Varloot, 19:352–353.

labyrinth. What will become of him? With no way of knowing, he abandons himself to the destiny that offers him only false hopes of a way out. Having taken just a few steps, he is brought back to the place where he began.[100]

Contradicting the central argument of *Le Paradoxe sur le comédien*, the harpsichord instructor tells his pupil that she first must feel the emotions aroused by the music's physical resonance and its mimetic structure, and then she can convey this emotion to others. The antithesis of the cold, dispassionate performer described in the *Paradoxe*, the harpsichordist of the *Leçons* must be entirely infused [*pénétrée*] with the enthusiasm generated by the music.

Finally, the philosopher and the instructor discuss the implications of representation in music. Here in the last section of the dialogue, the *philosophe* intervenes as the ultimate arbiter and interpreter of the event, and as the father – "do you understand, my daughter"? He explains that the source of music is in the heart and that its central purpose is "to speak to the soul and to the ear."[101] Next the *philosophe* claims that the image described by the instructor – that of a man lost in a labyrinth – is only one among many possible images which might be evoked by the same music: these particular musical progressions, interpreted differently by each listener, never remain meaningless. The harpsichord instructor follows suit by claiming that although music is certainly a representational art, the indeterminateness of sounds always leaves them open to interpretation: "every listener understands music according to the present state of his soul."[102]

This multiplication and superposition of images bears a striking resemblance to the semiotic polyphony which characterized the hieroglyph in Diderot's *Lettre sur les sourds et muets*. The harpsichordist's enthusiasm also recalls the poetic "spirit that ... enlivens every syllable" described in the *Lettre sur les sourds et muets*; both result from the human presence which realizes or activates the "text."[103] The performer draws this energy out and then transmits it to others. The musical or poetic hieroglyph of the *Lettre* is not ready-made or fixed, but depends on the listener or reader for its activation: "the understanding grasps the objects of representation, the soul is stirred by them, the imagination sees them, and the ear hears them."[104] In the *Leçons*, the choice of dialogue, whose open structure creates the effect of process (where representation is the product of an interaction, rather than being ready-made), supports the notion of interpretation as an interactive event in which both the performer and the spectator actively participate. By "telling" the music in two different ways,

[100] *Ibid.*, 19:353–354.   [101] *Ibid.*, 19:354.   [102] *Ibid.*, 19:354.   [103] *Ibid.*, 4:169.
[104] *Ibid.*, 4:169.

Diderot is able to exhibit the process of interpretation in narrative form. In the first instance, the performer partially "unpacks" the meaning of the sounds. By mixing musical terminology with the bare traces of plot and emotional content, Diderot renders in narrative the indefinite and mobile quality of the musical idea, which he had termed its "hieroglyph" in the *Lettre*. At the same time, he conveys the already rhetorical character of instrumental music. Then, by interpreting the musical hieroglyph as the story of a man in a labyrinth, Diderot gives one example of the way in which music is activated by the listener's engagement with it. For Diderot, it is the ambiguity of the musical hieroglyph – "so light and fleeting" – that gives it such power: "how can it be that of the three arts that imitate nature, the one whose expression is the most arbitrary and least precise is also the one that speaks most strongly to the soul? Could it be that, rather than directly revealing the object, it leaves more room for our imagination?"[105] There is only the most tenuous representational link between musical sounds and the objects of the world: "painting shows the object itself, poetry describes it, yet music scarcely evokes an impression of it."[106] Yet Diderot insists that the imprecision of music, its shifting hieroglyph, is precisely what empowers the spectator's imagination. In Diderot's *Leçons*, as in Sulzer's description of *caractère*, representations are completed by the spectator's experience, rather than being found, already made, in the artistic object. If music is more likely than ordinary language to arouse and express the passions, as Sulzer claimed in the supplement to the *Encyclopédie*, it is precisely because it leaves itself more open to interpretation.[107] In his review of a treatise on melodrama by Chastellux, Diderot directly links music's emotional power over the spectator with its ability to generate affect and to "turn on" the imagination through the senses: music has "the divine ability to move us, torment us, to bring the most varied nuances to our ears, and to make us imagine all kinds of apparitions."[108] The musical hieroglyph has the exceptional ability to propel the spectator's imagination in a multitude of directions; yet this impassioned state of "possession," as Diderot argues in his letter to Mademoiselle de la Chaux, is shared by all: "men have a reciprocal effect upon each other through the powerful image they each offer of the single passion that affects them all. This explains the uncontrollable excitement of our public festivals."[109]

---

[105] *Ibid.*, 4:207.   [106] *Ibid.*, 4:207.
[107] *Supplément à l'Encyclopédie*, s.v. "Accent (Art de la Parole)," 1:107.
[108] Diderot, "Observations sur un ouvrage intitulé *Traité du mélodrame ou Réflexions sur la musique dramatique*, par M. le chevalier de Chastellux," in *Œuvres complètes*, ed. Lewinter, 9:940.
[109] Diderot, *Œuvres complètes*, ed. Varloot, 4:207–208.

The resonance of the social body in the "public festival," triggered by music, recalls the speculative and erotic resonances set in motion between d'Alembert, Mlle. de l'Espinasse, and Bordeu in the *Rêve de d'Alembert*.[110] Just as bodily desire and intellectual discussion intermingle in the *Rêve de d'Alembert* and are conveyed to the reader, so the harpsichordist of the *Leçons* feels and understands the music and passes this affective understanding on to her listeners. The doctor–philosopher and the musician share a common objective: to tap and interpret resonances.[111] Although individual listeners are free to understand the music according to their own affective imaginations, a common and public experience results from the music. The material resonances of music could set minds in motion together, the music room or opera hall resonating like the beehive of the *Rêve*. Diderot's hieroglyph in the *Lettre sur les sourds et muets* and the musical example given in the *Leçons* offered new possibilities by recognizing that musical sounds – incomplete representational fragments which can only be completed by the listener – cannot be framed in terms of singular "truth," "reality," or "fiction." From this standpoint, the *Lettre sur les sourds et muets* and the *Leçons* could be considered as displaced supplements to, or commentaries on, the project of the *Encyclopédie*, as well as developing new aesthetic formulations.

Commentators have almost universally described a move in the late eighteenth and early nineteenth centuries away from language-based conceptions of music towards fledgling theories of autonomous art. I would argue, however, that a nuanced reading of the concern with sensibility found in medicine and music – a reading I have attempted in this chapter – tells a somewhat different story. What occurs towards the end of the eighteenth century is not so much an emancipation from language as a shift away from an aesthetic of singular referentiality and towards a rhetorical concern with affective response and interpretation. Rousseau describes this experience of music in a passage from *La Nouvelle Héloïse* where St. Preux is entranced by the operatic voice: "at each phrase, some image would enter my mind or some emotion my heart ... all the performers seemed animated with the same spirit ... at every moment I would forget the idea of music, of

<hr/>

[110] For two recent and sensitive readings of the *Rêve de d'Alembert*, see Rosalina de la Carrera, *Success in Circuit Lies: Diderot's Communicational Practice* (Stanford: Stanford University Press, 1991), 127–166; and Wilda Anderson, *Diderot's Dream* (Baltimore: The Johns Hopkins University Press, 1990), 42–76.

[111] "Diagnosis, then, would seem to consist in the delicate art of tapping the resonances created by sensibility in the body, resonances that resound all the more dramatically when this property is overexerted or pathologically diverted" (Vila, "Sensible diagnostics," 778–779).

song, of imitation; I believed I was hearing the voice of suffering, of anger, of despair; I believed I was seeing tearful mothers, betrayed lovers."[112] Representation remains as the aesthetic framework of these texts. What is interesting about Diderot's text, leaving Rousseau's novel and returning to the pedagogical text of the *Leçons de clavecin*, however, is that it bears witness to a displacement from imitation to communicative affect. The *Leçons* is less concerned with tracing the norms of a normative, referential, musical discourse as it is with a rhetoric of performance and reception. Diderot's text marks a shift from mimesis as content to mimesis as interpretive event. I have argued that this shift is corroborated by the simultaneous interest in music and sensibility found in both medical and musical treatises. The verbal paradigm is not abandoned; yet, the musical text becomes unconcerned with determinate content and opens itself, perhaps more than ever, to sensibility and the resonances of affect.

[112] "A chaque phrase, quelque image entrait dans mon cerveau ou quelque sentiment dans mon cœur ... tous les concertants semblaient animés du même esprit ... je perdais à chaque instant l'idée de musique, de chant, d'imitation; je croyais entendre la voix de la douleur, de l'emportement, du désespoir; je croyais voir des mères éplorées, des amants trahis" (Rousseau, *Œuvres complètes*, 2:133–134).

Conclusion

Having largely isolated the question of the origin of signs and culture from its theological underpinnings and having placed it within a secular and hypothetical framework, eighteenth-century writers contributed to the construction of what would later be called "les sciences humaines," the social sciences. Placing a common humanity at the center of this conjectural history, eighteenth-century essays on the question of origins attempted to explain the appearance of society and signifying practices by depicting a series of natural events which led to the conditions of the possibility of language and society. The majority of these narratives carefully avoided absolute breaks and fragmentation by claiming that all knowledge derives from our ability to perceive nature through sensation. Knowledge is continuous – a gradual building upon earlier principles, from the initial sense impressions of a hypothetical zero degree of humanity to the abstract constructions of geometry and philosophy. Condillac, in his *Essai sur l'origine des connaissances humaines*, invoked the metaphor of semiotic "chains or links" which had originally linked the objects of nature to simple ideas, and finally developed memory and complex thought.[1] Condillac's argument for the natural and simultaneous development of signs and culture established a paradigm for the study of the origin of language which remained in place into the early nineteenth century. Rousseau, while viewing the development of culture and society as a series of "natural" events, nonetheless marks a series of losses which at first appear insignificant but reveal themselves to be devastating. He also celebrates the brief moments of communality and passion that appear at specific junctures in the *Essai* and form the basis of a possible but unrealized social existence.

As I have argued throughout this study, music is given special emphasis, through its link to passion and language, in these narratives on the origination of culture. By virtue of its association with an "origin," music played a pivotal role in eighteenth-century discourse by articulating the mythical past of the origin with a vision of the

---

[1] Condillac, *Essay*, 46.

173

present and future. As the formative element of an original intersubjectivity through human sensibility, the musical voice articulates the passionate and violent demands of the individual within the initial constraints of the physical world and the social order. It serves as a "missing link," bridging conceptual gaps for eighteenth-century anthropology. By marking the emergence of the signifier, music also delivers a vision of the future directions and potentialities of culture.

The verbal paradigm is central to eighteenth-century conceptions of music as a semiotic form. While it may be possible to claim a shift within the verbal pardigm in the late eighteenth century – usually identified as a move from imitation to expression – one cannot claim that this shift constitutes a move away from a rhetorical approach to music. This is not to say that Rousseau or Diderot merely echo the neo-classical mimetic theory of their seventeenth-century predecessors. On the contrary, their texts may be said to represent limit cases in which the boundaries and definitions of musical representation are profoundly altered or stretched. As I argued in chapter 5, the increasing importance of sensation led to a shift in the focus of musical rhetoric during the late eighteenth century, not to its disappearance. The verbal paradigm, whatever its "faults" may be, gave music a particular place within the network of meanings and discourses that make up culture. In my attempt to reveal the continuity of the verbal paradigm, I have not intended to gloss over differences within eighteenth-century discourse, even within "Encyclopedic" discourse on music. I have pointed out that differing positions can be found in the writings of the Encyclopedists themselves. Whereas Diderot considers the unfathomable complexity of the musical object and views this complexity as an indication of music's place within the complicated (and often incompatible) networks of culture, d'Alembert is confident that "the true system of music" will eventually be discovered.[2] Yet I have sought to expose a larger set of concerns and a larger discourse on music that most eighteenth-century writers shared, contested, or engaged in some way.

Given its interest in the place of the body and of sensibility in knowledge, aesthetics could be said to have consummated that which the search for origins had initiated in its attempt to describe the place of sensibility and passion in knowledge. It is no wonder, then, that descriptions of the origin of language and culture share common ground with eighteenth-century reflections on music and musical theater. As David Wellbery has argued: "the Enlightenment attributes to art the capacity to renew the life of the culture by reactivating its most archaic mechanisms ... [if] the *telos* of Enlightenment culture is a

---

[2] D'Alembert, *Œuvres et correspondances inédites*, 140.

system of natural signs, then art becomes the locus where this *telos* is proleptically achieved."[3] Seen as a pre-linguistic, natural system of signs, music is both that which allows eighteenth-century writers to describe the origins of language and culture, and the means to imagine a new aesthetics based on the activation of this natural "language" of sensibility. Both a sensible force and a (virtual) representation, music activates the mechanism of intersubjective community which, at the origin of language, heralded the initial moments of society and culture. The experience of the senses leads to another, specifically communal, awareness. This idealized community – utopian mirror of the origin – is formed by subjects both present to themselves and present to each other within the participatory mimetic experience.

Guillaume André Villoteau's *Recherches sur l'analogie de la musique avec les arts qui ont pour objet l'imitation du langage* (1807) offers an interesting example of this fusion of origin and end, one with which I would like to conclude. Villoteau hoped that one day composers might tap the most "primitive" musical sounds in order to create the perfect music. As part of Napoléon's attempt to extend his vast empire, Villoteau traveled to Egypt along with a team of cultural explorers; among his many concerns in the *Recherches*, he attempted to bring his observations of Egyptian culture to bear on the question of music as a language. Of particular interest in this context is a chapter of commentary on Rousseau's *Essai sur l'origine des langues*, entitled "Jean-Jacques Rousseau in contradiction with himself in the various opinions that he has proffered on Music," in which Villoteau cites Rousseau's text at length. Although earlier in the *Recherches* he asserted that music adopted the individual character of each civilization, in a note of extended commentary on Rousseau's claim that music was "a language for which one has to have the Dictionary," Villoteau found that some of the most "primitive" cultures afforded a glimpse at what might have been an original and universal musical language.[4] The songs of the "Barabras" people, "mountain people of Nubia who live beyond the first falls of the Nile," seemed to fit this description: "these airs, in which art seems to be in its infancy, and which breathe the gentlest and most innocent melancholy, are nothing, in a way, but long modulated sighs, in which the voice is gently raised, and is slowly lowered, in imperceptible *intervals* of vaguely rhythmic sounds, only to begin again."[5] Villoteau compared these long, modulated sighs to the

---

[3] Wellbery, *Lessing's Laocoon*, 6–7. [4] Rousseau, *Essay*, 281.
[5] "Ces airs, où l'art paroît être dans sa première enfance, et qui respirent la plus douce et la plus naïve mélancolie, ne sont, en quelque façon, que de longs soupirs modulés, par lesquels la voix s'élève sans violence, et s'abaisse plus ou moins lentement par des

sounds children make before they learn to speak. As in Court de Gebelin's *Histoire naturelle de la parole* (1772), where the natural growth of the individual reproduced the general development of civilization, Villoteau's depiction of the Barabras shows civilization in its infancy. While providing a glimpse of universal origins, Villoteau's representation of Egyptian music simultaneously conjures up a sense of loss within modern Western society. The primitive or exotic stands as a figure of the lost purity of the origin; and in their role as documentation, they also justified Bonaparte's expansionism by marking Egypt – its music, its cultures – as confirming European civilization in its suspicion that its truths were indeed universal ones. Marked by the Encyclopedists and the Ideologues after them, Villoteau suggested that a modern composer could create a universal musical dictionary – "a veritable dictionary of musical language would present a collection of the various natural accents of expression, interpreted musically."[6] By analyzing and classifying the various musical properties of the natural voice, Villoteau claims, one is also engaged in the study of "the affections and passions of the human heart, of which they are the language."[7] The result of this analytical procedure would be the system of natural signs that eighteenth-century writers sought to reach through the search for origins. Origin and end thus ultimately coincide: "the modern composer or musician who has thus become familiar with the words of musical language, and who understands their proper use, would have arrived at the end of its development, and would reach the degree of perfection where art borders on nature at the extremity opposite its infancy."[8]

If the quest for origins allowed writers to imagine the semiotic foundation of a common humanity, it also launched efforts to rediscover, preserve, or re-create the original generative structure which began the process in the first place. Music had come full circle in its search for perfection. A system of natural signs might be achieved through music and, with it, an entirely new and revitalized society and culture in which the natural and the philosophical – that is, enlightened reason – would be perfectly united: "we will succeed in directing art simultaneously towards its greatest perfection and towards a goal useful for our happiness and for that of society."[9] Through their investigations of the origin of music, eighteenth-century writers were able to depict the beginning of semiosis, and at the same time to create a philosophical framework for articulating the utopian aims of their culture.

dégradations insensibles de sons vaguement cadencés, pour recommencer de même" (Villoteau, *Recherches*, 161n).
[6] *Ibid.*, 159–160n.   [7] *Ibid.*, 172.   [8] *Ibid.*, 160n.   [9] *Ibid.*, 171–172.

BIBLIOGRAPHY

Primary sources (before 1900)

Alembert, Jean le Rond d'. *Elémens de musique.* 1779. Plan-de-la-Tour: Editions d'Aujourd'hui [1984].

Œuvres et correspondances inédites. Geneva: Slatkine, 1967.

Preliminary Discourse to the Encyclopedia of Diderot. Trans. Richard N. Schwab and Walter E. Rex. Indianapolis: Bobbs-Merrill, 1963.

André, Yves Marie. *Œuvres.* Geneva: Slatkine, 1971.

Aristotle. *De Anima.* Trans. R. D. Hicks. 1907. Hildesheim: Georg Olms, 1990.

The Poetics. Trans. W. Hamilton Fyfe. Cambridge: Harvard University Press, 1927.

Arnaud, l'abbé François. *Lettre sur la musique à Monsieur le Compte de Caylus.* N.p.: n.p., 1754.

Augustine. *On Music.* Trans. Robert Catesby Taliaferro. In *Writings.* Vol. 2. Washington, DC: Catholic University of America Press, 1947.

Batteux, Charles. *Les Beaux arts réduits à un même principe.* Paris: Durand, 1746.

Bénigne de Bacilly. *L'Art de bien chanter.* 1679. Geneva: Minkoff, 1974.

Berard, Jean Antoine. *L'Art du chant.* 1755. New York: Broude Brothers, 1967.

Bergier, Nicolas. *La Musique speculative.* Cologne: Arno Volk, 1970.

Béthisy de Mezières [Jean Laurent de Béthisy]. *Effets de l'air sur le corps humain, considérés dans le son; ou Discours sur la nature du Chant.* Amsterdam, et se trouve à Paris, chez Lambert, 1760.

Blainville, Charles Henri. *L'Esprit de l'art musical ou reflections sur la musique.* 1754. Geneva: Minkoff, 1974.

Histoire générale, critique et philologique de la musique. 1769. Geneva: Minkoff, 1972.

Boileau, Nicolas. *Œuvres.* 2 vols. Paris: Garnier-Flammarion, 1969.

Bossuet, Jacques Bénigne. *Œuvres.* 12 vols. Bar-le-Duc: Guérin, 1863.

Bourdelot, l'abbé P., and Jacques Bonnet. *Histoire de la musique et de ses effets depuis son origine jusqu'à présent.* Paris: Cochart, 1715.

Boyé [Pascal ?]. *L'Expression musicale mise au rang des chimères.* Amsterdam: Esprit, 1779.

Brossard, Sébastien de. *Dictionnaire de musique.* Paris: n.p., 1705.

Buffon, Georges Louis Leclerc, comte de. *Histoire naturelle.* Ed. Jean Varloot. Paris: Gallimard, 1984.

Castel, Louis-Bertrand. "Suite et troisième partie des nouvelles Expériences d'optique & d'Acoustique." *Journal de Trévoux.* Vol. 35. 1735. Geneva: Slatkine, 1968. 454–462.

Chabanon, Michel Paul Guy de. *De la musique considérée en elle-même et dans ses rapports avec la parole, les langues, la poésie, et le théâtre*. Paris: Pissot, 1785.

Chastellux, François-Jean de. *Essai sur l'union de la poésie et de la musique*. A La Haye, et se trouve à Paris, chez Merlin, 1765.

Condillac, Etienne Bonnot de. *Essai sur l'origine des connaissances humaines*. Auvers-sur-Oise: Galilée, 1973.

An Essay on the Origin of Human Knowledge. Trans. Thomas Nugent. 1756. Gainesville, Florida: Scholars' Facsimiles & Reprints, 1971.

La Logique. New York: Abaris Books, 1980.

Œuvres. 23 vols. Paris: Chez les Libraires Associés, 1777.

Traité des animaux. Œuvres complètes. 16 vols. 1821–1822. Geneva: Slatkine, 1970.

Traité des sensations. London: De Bure, 1754.

Court de Gebelin, Antoine. *Histoire naturelle de la parole ou Origine du langage, de l'écriture et de la grammaire universelle*. Paris: n.p., 1772.

Crousaz, J. P. de. *Traité du beau*. 2 vols. Amsterdam: L'Honoré & Chatelain, 1724.

De Brosses, Charles. *Traité de la formation méchanique des langues*. 2 vols. Paris: Saillant, Vincent, Desaint, 1765.

Descartes, René. *Abrégé de musique*. Paris: Presses Universitaires de France, 1988.

Œuvres et lettres. Ed. André Bridoux. Paris: Gallimard, 1953.

Œuvres philosophiques. 3 vols. Paris: Garnier, 1963.

Les Passions de l'âme. Paris: Gallimard, 1988.

Diderot, Denis. *Œuvres complètes*. Ed. Roger Lewinter. 15 vols. Paris: Club Français du Livre, 1969–73.

Œuvres complètes. Ed. Jean Varloot. 25 vols. Paris: Hermann, 1975–86.

Dubos, abbé Jean-Baptiste. *Réflexions critiques sur la poésie et sur la peinture*. 2 vols. Paris: Jean Mariette, 1719.

Ducousu, Antoine. *La Musique universelle, contenant toute la pratique et toute la théorie*. Paris: Robert Ballard, 1658.

Encyclopédie ou dictionnaire raisonné des arts et des métiers. Ed. Denis Diderot and Jean le Rond d'Alembert. 28 vols. 1751–72. *Supplément à l'Encyclopédie ou Dictionnaire raisonné des sciences, des arts et des métiers*. [Ed. Jean-Baptiste-René Robinet.] 4 vols. 1776–77. Elmsford, New York: Pergamon, n.d. 5 vols. [*Encyclopédie* and *Supplément* together].

Estève, Pierre. *L'Esprit des beaux-arts*. Paris: Bauche Fils, 1753.

Nouvelle découverte du principe de l'harmonie. Paris: Jorry, 1752.

Eximeno, Antonio. *Dell'origine et della regole della musica*. 1774. Hildesheim: Georg Olms, 1983.

Frain du Tremblay, Jean. *Traité des langues*. Paris: Delespine, 1703.

Garcin, Laurent. *Traité du mélodrame*. Paris: Vallat-la-Chapelle, 1772.

Grimarest, Jean Léonor le Gallois de. *Traité du récitatif*. 1740. New York: AMS Press [1978].

Helvétius, Claude-Adrien. *De l'esprit*. Paris: Fayard, 1988.

Hoffmann, E. T. A. *E. T. A. Hoffmann's Musical Writings: "Kreisleriana," "the Poet and the Composer," Music Criticism*. Ed. David Charlton. Trans. Martyn Clarke. Cambridge: Cambridge University Press, 1989.

Huygens, Christian. *La Pluralité des mondes.* Trans. M. Dufour. Paris: Moreau, 1702.

Jones, Rowland. *The Origin of Language and Nations.* 1764. Menston, England: The Scolar Press, 1972.

Kant, Immanuel. *Critique of Judgment.* Trans. Werner S. Pluhar. Indianapolis: Hackett, 1987.

Kuhnau, Johann. *Six Biblical Sonatas.* New York: Broude Bros., 1953.

Laborde, Jean-Benjamin de. *Essai sur la musique ancienne et moderne.* 4 vols. Paris: Ph.-D. Pierres, 1780.

Lacépède, Bernard Germain Etienne de. *La Poétique de la musique.* 2 vols. Paris: Serpenti, 1797.

Lacombe, Jacques. *Le Spectacle des beaux-arts.* Paris: Hardy, 1758.

Lallemant, Jean Baptiste Joseph. *Essai sur le méchanisme des passions en général.* Paris: Le Prieur, 1751.

La Mettrie, Julien Offroy de. *Histoire naturelle de l'âme.* Oxford: n.p., 1747.

La Voye Mignot. *Traité de musique.* 1666. Geneva: Minkoff, n.d.

Le Cerf de la Viéville. *Comparaison de la musique italienne et de la musique française.* 1705–06. Geneva: Minkoff, 1972.

Leibniz, Gottfried Wilhelm. *Nouveaux essais sur l'entendement humain.* Paris: Garnier-Flammarion, 1966.

   Philosophical Papers and Letters. Ed. and trans. Leroy E. Loemker. 1956. Dordrecht: Reidel, 1970.

Le Pileur d'Apligny. *Traité sur la musique et sur les moyens d'en perfectionner l'expression.* Paris: Demonville, 1779.

Locke, John. *An Essay Concerning Human Understanding.* Oxford: Clarendon Press, 1975.

Mably, Gabriel Bonnot, abbé de. *Lettres à Madame la Marquise de P . . . sur l'opéra.* Paris: Didot, 1741.

Masson, Charles. *Nouveau traité des regles pour la composition de la musique.* 1699. New York: Da Capo Press, 1967.

Mersenne, Marin. *Harmonie universelle.* 1636. 3 vols. Paris: Editions du Centre National de la Recherche Scientifique, 1963.

   Questions harmoniques. Paris: Fayard, 1985.

Mirabeau, Honoré Gabriel Riquetti, comte de. *Le Lecteur y mettra le titre.* London: n.p., 1777.

Pascal, Blaise. *Pensées.* Paris: Garnier, 1964.

Plato. *The Republic.* Trans. G.M.A. Grube. Indianapolis: Hackett, 1974.

Rameau, Jean-Philippe. *Complete Theoretical Writings.* Ed. Erwin R. Jacobi. 6 vols. N.p.: American Institute of Musicology, 1968–69.

   Traité de l'harmonie. 1722. Madrid: Arte Tripharia, 1984.

Rémond de Saint-Mard, Toussaint. *Reflexions sur l'opéra.* The Hague: Neaulme, 1741.

Restif de la Bretonne, Nicolas-Edme. *La Mimographe.* 1770. Geneva: Slatkine, 1980.

Rousseau, Jean. *Traité de la viole.* 1687. Amsterdam: Antiqua, 1965.

Rousseau, Jean-Jacques. *Les Confessions.* Ed. Jacques Voisine. Paris: Garnier Frères, 1964.

   Confessions. 2 vols. London: J. M. Dent & Sons Ltd., 1931.

Correspondance complète. Ed. R. A. Leigh. 50 vols. to date. Geneva: Institut et Musée Voltaire, 1965–.

Dictionnaire de musique. Paris: Veuve Duchesne, 1768.

Ecrits sur la musique. Paris: Pourrat, 1838.

Essai sur l'origine des langues. Ed. Charles Porset. Bordeaux: Ducros, 1970.

Essai sur l'origine des langues. Ed. Jean Starobinski. Paris: Gallimard, 1990.

The First and Second Discourses together with the Replies to Critics and Essay on the Origin of Languages. Ed. and trans. Victor Gourevitch. New York: Harper & Row, 1986.

Œuvres complètes. Ed. Bernard Gagnebin and Marcel Raymond. 4 vols. Paris: Gallimard, 1959–.

On the Social Contract. Trans. Judith R. Masters. New York: St. Martin's Press, 1978.

Salvemini da Castiglione, G. F. M. M. *Discours sur l'origine de l'inégalité.* Amsterdam: Jolly, 1756.

Sentiment d'un harmoniphile, sur différens ouvrages de musique. Amsterdam, Paris: Jombert, Duchesne, Lambert, n.d.

Vico, Giambattista. *The New Science.* Trans. Thomas Goddard Bergin and Max Harold Fisch. Ithaca: Cornell University Press, 1968.

Villoteau, Guillaume André. *Recherches sur l'analogie de la musique avec les arts qui ont pour objet l'imitation du langage.* 2 vols. Paris: L'Imprimerie Impériale, 1807.

Warburton, William, Bishop of Gloucester. *Essai sur les hieroglyphes des Egyptiens.* Trans. Léonard des Malpeines. [1774.] Paris: Aubier, 1977.

Wilkens, John. *An Essay Towards a Real Character and a Philosophical Language.* London: John Martin, 1668.

Secondary sources

Aarsleff, Hans. *From Locke to Saussure: Essays on the Study of Language and Intellectual History.* Minneapolis: University of Minnesota Press, 1982.

Allen, Warren Dwight. *Philosophies of Music History.* New York: American Book Company, 1939.

Anderson, Wilda. *Diderot's Dream.* Baltimore: The Johns Hopkins University Press, 1990.

Auroux, Sylvain. "Condillac, inventeur d'un nouveau matérialisme." *Dix-Huitième Siècle* 24 (1992): 153–163.

"Empirisme et théorie linguistique chez Condillac." *Condillac et les problèmes du langage.* Ed. Jean Sgard. Geneva: Slatkine, 1982. 177–219.

La Sémiotique des encyclopédistes. Paris: Payot, 1979.

Bardez, Jean-Michel. *Philosophes, encyclopédistes, musiciens, théoriciens.* Geneva: Slatkine, 1980.

Barnouw, Jeffrey. "Feeling in Enlightenment aesthetics." *Studies in Eighteenth-Century Culture* 18 (1988): 323–341.

Barry, Kevin. *Language, Music and the Sign.* Cambridge: Cambridge University Press, 1987.

Benveniste, Emile. *Problèmes de linguistique générale.* 2 vols. Paris: Gallimard, 1974.

Bernstein, Leonard. *The Unanswered Question*. Cambridge: Harvard University Press, 1976.

Bonds, Mark Evan. *Wordless Rhetoric: Musical Form and the Metaphor of the Oration*. Cambridge: Harvard University Press, 1991.

Boulez, Pierre. *Points de repère*. 2nd edition. Paris: Christian Bourgois, 1985.

Buelow, George J. "Music, rhetoric, and the concept of affections: a selective bibliography." *Notes* 30 (1973–74): 250–259.

Cannone, Belinda. *Philosophies de la musique: 1752–1789*. Paris: Aux Amateurs de Livres, 1990.

Carrera, Rosalina de la. *Success in Circuit Lies: Diderot's Communicational Practice*. Stanford: Stanford University Press, 1991.

Castarède, Marie-France. *La Voix et ses sortilèges*. Paris: Les Belles Lettres, 1987.

Christensen, Thomas. "Diderot, Rameau and resonating strings: new evidence of an early collaboration." *Studies in Voltaire and the Eighteenth Century*, forthcoming.

   "Music theory as scientific propaganda: the case of d'Alembert's *Elémens de musique*." *Journal of the History of Ideas* 50.3 (1989): 409–427.

   Rameau and Musical Thought in the Enlightenment. Cambridge: Cambridge University Press, 1993.

Cohen, Albert. *Music in the French Royal Academy of Sciences*. Princeton: Princeton University Press, 1981.

Cohen, H. F. *Quantifying Music*. Dordrecht: Reidel, 1984.

Corbett, John. "Free, single, and disengaged: listening pleasure and the popular music object." *October* 54 (1990): 79–101.

Cornelius, Paul. *Languages in Seventeenth- and Early Eighteenth-Century Imaginary Voyages*. Geneva: Droz, 1965.

Coward, Rosalind, and John Ellis. *Language and Materialism: Developments in Semiology and the Theory of the Subject*. London: Routledge, 1977.

De Man, Paul. *Blindness and Insight: Essays in the Rhetoric of Contemporary Criticism*. Minneapolis: University of Minnesota Press, 1983.

Derrida, Jacques. *L'Archéologie du frivole*. [Introduction.] *Essai sur l'origine des connaissances humaines*. By Etienne Bonnot de Condillac. Auvers-sur-Oise: Galilée, 1973.

   The Archeology of the Frivolous. Trans. John P. Leavey, Jr. Pittsburgh: Duquesne University Press, 1980.

   De la grammatologie. Paris: Editions de Minuit, 1967.

   Of Grammatology. Trans. Gayatri Chakravorty Spivak. Baltimore: The Johns Hopkins University Press, 1976.

   Marges de la philosophie. Paris: Editions de Minuit, 1972.

Didier, Béatrice. "Aspects de la pédagogie musical chez Diderot." *Colloque international Diderot*. Ed. Anne-Marie Chouillet. Paris: Aux Amateurs de Livres, 1985.

   La Musique des lumières. Paris: Presses Universitaires de France, 1985.

Doolittle, James. "A would-be *Philosophe*: Jean Philippe Rameau." *PMLA* 74.3 (1959): 233–248.

Duchez, Marie-Elisabeth. "D'Alembert diffuseur de la théorie harmonique de Rameau: déduction scientifique et simplification musicale." *Jean d'Alembert, savant et philosophe: portrait à plusieurs voix*. Ed. Monique Emery and

Pierre Monzani. Paris: Editions des Archives Contemporaines, 1989. 475–96.

"Principe de la mélodie et origine des langues: un brouillon inédit de Jean-Jacques Rousseau sur l'origine de la mélodie." *Revue de Musicologie* 60.1–2 (1974): 33–86.

"Valeur épistémologique de la théorie de la basse fondamentale de Jean-Philippe Rameau: connaissance scientifique et représentation de la musique." *Studies on Voltaire and the Eighteenth Century* 245 (1986): 91–130.

Ducrot, Oswald, and Tzvetan Todorov. *Dictionnaire encyclopédique des sciences du langage*. Paris: Editions du Seuil, 1972.

Eco, Umberto. *Sémiotique et philosophie du langage*. Trans. Myriem Bouzaher. Paris: Presses Universitaires de France, 1988.

La Structure absente. Trans. Uccio Esposito-Torrigiani. Paris: Mercure de France, 1972.

Ehrard, Jean. *L'Idée de nature en France dans la première moitié du XVIIIe siècle*. 2 vols. Paris: SEVPEN, 1963.

Escal, Françoise. "D'Alembert et la théorie harmonique de Rameau." *Dix-Huitième Siècle* 16 (1984): 151–162.

Ettelson, Trudy Gottlieb. "Jean-Jacques Rousseau's writings on music: a quest for melody." Ph.D. dissertation, Yale University, 1974.

Fouquet, Paul. "J.-J. Rousseau et la grammaire philosophique." *Mélanges de philologie offerts à Ferdinand Brunot*. Paris: Société Nouvelle de Librairie et d'Edition, 1904. 115–136.

Gans, Eric. *The Origin of Language: A Formal Theory of Representation*. Berkeley: University of California Press, 1981.

Girard, René. *Des choses cachées depuis la fondation du monde*. Paris: Grasset, 1978.

Grosrichard, Alain. "La voix de la vérité." *Littérature et opéra*. Ed. Philippe Berthier and Kurt Ringger. Grenoble: Presses Universitaire de Grenoble, 1987. 9–17.

Habermas, Jürgen. *The Philosophical Discourse of Modernity*. Trans. Frederick G. Lawrence. Cambridge: MIT Press, 1987.

Hacking, Ian. "How, why, when, and where did language go public?" *Common Knowledge* 1.2 (1992): 74–91.

Hennion, Antoine. "Rameau et l'harmonie: comment avoir raison de la musique." *Actes de Jean-Philippe Rameau: colloque international*. Ed. Jérôme de la Gorce. Paris: Champion-Slatkine, 1987. 393–407.

Huet, Marie-Hélène. *Monstrous Imagination*. Cambridge: Harvard University Press, 1993.

Juliard, Pierre. *Philosophies of Language in Eighteenth-Century France*. The Hague: Mouton, 1970.

Kavanagh, Thomas M. Introduction. *The Limits of Theory*. Ed. Thomas M. Kavanagh. Stanford: Standford University Press, 1989. 1–22.

Kintzler, Catherine. *Jean-Philippe Rameau: splendeur et naufrage de l'esthétique du plaisir à l'âge classique*. Paris: Le Sycomore, 1983.

Poétique de l'opéra français de Corneille à Rousseau. Paris: Minèrve, 1991.

Knight, Isabel F. *The Geometric Spirit*. New Haven: Yale University Press, 1968.

Koana, Akiko. "La Théorie musicale dans l'épistémologie de Condillac." *The Reasons of Art: l'art a ses raisons.* Ed. Peter J. McCormick. Ottawa: University of Ottawa Press, 1985. 448–451.

Kramer, Lawrence. *Music as Cultural Practice: 1800–1900.* Berkeley: University of California Press, 1990.

Kristeva, Julia. *Language the Unknown.* Trans. Anne M. Menke. New York: Columbia University Press, 1989.

Launay, Denise, ed. *La Querelle des bouffons: textes des pamphlets.* 3 vols. Geneva: Minkoff, 1973.

Launay, Michel, and Michèle Duchet. "Synchronie et diachronie: l'*Essai sur l'origine des langues* et le second *Discours.*" *Revue Internationale de Philosophie* 82.4 (1967): 421–442.

Lenneberg, Hans. "Johann Mattheson on affect and rhetoric in music (II)." *Journal of Music Theory* 2.1 (1958): 193–236.

Lesure, François, ed. *Textes sur Lully et l'opéra français.* Geneva: Minkoff, 1987.

Levi, Anthony. *French Moralists: The Theory of the Passions 1585 to 1649.* Oxford: Clarendon Press, 1964.

Lindenberger, Herbert. *Opera, the Extravagant Art.* Ithaca: Cornell University Press, 1984.

Maniates, Maria Rika. "'Sonate, que me veux-tu?': the enigma of French musical aesthetics in the 18th century." *Current Musicology* 9 (1969): 117–140.

McDonald, Christie Vance. "En harmoniques: l'anagramme de Rousseau." *Etudes Françaises* 17.3–4 (1981): 7–21.

"Jacques Derrida's reading of Rousseau." *The Eighteenth Century: Theory and Interpretation* 20 (1979): 82–95.

Murat, Michel. "Jean-Jacques Rousseau: imitation musicale et origine des langues." *Travaux de Linguistique et de Littérature* 18.2 (1980): 145–168.

Nattiez, Jean-Jacques. *Musicologie générale et sémiologie.* Paris: Christian Bourgois, 1987.

Nettl, Bruno. "Mozart and the ethnomusicological study of Western culture: an essay in four movements." *Disciplining Music: Musicology and its Canons.* Ed. Katherine Bergeron and Philip V. Bohlman. Chicago: University of Chicago Press, 1992. 137–155.

Neubauer, John. *The Emancipation of Music from Language.* New Haven: Yale University Press, 1986.

Niklaus, Robert. "Diderot and the *Leçons de clavecin et principes d'harmonie* par Bemetzrieder." *Modern Miscellany.* Manchester: Manchester University Press, 1969. 180–194.

Norris, Christopher. *Contest of Faculties: Philosophy and Theory after Deconstruction.* London: Methuen, 1985.

What's Wrong with Postmodernism. New York: Harvester Wheatsheaf, 1990.

Oliver, A.-R. *The Encyclopedists as Critics of Music.* New York: Columbia University Press, 1947.

Paxman, David B. "Abstraction in eighteenth-century language study." *Journal of the History of Ideas* 54.1 (1993): 19–36.

Porset, Charles. "L'"inquiétante étrangeté' de l'*Essai sur l'origine des langues*:

Rousseau et ses exégètes." *Studies on Voltaire and the Eighteenth Century* 154 (1976): 1715–1758.

ed. *Varia linguistica*. Bordeaux: Ducros, 1970.

Powers, Harold S. "Language models and musical analysis." *Ethnomusicology* 24.1 (1980): 1–60.

Reiss, Timothy J. *The Discourse of Modernism*. Ithaca: Cornell University Press, 1982.

"Problems in logic and rhetoric." *A New History of French Literature*. Ed. Denis Hollier. Cambridge: Harvard University Press, 1989. 278–284.

Richebourg, Louise. *Contribution à l'histoire de la Querelle des bouffons*. Philadelphia: n.p., 1937.

Robrieux, Jean-Jacques. "Jean-Philippe Rameau et l'opinion philosophique en France au dix-huitième siècle." *Studies on Voltaire and the Eighteenth Century* 238 (1985): 269–395.

Rosow, Lois. "How eighteenth-century Parisians heard Lully's operas: the case of *Armide*'s fourth act." *Jean-Baptiste Lully and the Music of the French Baroque: Essays in Honour of James R. Anthony*. Ed. John Hajdu Heyer. Cambridge: Cambridge University Press, 1989. 213–237.

Rousseau, Nicolas. *Connaissance et langage chez Condillac*. Geneva: Droz, 1986.

Sadie, Stanley, ed. *The New Grove Dictionary of Music and Musicians*. 20 vols. London: Macmillan, 1980.

Said, Edward W. *Beginnings: Intention and Method*. New York: Columbia University Press, 1985.

Musical Elaborations. New York: Columbia University Press, 1991.

Seay, Albert. *Music in the Medieval World*. Englewood Cliffs: Prentice-Hall, 1975.

Sgard, Jean, ed. *Condillac et les problèmes du langage*. Geneva: Slatkine, 1982.

Corpus Condillac. Geneva: Slatkine, 1981.

Sisman, Elaine R. *Haydn and the Classical Variation*. Cambridge: Harvard University Press, 1993.

Slaughter, M. M. *Universal Languages and Scientific Taxonomy in the Seventeenth Century*. Cambridge: Cambridge University Press, 1982.

Snyders, Georges. *Le Goût musical en France aux XVIIe et XVIIIe siècles*. Paris: Vrin, 1968.

Starobinski, Jean. *Jean-Jacques Rousseau: la transparence et l'obstacle*. Paris: Gallimard, 1971.

Le Remède dans le mal. Paris: Gallimard, 1989.

Steblin, Rita. *A History of Key Characteristics in the Eighteenth and Early Nineteenth Centuries*. Ann Arbor: UMI Press, 1983.

Stevens, Jane R. "The meanings and uses of *caractère* in eighteenth-century France." *French Musical Thought, 1600–1800*. Ed. Georgia Cowart. Ann Arbor: UMI Press, 1989.

Subotnik, Rose Rosengard. *Developing Variations: Style and Ideology in Western Music*. Minneapolis: University of Minnesota Press, 1991.

Thomas, Downing A. "Musicology and hieroglyphics: questions of representation in Diderot." *The Eighteenth Century: Theory and Interpretation*, 35.1 (1994): 64–77.

Tiersot, Julien. *J.-J. Rousseau*. Paris: Félix Alcan, 1912.

Todorov, Tzvetan. *Théories du symbole*. Paris: Editions du Seuil, 1977.

Vartanian, Aram. "Derrida, Rousseau, and the difference." *Studies in Eighteenth-Century Culture* 19 (1989): 129–151.

Diderot and Descartes: A Study of Scientific Naturalism in the Enlightenment. Princeton: Princeton University Press, 1953.

Vendrix, Philippe. *Aux origines d'une discipline historique: la musique et son histoire en France aux XVIIe et XVIIIe siècles.* Geneva: Droz, 1993.

Verba, Cynthia. *Music and the French Enlightenment: Reconstruction of a Dialogue: 1750–1764.* Oxford: Clarendon Press, 1993.

Vidler, Anthony. "The return to the origins: rituals of initiation in late eighteenth century France." *The Princeton Journal* 1 (1983): 116–125.

Vila, Anne C. "The sensible body: medicine and literature in eighteenth century France." Ph.D. dissertation, The Johns Hopkins University, 1990.

"Sensible diagnostics in Diderot's *La Religieuse.*" *MLN* 105 (1990): 774–799.

Walser, Robert. *Running With the Devil: Power, Gender, and Madness in Heavy Metal Music.* Hanover: Wesleyan University Press / University Press of New England, 1993.

Wellbery, David E. *Lessing's Laocoon: Semiotics and Aesthetics in the Age of Reason.* Cambridge: Cambridge University Press, 1984.

Wells, G.A. *The Origin of Language: Aspects of the Discussion from Condillac to Wundt.* La Salle, Illinois: Open Court, 1987.

Wokler, Robert. "Rameau, Rousseau and the *Essai sur l'origine des langues.*" *Studies on Voltaire and the Eighteenth Century* 117 (1974): 179–238.

"Rousseau on Rameau and revolution." *Studies in the Eighteenth Century IV.* Ed. R. F. Brissenden and J. C. Eade. Canberra: Australian National University Press, 1979. 251–283.

Social Thought of Jean-Jacques Rousseau. New York: Garland Publishing, 1987.

Zaslaw, Neal. "The first opera in Paris: a study in the politics of art." *Jean-Baptiste Lully and the Music of the French Baroque: Essays in Honour of James R. Anthony.* Ed. John Hajdu Heyer. Cambridge: Cambridge University Press, 1989. 7–23.

Index

actor, 66, 148–149, 161
  see also listener; spectator
aesthetic ideology, 18–19
aesthetics, 1, 8, 10–11, 12–13, 32, 55n66, 89,
  117, 125–126, 141, 145–146, 147, 152,
  154, 155, 158, 166–167, 171–172,
  174–175
absolute, 5–7, 23, 19–20
  see also autonomy; expression;
  imitation; mimesis
affect, 6, 65, 108, 129, 142
  see also melody: and affect; music;
  passions
Affektenlehre, 70
airs de cour, 22
Alembert, Jean le Rond d', 2, 16, 18, 32, 33,
  44, 72–73, 127, 163n77, 171, 174
  "Discours préliminaire," 1, 16, 18, 58n7,
  73, 94, 123n101, 124, 125, 165–166
  Elémens de musique, 73, 96
  and *Encyclopédie*, 94–96
  "Fragment sur la musique," 163n77
  "Réflexions sur la théorie de la
  musique," 94–95
Allen, Warren Dwight, 35
Americans, native, 48
  see also music: American
analogy, 25n40, 43, 60, 62, 76, 100, 123,
  131–134, 164
analytico-referential discourse, 32
André, Yves Marie, 39, 40, 175
animals
  and communication, 26, 53–54, 56, 152
  and humans, 9, 38, 98–99, 104, 112, 152,
  155–158
  and origins of music, 50–51, 63
  see also music: and noise
  anthropology, 2, 9, 15, 45n45, 47, 49, 54,
  56, 63, 95, 108, 110, 125, 138, 141, 143,
  174
  generative, 51n56

paleoanthropology, 38
  see also fiction: anthropological; missing
  link
antiquity, 9, 52–53, 78–80, 100, 114, 130,
  147, 165
  see also languages; music: of antiquity
archeo-teleology, 138
architecture, 45n45, 165, 166
  see also music: and architecture
Aristotle, 57, 60, 62, 81, 149, 150, 154,
  162
Arnaud, l'abbé François, 24
articulation, 45–46, 71, 106–113, 118, 120,
  121–123, 127, 135, 141
  see also language; vocal accent
artifice, 124n103, 131n118
Auroux, Sylvain, 41, 46n, 58, 61, 67, 68
authenticity, 20, 145
auto-affection, 128
autonomy, 6–7, 12, 14, 25, 171
  see also aesthetics: absolute

Babbitt, Milton, 12
Babel, 35
Bacon, Francis, 94, 147
Baïf, Jean-Antoine de, 20–22, 29
Bardez, Jean-Michel, 6
Barnouw, Jeffrey, 166
Batteux, Charles, 28, 44, 115, 123–124, 127,
  132n120, 142
Baumgarten, Alexander Gottlieb, 145n6,
  166
Beauzée, Nicolas, 41n27, 42n33
Bemetzrieder, Anton, 16, 167
Bénigne de Bacilly, 24
Benveniste, Emile, 13, 17
Berard, Jean Antoine, 160
Bergier, Nicolas, 23, 29, 30
Bernstein, Leonard, 14
Béthisy de Mézières, 157
Bible, 46, 48, 59, 52, 63

186

language *cont.*
grammar, 121, 141
and habit, 59, 67–68, 74
illogical, 80
and law, 42, 102
and loss, 34, 80–81, 113, 122, 141
and love, 100, 102, 104, 111–112, 120
and mathematics, 60
and oppression, 90
and pleasure, 105, 109, 111–112
prelinguistic, 10n24, 61, 102, 153
and psyche, 69, 90
public, 104–105, 114
public vs. private, 8n22
and reason, 35, 67, 107, 110–114, 121,
   138, 139n132, 141
and repression, 120
and silence, 100, 113–114
and sonority, 90, 106–107, 112–113, 115,
   121–122, 137
and syntax, 13, 61, 120
and temporality, 59, 78, 100–101, 107,
   109–110, 112
travelers' accounts of, 110
universal, 9, 35, 38
utterances, 45, 65–66, 103–104, 106,
   108–109, 113, 118
visual, 38, 79, 99–102, 107
and vocalization, 45, 53, 67, 69–70, 79,
   106
vowels, 108, 111
see also articulation; eloquence; gesture;
   music: as discourse; music: as
   rhetoric; music: verbal paradigm for;
   recitative; rhetoric; vocal accent
languages
Arabic, 110, 136
Chinese, 77–78, 106–107, 110, 136
French, 21, 79–80, 90, 96, 107, 111,
   114n90
Greek, 21n30, 77, 78, 80, 110, 114n90,
   116, 117
Latin, 61, 79, 117
Polish, 110
Lassus, Orlando, 21
Launay, Michel, 85–86
Le Brun, Antoine-Louis, 146
Le Cerf de la Viéville, 36
Leibniz, Gottfried Wilhelm, 16, 37, 61
Le Jeune, Claude, 21
Le Pileur d'Apligny, 124
Lessing, Gotthold Ephraim, 140
Levi, Anthony, 150

Lindenberger, Herbert, 120n100
linguistics, 13–14
listener, 6, 25, 26, 28–29, 66, 101, 107, 115,
   122–123, 126, 128, 140, 142, 145, 158,
   163, 167, 169–171
see also actor; spectator
literary studies, 2
logocentrism, 17, 18, 88
logos, 17, 18, 55, 138, 163
Lorenzi, [Jacques Roland] chevalier de,
   86
Lucretius, 9, 40, 50, 51, 53
Lullistes, 4
Lully, Jean-Baptiste, 4–5, 36n8, 147, 149
   Armide, 96, 159n62, 164

major triad, 75, 92
   see also corps sonore
Malesherbes, Chrétien-Guillaume de
   Lamoignon de, 84, 86
Maniates, Maria Rika, 6, 55n66
Marais, Marin, 160
Marpurg, Friedrich Wilhelm, 32
Masson, Charles, 29–30, 31, 85
materialism, 42, 126, 132, 156, 158, 171
   see also empiricism; sensationalism
Mattheson, Johann, 28–31
Maupertuis, Pierre-Louis de, 8, 17n22, 153
Mazarin, Jules, 4
McDonald, Christie, 10n24, 83n4, 88,
   110n81
médecins-philosophes, 152
medicine, 10–11, 24n40, 143–144, 146, 152,
   154–159, 167, 171, 172
   see also music: as cure; passions
melody, 21, 56, 73, 78, 108, 112, 146, 148
   and affect, 28, 30, 119–120, 123–129, 133,
   155–156
   and culture, 123–125, 128–129, 131,
   137–139
   as feminine, 29
   and harmony, 90, 92–93, 97, 102, 122,
   132–136, 141
   and language, 115–116, 141
   loss of, 121–122, 141–142
   origins of, 50, 53–54, 84, 122
   and voice, 24, 115, 118
   see also harmony; music; passions;
   vocal accent
memory, 5, 39, 59, 65, 67, 77, 79, 94,
   130–131, 132, 173
   see also origin
Mendelssohn, Moses, 140

Printed in the United States
65693LVS00006B/247-255